# Issues in American Advertising

## Media, Society, and a Changing World

**Edited by Tom Reichert**

ISBN: 978-1-887229-35-7
© 2008 Tom Reichert

Published by The Copy Workshop
A division of
Bruce Bendinger Creative Communications, Inc.

Cover Design: Gregory S. Paus

All rights reserved. Printed in the USA.
Editor: Bruce Bendinger
Assistant Editor / Compositor: Patrick Aylward

**The Copy Workshop**
• 2144 N. Hudson • Chicago, IL 60614
• TEL: 773-871-1179 • FAX: 773-281-4643 •
thecopyworkshop@aol.com • www.adbuzz.com

# Table of Contents

Foreword     v

Preface     vii

Introduction     1

## Law and Regulation:
## Puffery, Privacy, and Problematic Products

**1**    **Puffery:** A Controversial Type of Ad Claim     15
     **By Ivan Preston, University of Wisconsin**

**2**    **Shhhh, That's Private:** How Advertisers Today     29
     Can Leave You Feeling Exposed
     **By Jef Richards, University of Texas at Austin**

**3**    **Sex, Drugs, and the Evening News:**     41
     DTC Pharmaceutical Drug Advertising
     **By Wendy Macias, University of Georgia,**
     **and Liza Stavchansky Lewis, University of Texas at Austin**

**4**    **Alcohol Advertising:** The Effectiveness and Future     57
     of Self Regulation
     **By Stacey Hust, Washington State University**

**5**    **The Two Faces of Tobacco Advertising:**     71
     Marketing Triumph or Social Evil?
     **By Hye-Jin Paek, University of Georgia**

**6**   **Sweet Innocents or Savvy Consumers:** Exploring          85
        the Controversial Practice of Advertising to Children
        **By Catharine M. Curran, University of Massachusetts Dartmouth,
        and Joël Bree, University of Caen**

## Media:
## New Media Tools, Product Placement, and Saturation

**7**   **From Viral Videos to the Third Screen:**                 103
        Welcome to the New Media Ad Game
        **By Tom Reichert, University of Georgia**

**8**   **Pay to Place:** Product Placement Comes on Strong        126
        **By Tom Reichert, University of Georgia**

**9**   **How Advertisers Want to Cozy Up between You and Your**   138
        **Friends:** Word-of-Mouth and Social Networking in the Digital Age
        **By Jacqueline Lambiase, University of North Texas**

**10**  **All Ads, All the Time:** Are We at the Tipping Point of  152
        Advertising Saturation?
        **By Jay Newell, Iowa State University**

## Representation and Recruitment:
## Women and Minorities

**11**  **Women in Advertising:** Representation and               169
        (Lack of) Possibilities
        **By Tom Reichert, University of Georgia**

**12**  **Wanted:** Sense and Sensitivity Regarding Race and       183
        Ethnicity in Advertising
        **By Caryl Cooper, University of Alabama**

**13** **New Opportunities for Minorities:** Today, Growth Is in                    **196**
Multicultural Agencies and Media, Not on Madison Avenue
**By Jami Fullerton, Oklahoma State University,**
**Alice Kendrick, Southern Methodist University,**
**and Tom Reichert, University of Georgia**

## Content and Effects:
## Sex, Celebs, and America

**14** **Sex in Advertising:** Appeals to One of Our Basic Instincts        **211**
**By Tom Reichert, University of Georgia**

**15** **Celebrity Endorsement:** A Double-Edged Sword               **224**
**By Sejung Marina Choi, University of Texas at Austin**

**16** **Political Advertising:** A Formidable Weapon in                **239**
Battleground States and Beyond
**By Tom Reichert, University of Georgia**

**17** **Can Advertising Sell America?** Winning Hearts and         **253**
Minds in the Muslim World
**By Jami Fullerton, Oklahoma State University,**
**and Alice Kendrick, Southern Methodist University**

**18** **Beyond Obligation:** Advertising's Grand Potential to Do Good        **265**
**By Glenn Griffin, Southern Methodist University,**
**and Deborah Morrison, University of Oregon**

**19** **If It Feels Good, Watch It:** Emotion in Advertising          **282**
**By Tom Reichert, University of Georgia**

**Index**                                                          **295**

**About the Contributors**                                         **305**

# Foreword

EYE CANDY. ANNOYANCE. A chance for a trip to the fridge. A road bump to desirable web content. Wallpaper for everyday life. Inescapable.

While people often are dismissive of advertising, they occasionally express admiration for an effectively clever ad, an ad that has worked its way under their skin.

Think of advertising as a class clown. It works in much the same way as a passive-aggressive, capitalistic dream-machine that touches our emotions and affects us and our culture profoundly. It works us over, sometimes with subtlety and sometimes with aggravating persistence.

This book provides the back story for the workings of this powerful cultural and commercial institution.

Why is advertising's backstory important, when its front story is already so overexposed? After all, it is easy to view an ad, to quickly scan its visual images and textual copy, and to get the general idea. Everyone has this sort of basic advertising literacy.

Yet in this up-to-date book, Tom Reichert uses his fluency in advertising culture to help us gain more literacy about the industry and its tactics.

Advertising is wily, using many disguises from product placement in television programming to viral videos on YouTube.

Advertising carries emotional content designed to make us laugh or to stir sexual desires. And of course, it seeks to influence our political beliefs and actions.

Through professional and academic perspectives, Reichert and other scholars give us a roadmap to understand product placement, celebrity endorsements, emotional and sexual appeals, political ads, and branding. Social responsibility, ethics and legal issues—ranging from privacy to tobacco advertising regulations—are discussed across several sections of this book. Also tackled are the continuing problems of gender and race stereotyping within ads, along with recruitment and retention of minorities to the profession. Scholars also dissect ad content presented through emerging media forms.

These chapters provide in-depth information about current topics that are usually mentioned too briefly in larger introductory books.

Combining your own advertising literacy with the information in this book, you'll gain understanding of industry trends and be ready to discover how they affect your mediated experiences.

Some in the industry have proclaimed advertising as diminishing, as less important or less effective than public relations, as the less respectable protégé of marketing.

This short volume shows us the range and limits of advertising's power, as well as its transformation and transmutation in the digital age.

—Jacqueline Lambiase
Associate Professor in the Mayborn Graduate School of Journalism
and Department of Journalism at the
University of North Texas

# Preface

WHAT'S THE OLD SAYING: "Don't mention sex or politics in polite conversation?" Apparently, that advice has gone unheeded, at least in the conversation commonly referred to as advertising.

So as not to disappoint, this book contains in-depth discussions of both sex and politics, and many other important topics in contemporary advertising. These discussions, however, are written to illuminate rather than to titillate.

## Mixed Emotions

For many people, advertising evokes mixed emotions. On one hand, they say that they can't stand its intrusiveness. Countless surveys continue to indicate that people consider ads to be creeping into every part of their lives.

Indeed, many online marketers are tracking individuals' behavior through cookies, ISP addresses, and other means.

On the other hand, people buy magazines and newspapers because they enjoy the ads and find them informative and useful. People also still search and place classified ads in newspapers and online sites. And a recent study revealed that most people with ad-skipping devices such as TiVo still watch the commercials.

## Big Issues

Many of the chapters in this book touch on consumers' love/hate relationship with advertising. But more important, this book delves into the big issues influencing the look and delivery of today's advertising.

Broadly, these issues pertain to law and regulation, media and new technology, minority representation and recruitment, and the content and effects of various products, creative strategies, and campaigns.

The first edition touched on six pressing issues and served as a reader for my Introduction to Advertising course. I found that students need timely, in-depth discussions of pressing advertising issues. Given the quick pace of change, especially in the media area, such time-sensitive topics are difficult to include in even the best Intro books.

The opportunity arose to write and edit a much more comprehensive edition that can be used for a wider array of classes, especially Issues and Ad & Society courses.

The new edition—the one you have in your hands—is the result.

To provide the additional coverage, I went to the source; experts.

As a result, the book now covers 19 separate issues that are written by knowledgeable scholars. These contributors include Ivan Preston, Jef Richards, Wendy Macias, Liza Stavchansky Lewis, Stacey Hust, Hye-Jin Paek, Catharine Curran-Kelly, Jacqueline Lambiase, Jay Newell, Caryl Cooper, Jami Fullerton, Alice Kendrick, Glenn Griffin, Deborah Morrison, Joël Bree, and Sejung Marina Choi.

The issues I've chosen to include are particularly notable because they (1) receive scant attention or are misunderstood by consumers, reporters and, in some cases, advertisers, (2) they are controversial and/or substantial and demand much attention, or (3) they are relatively new and morphing so quickly that conventional wisdom is out of date.

These issues are organized within four broad sections. One section involves law and regulation, as well as the advertising of tobacco, alcohol, and pharmaceuticals.

Another section addresses media issues, and ranges from the tools and strategies available with new technology, to media saturation, and the power of social-network and word-of-mouth advertising.

The third section addresses the representation of women and minorities in advertising as well as multicultural opportunities for minorities.

The last section covers a range of topics that involve both controversial practices such as sex in advertising and the use of emotion, to the selling of politics and the American way of life. This section also includes a chapter that reveals the dark side of celebrity endorsements, as well as the upside of socially conscious marketing.

Each chapter provides a nuts-and-bolts synopsis of the issue it covers. Each chapter provides a historical context, a sense of prevalence, related research findings, and important implications and potential ethical dilemmas. Each chapter also includes definitions of key terms and features such as references and recommended readings and online resources.

## What You'll Get Out of This Book

If you're an advertising student, I'm confident that you'll find these issues interesting. In addition, I'm confident that in your first job—or entire career for that matter—you'll confront the issues discussed in the following chapters. Investing the time now to understand these issues will allow you to make better, more informed, decisions when you tackle them in the workplace or subsequent advertising courses.

If you're simply a consumer with no plans for a position in advertising or marketing, you'll also find this book particularly useful.

It'll help you cope. Estimates are that you view hundreds of ads a day, that you spend at least 12 hours a day enjoying media—much of it ad-supported—and that you saw something like 350,000 TV commercials by the time you turned 18. Quite simply, you are surrounded by advertising and taking the time to understand what it is, how it works, and why it is creeping—unannounced—into programming, books, and video games can help you become a fully informed participant—instead of a vulnerable consumer—in the marketing process.

Finally, if you're a teacher, you can use this book in several ways.

First, and most obviously, this book can be used as a stand-alone text for your courses that focus on contemporary advertising issues as well as advertising and society courses.

Second, you can include it as a supplement to the primary text you require for other advertising courses. I continue to use *Issues in American Advertising* in my Intro course.

You can design special one-day lectures around the issues in this book.

In my introductory advertising course, for instance, I may designate a class period for each topic. On that day, I show a related video or I organize the students into small groups to discuss the questions at the end of each chapter. To ensure engagement, I assign the questions so that students submit typewritten answers to the corresponding questions the day of discussion. Or I might ask my students to provide a brief report on their visits to the websites also listed at the end of each chapter.

## reichert@uga.edu

No matter who you are, I encourage you to contact me with any questions or concerns you might have regarding something you read in this book. You are certainly entitled to disagree with my conclusions. If so, let me know. Similarly, if you find an omission or error, please bring it to my attention. You can contact me at the College of Journalism & Mass Communication, University of Georgia, Athens, GA 30602, or by e-mail (reichert@uga.edu).

# Introduction
# Today and Tomorrow:
## Issues Confronting Advertisers

HAVE YOU SEEN THE "Beer Cannon"? If not, you should check it out on YouTube. Created by marketers for Milwaukee's Best Light, the cannon fires sand-filled cans of MBL at unmanly objects such as a bottle of wine, a flower bouquet, and china.

Word of the "Beer Cannon" has spread such that as of October 2006 the video had received over 3 million hits, which earned it a prominent story in *Advertising Age*. By all accounts, this video-gone-viral is a major success story.

### Instead of Expensive Media Buys

Instead of placing expensive media buys, MBL's agency generated high levels of awareness by simply producing a creative short and making it available for viewing on the web.

But, unfortunately for MBL, that wasn't the end of the story. The *Ad Age* article also described how, despite the video's recent popularity, sales of Milwaukee's Best were down 7.5% over the past year.

As Jeremy Mullman (2006, p. 3) observed, "…viral sensations don't always immediately translate into sensational sales."

Milwaukee's Best is not alone. All marketers are deciphering the roles of online and emerging media in brand promotion.

A similar challenge is how best to combine digital advertising with traditional delivery to maximize returns and stave off aggressive competition.

Despite the sales lull, MBL does appear to be on the right track. Instead of simply posting an intriguing video, the beer brand is now blending its videos into an integrated campaign that includes television commercials showing import beer drinkers being crushed by giant beer cans and other metrosexual-themed ads in which the protagonists (e.g., men driving scooters) also get crushed.

## Essential Issues and Trends

New media tools and media trends are essential to grasp, but future advertisers (and consumers) should be aware of other advertising practices as well.

Several of the most important and controversial issues in advertising are discussed in the following chapters.

In my opinion, awareness and understanding of each issue is crucial for anyone creating, studying, or even exposed to advertising.

# Advertising = A Big, Evolving Business

As we know, advertising is a substantial business.

We know it's big because we see it all around us. But few of us outside the ad biz know how truly big it is.

## Over $280 Billion

Consider, for example, that in 2007 over $280 billion was invested in US advertising. It is difficult to image that this enormous pile of money produces messages that fail to affect us in a variety of ways.

Sure, ads make us think differently about products. Ads also remind us of products and they imbue those products with personalities.

Our feelings, too, are affected by ads that make us laugh, that make us cringe, and that make us yearn for an imagined ideal.

But aside from affecting our hearts and minds, advertising has the power to take action. Ads prompt us to pick up the phone, to make an online transaction, or—though increasingly rare—they encourage us to visit a retail location to make a purchase in person.

Ads can also convince us to vote for a political candidate or a particular ballot initiative. Or, more frequently, they work to make us not vote for the other candidate. Several of the chapters in this book provide a good look into the effects, complexities, and issues surrounding advertising that tries to change how we feel, think, and behave.

### A Major Transition

Not only is advertising a big industry, but it's an industry that is in the midst of a major transition.

It goes without saying that traditional advertising is more sleek and visually arresting than ever before. But the traditional avenues of delivering those captivating messages are changing, partly as a result of new media influences and partly as the result of audiences whose attention is increasingly stretched from a dizzying array of media options.

"Reaching a target audience isn't as simple as cranking out a 30-second spot, and more and more marketers are reacting by shifting budgets into interactive media," notes *Ad Age* writer Matthew Creamer (2006, p. 71).

In addition, marketers are increasingly utilizing what Joe Cappo, the author of *The Future of Advertising*, refers to as below-the-line advertising. These alternative options include promotion, public relations, event marketing, and sponsorship. "Advertising has lost a considerable amount of influence to other forms of marketing communication," says Cappo (2003, p. 87).

Similar to the Milwaukee's Best effort described earlier, a host of online tools such as blogging and podcasting are allowing marketers to let consumers spread the brand's message—for free.

## Four General Sections

Overall, the chapters in this book are arranged into four general sections. Here is a sneak preview.

# 1. Law and Regulation: Puffery, Privacy, and Problematic Products

Today, there is increased scrutiny over both the claims and types of products that can be advertised. The chapters in this section tackle several regulatory issues and the controversy surrounding the promotion of products including prescription drugs, alcohol, and tobacco.

## "This Is the Best Book Ever!"

As an optimistic editor, I can only hope you find truth in this bold claim. As a realist, I realize you'll recognize the statement as a common claim in advertising. The statement is technically a form of "puffery." Deceptive and misleading ads are illegal, but "puffs"—subjective superiority claims—are allowable.

Ivan Preston, University of Wisconsin professor and the expert on puffery, describes the types of subjective claims in advertising and implications of their use.

## Privacy Please

Do you have a Google mail account?

Are you a member of an online social network?

Do you use a credit card?

If so, you and many consumers like yourself are trading away information that includes your identity and behavior patterns. When you use credit cards, shop online, or engage in online communities like Facebook and MySpace, the opportunity exists to track both your purchases and network of friends.

Jef Richards, a privacy expert and University of Texas at Austin professor, sounds the warning in his chapter as he describes how marketers collect our information and what they do with it. Richards touches on landmark legislation and tells us why, especially in today's era of online database-driven marketing, consumers may be divulging more than they should be.

## RX Drug Ads

Prescription drug ads are one of the fastest growing categories of consumer advertising. Large and small pharmaceutical companies are creating demand for their medications by going straight to consumers and encouraging them to ask for specific drugs when talking to physicians.

Although research is showing that drug ads can educate consumers about health issues and illness, some groups are more concerned with marketers tampering with the sacred relationship between patient and physician.

University of Georgia professor Wendy Macias and University of Texas at Austin's Liza Stavchansky Lewis outline both sides of this debate as well as other important issues surrounding prescription drug advertising.

## Alcohol Ads

Mass communication scholar Stacey Hust provides a detailed description of the issues surrounding the promotion of alcohol. Currently, there are no legal restrictions on beer, wine, and distilled spirits advertising, as media and alcohol industry groups work together to dictate when, what, and where ads are published or aired.

Despite efforts at self-regulation, policymakers are keeping a close eye on this category of advertising, especially with new research—some of it conducted by Hust—showing high levels of exposure among underage drinkers.

## Tobacco Ads

It's been a long time since cigarette ads appeared on television screens. They also are absent from outdoor displays, and images of frolicking smokers are slowly disappearing from ad pages in magazines. Despite this retreat, tobacco advertising and promotion budgets show consistent growth and recently topped over $15 billion.

Hye-Jin Paek, a persuasion researcher at the University of Georgia, tells us where that money is going as tobacco marketers continue to find ways to sell their products.

Paek also recounts the story of tobacco's historically large, influential, and innovative role in the development of consumer advertising, as well as legislation and antismoking efforts designed to curb the use of this potentially deadly product.

## Advertising to Kids

As rates of childhood obesity increase, so does scrutiny of the type and amount of ad appeals directed to kids.

Catharine Curran, a professor at the University of Massachusetts at Dartmouth, and Joel Brëe, a professor at the University of Caen, outline the major fault lines and criticisms of promotion directed to children. These issues include food advertising, Channel One, and the "pester power" of ads encouraging kids to needle their parents about specific products.

Additionally, the authors reveal the age children are able to differentiate advertising and programming, and when they become critical consumers of advertising messages.

# 2. Media: New-Media Tools, Product Placement, and Saturation

A second set of issues pertain to areas of advertising that are changing so fast (product placement and emerging media) that conventional wisdom is often dated.

How are advertisers adjusting and taking advantage of new technology and digital options in the face of increased scrutiny and diffidence to advertising? Section two describes the fluctuating media landscape and discusses how advertisers are reaching consumers with an increasingly wide assortment of tools.

## Emerging Media

There are many innovative tools that marketers are using to their advantage to reach customers. These tools include blogging, podcasting, producing viral videos, and sponsoring downloaded content that appears on mobile phones.

As previously mentioned, a media revolution is occurring and successful marketers are adapting. The old rules still have applicability but new rules are being forged. In this chapter I highlight some of these rules and describe media professionals who are recognized for their forward thinking and their ability not only to adapt, but to grasp, today's media marketplace.

## Product Placement

What if I told you that Milwaukee's Best paid me a hefty fee to mention its brands within the pages of this book? Actually, according to recommendations within the industry, I shouldn't disclose that information because product placement is less effective if its use is glaringly apparent.

Such practices are not unheard of. Several authors have been commissioned to write books about—or to mention within the pages of their books—specific brands. Increasingly, product placement is becoming a sizeable practice in the worlds of marketing and entertainment.

We see branded products making their way into television programming, movies, and video games. Product placement is growing as more marketers are looking for nontraditional approaches to reach consumers. The effects of this intrusion also are discussed in this chapter.

## Tapping Friend Networks and WOM

Whereas Jef Richards writes about privacy issues related to Facebook use, Jacqueline Lambiase, a professor in the Mayborn Institute of Journalism at the University of North Texas, describes in detail how marketers are tapping social networking sites to sell their wares. Each week, headlines herald new ad models for these sites that will target networks of consumers—even individuals—instead of the mass audiences of traditional media.

Just as important, Lambiase provides a foundation for understanding the "word-of-mouth" phenomenon that is gaining a new dimension with online communication. In addition to defining pertinent terms, she also describes the issues surrounding this viral, but highly credible, form of communication.

## "No More Media, Please!"

New-media tools. Digital technology. Enhanced connectivity.

Marketers are salivating at new opportunities to surround consumers with more effective selling messages.

"But enough is enough," say many consumers. They are reporting that they are tired of being harassed with promotional messages at every turn, often describing it as a cacophony of solicitation.

Jay Newell, a professor at Iowa State University, describes the current state of media saturation and tells us what it means for the future of advertising. In the process, Newell tells us how we've gotten into this mess and what can be done about it.

# 3. Representation and Recruitment: Women and Minorities

Historically, advertising images of women and minorities have either been absent or not representative of reality. Moreover, research indicates that these images (or lack thereof), can influence perceptions about the abilities of individuals within these groups.

The chapters in this section address these issues while both updating what we know and making it relevant. In addition, one chapter describes how several groups have found themselves excluded from the ad game.

## Representation of Women

How women are represented in advertising is an important issue. Since the 1960s feminists and media critics have rightfully complained that women are miscast in mainstream advertising.

In the early days, women shown in ads were limited to the home, traditional female occupations such as nurses or teachers, or as alluring objects. Critics of advertising pointed out that these images were contrary to the reality of women's lives and that such representations limited what society deems appropriate roles for women.

You might be surprised that little has changed over the years. Dove and Nike are offering enlightened images that touch women's lives, but research continues to show that distortion is still the norm.

Consider, for instance, that in 2005 women represented 40% of small business owners but a recent analysis revealed that only 3% of ads containing images of women were categorized as progressive.

In this chapter, I also describe some of the social effects of these miscast images.

## Representation of Minorities

In addition to women, minorities also are misrepresented in advertising. Historically, they were either absent or stereotyped in disparaging ways.

University of Alabama professor Caryl Cooper writes about these issues also while providing insights into representation today and in the future, especially as the marketplace becomes more diverse, and the current racial majority is soon to become a minority.

## Multicultural Opportunities

Not only are minorities underrepresented in ads, they also are absent behind the scenes. In fact, the large general-market agencies on Madison Avenue recently were rebuked for their low numbers of minority employees, especially in upper-level management positions.

Jami Fullerton at Oklahoma State University and Alice Kendrick at Southern Methodist University provide context for this issue and tell us the reasons for the low numbers. As important, the authors provide several solutions for improving the situation; some of those solutions coming from their work on the Most Promising Minority Students initiative.

Last, Fullerton and Kendrick describe the growth in multicultural agencies and media. Currently, these entities are offering more opportunities for America's minority applicants than major market agencies.

# 4. Content and Effects: Sex, Celebs, and America

The forth section contains chapters that address a variety of important issues from sex and celebrities to politics and social responsibility.

Through my own research, I've discovered that sexual ads, as well as the ads of political candidates, are not fully understood by most consumers (or voters). Two of the chapters in this section seek to reveal the nature, prevalence, and effects of these two types of ads.

Several other issues are included because they spark debate and have real-world implications.

## More Than Attention-Getting

As mentioned, sex in advertising is an issue that is widely recognized but shockingly misunderstood. Many people consider sex to be used simply as an attention getter. While technically true, the ability of sex to promote products is far more complex than just attracting attention.

For one, sexual appeals provide enticing reasons for buying: "Buy and use our brand and others will find you irresistible!"

Second, sexual appeals imbue brands with sexual personas that, for some products, consumers seek and are willing to pay for. These uses of sex, and other considerations, are discussed in this chapter.

## Celebrity Endorsement

Without a doubt we live in a celebrity-crazed culture. The popularity of fanzines and celebrity websites (e.g., TMZ.com) remind us of our insatiable fascination with the lives of entertainment and sports figures.

It's no surprise that advertisers tap into this fascination to promote their products.

University of Texas at Austin professor Marina Choi explores this relationship while also describing the pitfalls of celebrity endorsement—most notably, the criminal prosecution of NFL quarterback Michael Vick. Bad behavior is certainly a concern as more endorsers are hired to differentiate parity products.

## Political Advertising

Next, few people realize that a certain type of advertising—that which features candidates and initiatives—directly influences democracy in the United States.

These same people also fail to realize that political ads represent the bulk of all campaign expenditures.

For instance, 68% of all dollars spent on the 2004 presidential campaign went to advertising. Even more striking, political ads are the primary source of information in campaigns regarding the candidates and the issues, and people consider political advertising to be completely truthful.

## Selling America

Advertisers can brand products and services, but can they brand the USA? Or, can advertisers stem anti-American sentiment, especially when the audience is hostile?

In their second chapter in this book, Jami Fullerton and Alice Kendrick answer these questions by sharing insights from their book *Advertising's War on Terrorism: The Story of the U.S. State Department's Shared Values Initiative*.

In this chapter, the authors describe the Shared Values Initiative—essentially an ad campaign touting the best of America to the Muslin world.

Based on Fullerton and Kendrick's own research, the campaign was effective. Unfortunately, the SVI campaign was terminated after only a few months; not because of the campaign's outcomes but because of politics.

## Social Responsibility

"Green" is in. It seems as if everyone is aware of climate chaos and carbon footprints. In addition, marketers are scrambling to demonstrate that their brands are environmentally friendly. But green is not the only socially responsible issue that is gaining attention.

The role of social responsibility in advertising is discussed by Southern Methodist University's Glenn Griffin and University of Oregon's Deborah Morrison. They describe how advertisers are communicating their accountability and ability to be good stewards to consumers.

## Tugging on the Heart Strings

Yet another issue of increasing interest is the effectiveness of emotion in advertising. Advertising wasn't always as evoking emotion as it is today.

For example, early ads were primarily, if not exclusively, information-based. Merchants described in text-heavy ads what they had for sale, how much it cost, when it was available, and where it could be purchased.

Today, many of those elements are absent as commercials seek only to trigger emotions. Translating the effectiveness of emotions when it comes to motivating consumer behavior—and determining how to measure that effectiveness—represents an important initiative within the advertising industry.

# References and Recommended Reading

Cappo, Joe (2003). *The Future of Advertising*. New York: McGraw-Hill.

Creamer, Matthew (2006, October 9). ANA confab offers more than tee times. *Advertising Age*, p. 1, 71.

Garfield, Bob (2007, March 26). Chaos scenario 2.0: The post advertising age. *Advertising Age*, p. 1, 12-14.

Mullman, Jeremy (2006, October 9). What do they have to do, shoot it out of a cannon? Oh, wait… *Advertising Age*, p. 3, 74.

# Section 1

# Law and Regulation:
## Puffery, Privacy, and Problematic Products

# Puffery
## A Controversial Type of Ad Claim

### By Ivan L. Preston

PUFFERY IS THE LEGAL TERM for ad claims that state opinions rather than facts and that are excused from legal control even when the advertiser disbelieves them. The controversy created by such incongruity is the topic discussed here, with emphasis on the consequences it produces for advertisers, regulators, and consumers.

Before examining puffery directly, I'll identify two contexts in which it operates.

## The Mass Communication Context

*"...the best shave ever" is one of the most common forms of puffery.*

Students in programs originally founded in journalism typically study mass media information, including advertising and PR along with news. The programs are best known for training in creating and distributing messages, but also discuss effects on the audience. The latter, being human behavior, is a branch of psychology. Many faculty, including myself, are especially interested in consumers' perception behavior—what people see a news story or ad to be telling them.

A key understanding is that the sender cannot fully control that. Expose 100 people to a message and you almost always find two or more messages actually communicated. Theoretically, every single one of the hundred may see content that none of the other 99 do.

That's because people see both explicit and implied messages. When we see an ad saying words it actually states, that's an explicit message. When we see words not actually stated, that's an implied message, an implication. What's implied may differ because we each interpret the explicit content to create perceptions of additional content that exist only in our separate heads.

It's human nature to feel that everyone else saw exactly what I saw. Actually, though, the only good way to know what others saw is to obtain their own statement of it. Looking just at the ad or just into your own head doesn't do it.

## The Legal Context—Deceptive Claims

Given the above, I was pleased to learn that the legal and self-regulators define deceptive claims exactly so (Preston, 1989). As a researcher, though, I questioned their method of identifying consumer perceptions, and by luck I got a chance to act on that when the chief regulator, the Federal Trade Commission, asked me in 1971 to be an expert witness in a case.

In prosecutions, the FTC charges that what consumers are led to see claimed about a product or service is contrary to the truth. So they must present evidence about the features or benefits consumers see claimed, which was what my role involved, along with evidence about the actual features or benefits. If there is a discrepancy between the claim and the reality, the claim is ruled deceptive and the advertiser must stop saying it either explicitly or impliedly.

I was concerned that expert opinion about perceptions is less direct and so less good than getting reports directly from consumers via surveys. The regulators had never created a survey for a case, but they accepted my proposal to do one, and the evidence played an important role. Surveys soon became regular practice, and are still considered the best evidence of what consumers see a message saying.

I also discovered, though, that the regulators were doing something different, and very strange, with puffery.

## Defining Puffery

In regulation it's called puffery or puffs, but evaluations or opinions is what it is. In contrast to facts, which are about products, what they are or do or look like, puffery is about their sellers' opinions of the appropriate evaluations consumers should give their products. Naturally such evaluations are always positive, often exaggeratedly so.

1: "Best." The strongest puff of course is "best," which means no competitor equals you. Nestlé says it makes the very best chocolate; Gillette is the best a man can get; Goodyear has the best tires in the world. Other ways of saying best include terms such as most comfortable, longest lasting, tastiest—anything that says you're superior to all others on some feature or overall.

2: "Best Possible." Nothing cleans stains better than Clorox. This is also a claim to be at the top, except that it allows for others to be equally good. It's a clever claim because research shows many consumers think it means better than all others.

3: "Better." You are better than another, or better than many, or just better. Advil works better. It is not an explicit claim to be superior to all others, though it may imply that. It's often used when competing mainly against just one other brand.

4: "Specially Good." This involves strong statements such as great. Weber says its barbecue grill is great outdoors. Coty calls its perfume extraordinary. Many products claim to be wonderful or fantastic. Bayer aspirin works wonders. Though not saying so explicitly, such claims may imply best or better.

pickles. process, crunchy.

THE WORLD'S MOST EXCELLENT PICKLE.

©2007 Kraft Foods

*"Excellent" pickles is a variation of the "best" category of puffs.*

5:  "Good." This is just plain good. You're in good hands with Allstate. Campbell's Soup is M'm M'm good. These are weaker, lower on the scale, but they are still opinions that express positive valuations.

The headline in this Ritz ad is an example of a "subjective" claim.

6: "Subjective Claims." These use words that are not explicitly evaluative, but consumers are welcome to take them as valuations. A sports network refers to itself as Sports Heaven. A candy maker says there's a smile in every Hershey Bar. Various cars are sexy or the sexiest.

## Regulatory Treatment of Puffery

Only with explicit fact claims do regulators gather evidence to find if there is additional content that consumers see being implied. For puffery they begin with identifying explicit claims that are not factual but rather are words or phrases of evaluation. Then—this is the strange part—rather than examining consumer perceptions of that, they apply a very old legal decision that such words, puffery, are perceived by consumers as meaningless.

The law assumes that such opinions, evaluations, say nothing factual, including nothing implied, and thus state no claim. If there is no claim, there is nothing about which the question of deception can be asked, and so puffery cannot be deceptive. The result is that advertisers have a very strong puffery defense against charges of deception.

## A Counter-Argument Involving Evidence of Consumer Perceptions

Because they don't, as with explicit and implied fact claims, look at consumers or anywhere else for evidence on how puffs are perceived, regulators may not always be correct in saying consumers never take puffery as making fact claims. They merely assume that conclusion by relying on a precedent that is very old and solidly established but also outdated and just wrong for today's marketplace.

The first legal decision supporting the treatment of claims of evaluation came in England in 1602. A man bought an investment, relying on the seller's evaluation, and then sued for being deceived by that. He lost, and the principle created was that people should make and rely on their own evaluations and avoid reliance on anyone else's. That was fine in 1602, but while over 400 years later we have the same rule, we do not buy and sell under the same conditions.

Various developments contradict the idea that consumers must use only their own opinion. In earlier times people bought things they were familiar with, from people who lived in the same place, and presumably all parties were experts. That recognition of buyers being equal to sellers prompted the law to require that they must be. The prevailing belief became that only you can create your evaluation of something. You can't ask others about it, because it's your statement about you, and only you know about you.

Today's marketplace, however, typically no longer involves equal parties, but rather has expert makers/sellers and inexpert consumers. Since opinions better than your own are available, why shouldn't you protest the idea of relying only on your own? Certainly for complex items such as cars, computers, and cell phones, we must rely on others. Some experts we can use are third parties such as *Consumer Reports*, but the parties we most need to rely on and trust are the sellers. That makes the idea that we must distrust their puffery seem inappropriate; the law is going against what we need.

Of course there are opinions about personal tastes; I tell you I prefer Coke, and you say you like Pepsi better. I call those taste puffs, and since, concerning mine, I am not just the most expert but the only expert, there is no sense in relying on anyone else. However, puffs in advertising typically do not operate that way and so they don't contradict the conclusion of a major shift from equality to inequality over the 400 years.

Another change is what we've learned about people's responses. The field of psychology began only in the 1800s, and from it we now know an opinion usually isn't just an opinion, because we can see any opinion to imply a fact. Don't opinions typically imply at least the fact that their speakers believe them and so have a factual basis for their belief?

Puffery typically states no factual basis explicitly. Rather than saying "Our brand is best because...," followed by the basis, it usually just says "Our brand is the best." And when I see no basis given, I generally believe there is none available, because otherwise the advertiser would use it. Factual support for a puff has more persuasion, more selling power than the puff.

If you have the factual support, you may not even need the puff. State factually that your brand performs in some way that no other brand does, and you'll imply that it's better or best. Implying could actually be more effective, because consumers are creating the claim in their own minds rather than seeing you trying to create it for them.

Of course, if consumers see puffery with no accompanying facts, and take it to claim impliedly to be supported by fact, that sometimes may be false. Those consumers could be deceived and potentially harmed by relying on that.

The most fuel-efficient auto company in America.

EnviroNMeNTology

HONDA
The Power of Dreams

*Unlike puffs, the headline in this Honda ad is an "objective" claim supported by evidence in small print at the bottom.*

So a variety of results is possible. Some puffs will prompt consumers to see a false implication, and the consumers will reject it, leaving no deception or harm. Other times they will see an implication of support that is true, and again there's no problem. Some puffs will be seen by consumers to imply nothing factual and those puffs could appropriately be treated by the traditional rule. You can see from the possibilities that puffs should not be pre-judged.

The six types of puffery are relevant here because I think testing would show that the strongest puffs, especially number one, are most likely to prompt false perceptions. Those at the bottom are least likely. Examples such as the smile in the candy bar seem more likely to be seen as fanciful or joking rather than serious. But still, some of number six might deceive and some of number one might not. Results can vary because ads and consumers vary so much.

Obviously, then, I don't call all puffs deceptive; I say only that the legal and self-regulators are wrong in assuming they are all not deceptive. Communication theory and research show that people get different messages, and all I add is that the same should be shown with puffery. There is some research on messages that supports my point, and not any that opposes it. But the regulators keep on saying every puff means the same thing to every consumer. No evidence; ancient precedent; weak argument!

The argument is weak by being circular, which is saying something is A because it's B but also it's B because it's A, which proves nothing about whether either A or B is true. The regulators say a claim that's meaningless to consumers is puffery, which makes you think they get evidence of meaninglessness. But what they actually do goes oppositely: they look only at the explicit wording, not any response to it. They then say that since it's explicitly evaluative it must be meaningless, which is often wrong. Finally, they use illogical circularity to conclude that since the evaluative claim is meaningless it must be puffery.

Given their prejudging, the regulators simply don't know what they're talking about. By ignoring evidence on consumer response they assure their assumption of meaninglessness will never be contradicted. It's curious that they don't have the same standard of verification for themselves that they routinely impose on advertisers.

Deciding on facts by predetermined assumption supposedly ended when science began. Suppose you claimed to be an astronomer, and you wrote about stars while never looking at any. We call such people astrologers, not astronomers. They say they read your future from the stars, but they just make it up. So I think the regulators are the astrologers of puffery. As a result, puffery can be factually false yet legal. It can be fraudulent, meaning deliberately, knowingly false, which means the speaker knows consumers may rely on the claim and be hurt. Fraud is thought especially serious in most areas of law, but not here.

## Reasons Why the Puffery Rule Is Still With Us

There are reasons, not necessarily good ones, for why the puffery rule lives on despite these problems. One is because the change from equality to inequality of buyers happened very slowly over the centuries. That enables sellers to ignore that it has happened, and to think of puffing as something like a birthright, a privilege they've always had and can't imagine anyone removing.

Another reason is that advertisers seem to have a strong desire to get all the freedom of speech they can. Yes, we all feel that way, but this strikes me as an obsession in the sense that they seem to want freedom simply for its own sake rather than any real need. Consider that, if the puffery rule were removed, advertisers and marketers would all be as equal with each other as they were before. Nobody would get an advantage. But I never see them discussing that; they just want the greatest freedom anyway.

Perhaps that attitude comes from the fact that deception is prohibited only in commercial speech, which involves exchanging goods or services for money. The greater portion of speech directed to the public is noncommercial, even when in ads. Political candidates run many ads, of which quite a few are shown to contain lies, but there's no regulation of that as deceptive. Commercial speakers, therefore, may feel unfairly singled out as the only ones restrained in this way.

A third reason is that regulators are most likely to make changes when they get objections, and advertisers are the biggest source of those they

No other blush looks more natural.
Or comes in such a clever package.

New Mineral Sheers™ Blush.

*The headline for this blush contains two "best" puffs.*

get. But advertisers have no objection to the puffery rule, so the regulators feel scant pressure to change it. On the other hand, advertisers become a huge source of objection whenever anyone wants to eliminate or narrow the puffery rule. A few years ago lawyers writing changes in the Uniform Commercial Code decided to place the burden on the advertiser to show a claim is puffery, rather than keeping it on the consumer to show it's not puffery. Lobbyists from advertising's national organizations rushed to those meetings and complained loudly until the lawyers gave in and cancelled the change.

## Should Advertisers Want to Consider Eliminating the Rule?

So advertisers retain the puffing privilege, but let's examine why they want it so badly. Again, I think it's partly just because they can. But also many of them must think puffery works. They ignore the regulatory position that it's factually meaningless and thus doesn't work. They appreciate that the latter is what makes puffery permissible, but, if advertisers actually believed that, they would never use it. Isn't it an odd combination of things? Puffery is legal because it doesn't work, but it's used because it does. Advertisers are smart people, and better informed about consumer response than regulators are, and as a result they win on both sides of the argument.

However, to say "they win" means only that they keep the right to puff. But let's see what they might be losing from using it. The Gallup Poll does mostly political polling, but every year asks people to rate "the honesty and ethical standards of people in [various] fields." Each field is rated as very high, high, average, low, or very low. The rankings are determined by the combined percentage of very high plus high. Advertising gets those ratings only around 10 percent of the time. The number of fields varies from year to year, but whatever the number, ad people usually rank ahead only of car salesmen (Gallup, 2007).

Gallup does not ask people why they rate as they do, but it's reasonable to think puffery is involved. Certainly the presence of the rule gives consumers an objective basis for thinking ads are often dishonest. False factual

23

claims could also be a reason, but those are subject to being removed by regulation and lasting only briefly, while puffery goes on forever.

Because of puffery, when ad people go into their offices they walk into a culture that permits and thus encourages lying. That doesn't mean they all lie, but when they ask lawmakers to help them keep the rule, they certainly indicate that they want to retain the opportunity. Such actions make it impossible to claim they're doing all they can to keep falsity out of their work. In fact, they're doing all they can to keep that possibility alive.

The stakes seem even higher when you consider that using false puffs, which are relatively small lies, may lead sellers to try greater and more harmful ones, which means the topic is not just puffery but potentially also other deceptions, which the regulators detect and prosecute numerous times every year. It's easier to slide into more serious lying when you start from the level of puffery than from the higher standard of tolerating no falsity at all. That makes the puffery rule way more powerful and significant than you might otherwise think.

Another way to see how puffery can hurt advertisers lies in how they see meaninglessness as a defense. They say: we weren't being false; our claim was merely meaningless, and therefore harmless. Apparently they believe that when consumers treat it as meaningless, everything is OK. I think that's not accurate, because consumers want and need information.

We could agree that being meaningless, which means noninformative, is better than being meaningful and false, which means misinformative. However, switching to being noninformative rather than misinformative only raises claims from being harmfully false to the higher level of being merely worthless. Either way consumers are not getting the information they need. So while meaninglessness may work as a legal defense, it hurts consumer reaction by amounting to a public demonstration of unwillingness to be informative, not a positive thing for advertisers.

Another aspect is that advertising becomes less effective when consumers become more skeptical or outright distrustful of it, and the advertisers themselves provoke that. It's odd to see how they work against themselves that way. Yes, there's a good side to skepticism, with sellers, regulators, and even consumer advocates arguing that consumers should watch out. Remember the phrase "caveat emptor," which means "Let the buyer beware." There seems to be less tendency, however, to acknowledge any disadvantage to skepticism, such as making shopping unsatisfactory to people even when they don't get fooled. In the long run an industry position that consumer skepticism is all that's needed to take care of problems of deceptiveness may have a net negative effect.

## What I Wish the Law Would Do

I feel the law should treat puffery just as it treats fact claims. That means finding out what claims mean to consumers, both explicitly and impliedly, and finding whether any of that is factual and so can be examined for truth or falsity, and finding out whether any of that is false, and prohibiting that falsity.

That's not as bad as it sounds because it means puffery is an issue only when deception is, and deception is an issue only when there's a claim. Not all ad content is a claim. A lot of it is intended only to get attention so consumers will stay with the ad long enough to see the claim. Other ad content shows sheer enthusiasm, such as appeals to action like, "Look at this deal," or, "You should try our brand." Such statements may just dramatize the product without saying anything factual about what it's made of, or what it does, or what benefit it gives. Remember: no claim, no problem.

The only puffery I would prohibit is the kind that has no supporting facts and thus give the speaker no basis for believing it, and especially that for which facts exist that give the speaker a basis for disbelieving it. I think a lot of it is that way, but when it's factually supported and true it should have none of the negative results I've discussed. Yes, I've also criticized

*Is the headline in this Sephora ad an "opinion" claim? If so, what type?*

25

puffery that is merely meaningless and noninformative, and have suggested that regulators and advertisers might discourage that. Concededly, though, being meaningless is not against the law.

I also recommend expressing concern for those advertisers that seem to be ignored because the law restricts its consideration of puffery's consequences to only two groups: advertisers who puff and consumers. Why not also consider those advertisers who are puffed against! Puffs are comparisons, and when they raise the puffer higher on the scale, they hurt competitors by pushing them down the scale. The latter are just as much part of the industry, yet puffery law doesn't acknowledge them.

A loan company, IOwn, claimed to have the "best loans on the web." A competitor, E-Loan, asked the self-regulators to stop that, because it felt hurt by consumers thinking IOwn's loans had features no one else offered. The case record found IOwn unable to identify any such thing, thus demonstrating that its puff was impliedly false. E-Loan was being pushed down the scale unfairly, but the self-regulators, without asking consumers, said it was only puffery that meant nothing to anyone.

I called the owner of E-Loan, and he was really angry. He felt cheated to be called less good when he knew he was not less good. And he was very negative toward the self-regulator which presumably was conducting its business in order to help advertisers. When a policy helps one company only by hurting another, what good is that for the total group? And if multiple competitors are hurt, the ratio of disservice to service increases.

Further, aside from regulatory actions, advertisers and their national organizations might disavow puffery on their own as a matter of ethics. The Gallup evidence about honesty and ethics suggests that this excellent field might use its own initiative to make itself even more effective.

## A Final Point

The late Bill Arens, author of a much-used ad text, said this: "Using puffery means you're creatively lazy; you haven't tried hard enough to find claims of real worth. You can make yourself look better than that."

## Questions and An Exercise

1.   How many puffs can you find in one magazine or one hour of television?

2.   Consider the following statements. Then form your opinion about each statement, consider how often each may happen, and decide what you think about being a puffer.
     a.   If your puffery has factual support, you don't need it.
     b.   If your puffery has no support and consumers rely on it and are harmed, they will think more negatively of you and of advertising in general.
     c.   If your puffery has no support and consumers reject it, they will think more negatively of you and of advertising in general.

3.   Write some ad copy that features a puff. Then rewrite it to feature fact claims instead. (You may have to assume some facts, but perhaps you can find a real situation for which you know the facts.)

## References and Recommended Readings

I am author of these items except one. I draw from the first two so much that I've omitted the dozens of citations that could be given. The third item and the Web site item are cited in the text.

Preston, I. L. (1998). Puffery and other 'loophole' claims: How the law's 'Don't Ask, Don't Tell' policy condones fraudulent falsity in advertising. *Journal of Law and Commerce*, 18 (Fall), 49-114.

Preston, I. L. (1996). *The great American blow-up: Puffery in advertising and selling* (revised edition). Madison, WI: University of Wisconsin Press.

Preston, I. L. (1989). The FTC's identification of implications as constituting deceptive advertising. *University of Cincinnati Law Review*, 57 (4), 1243-1310.

Gallup (2007). *Honesty/Ethics in Professions*. Retrieved May 9, 2007, from: http://www.galluppoll.com/content/default.aspx?ci=1654

# Shhhhh..., That's Private!
## How Advertisers Today Can Leave You Feeling Exposed

## by Jef I. Richards

THINK THAT PRIVACY ISSUES DON'T AFFECT YOU? What if you found out that you were paying full price for clothing purchased online while your best friend was buying clothes on the same site for half the price? Or imagine that your credit card company was selling detailed information about your purchases to other companies: what you bought, how often you bought it, and how much you spent. These examples involving privacy are not fiction but reality for millions of people whether they realize it or not. Usually people have no idea that advertisers are monitoring their private information so they can reach you with more effective ads. In this chapter I want you to see how intimately these advertisers know you, and I hope that you'll think about just how far they should go in their attempts to seduce you.

## What is Privacy?

Most of us learn about privacy as young children, about the same time we are learning the merits of modesty. Our concept of privacy then is all about our body and bodily functions. But by the time we reach our teens, privacy extends to "secrets" between friends and emotions we would prefer to hide from others. Once we reach adulthood, we begin to distinguish between our professional lives and our "private" lives, alluding to the desire to leave work at the office, away from home and family. By that time we also have bank accounts and passwords that are extremely valuable, *only* because they are unknown by others. Without privacy our lives would be chaos, or disaster, not to mention embarrassing.

For most of those conceptions of privacy, what we try to keep private is information, whether it is information about our bank accounts, our marital problems, or the appearance of our unclothed bodies. And information is the coin of the advertising realm. The more sellers know about a prospective customer, the more effective their sales pitches can be. And the customer may even want a seller to know certain facts. If I have a disease, I want the pharmacist to know about it so she can sell me the proper medication. I might not, though, want my insurance company to have that information, because it might choose to raise my rates or even cancel my health coverage. I want control over those "private" facts. Therein lies the problem. We have very little control over, or legal protection of, those facts.

## The "Rights" of Privacy

In the United States, the Constitution defines our personal rights, like the right of free speech, but nowhere in that document is privacy mentioned. Well, back in 1890 two influential lawyers, Samuel Warren and Louis Brandeis, made a convincing legal argument that people have a right to be left alone. They were, in effect, the inventors of the "right to privacy." In the years that followed, the courts picked up the Warren & Brandeis ideas and found reasons to protect certain rights associated with privacy. It no doubt helped that Brandeis subsequently became a Justice of the Supreme Court, and voiced some of his thoughts about privacy in that role. In fact, in *Olmstead v. United States* (1928), the nation's first wiretapping case, Brandeis argued that government had discovered new technologies for spying on its citizens. He feared what government might do if psychiatric sciences ever allowed it to read minds or emotions.

Since that time privacy has been expanded to encompass more than simply being left alone. As Lansing and Halter (2003) point out, at least four separate categories of privacy are well-established legal issues. First, growing out of that "right to be left alone" is the idea that people have a right to prevent unreasonable *intrusion* upon their seclusion. Secretly tapping your telephone, searching your car, and getting copies of your medical records are good examples of how this right can be violated. Some modern versions of intrusion used by many advertisers are junk mail, e-mail spam, telemarketing, and pop-up Internet ads.

Second is the right to prevent *appropriation* of your name or likeness. If an advertiser puts your picture in an ad or suggests you endorsed their product without your permission, they would be violating your privacy through appropriation. Celebrities often deal with this right when advertisers try to use the image of a famous person in their promotional efforts.

Third is the right to prevent publishing of *private facts* about your life. If a photographer were to take pictures of you sunbathing nude in your backyard and publish them in the local newspaper, that probably would be an invasion of your privacy. Yes, this actually happens to some celebrities, but they've made themselves into "public figures," so it may not be reasonable for them to expect the same amount of privacy as you. Perhaps a more realistic concern for you is all of the information advertisers do gather about your life—where you shop, what you buy, how much you spend, where you bank—and pass on to others. This is becoming a major concern, and one that is discussed at greater length in the following pages.

The fourth type of privacy is one that may not immediately seem like "privacy" at all. It is the right not to have your name or likeness published in a *false light*. In this instance, for example, your picture and a story about you appear in a newspaper. Everything in the story is accurate, but your picture appears next to a headline for another story about a criminal being caught, and the juxtaposition of your picture to the headline makes readers think that you were the criminal. This probably is the least common problem in privacy.

The extent to which each of those four privacy rights is legally enforceable varies from state to state and country to country, but the ideas behind them are found in several specific rights granted by statutes in the US. A federal law prohibiting government from tapping your telephone is clearly derived from the thinking behind the first right mentioned above, the intrusion right. That law, in fact, was one of the first statutes in the US to specifically deal with privacy rights.

Most privacy-related statutes have been passed since 1970, and they form a legal patchwork. Today we have laws preventing the government from digging through our bank records, while protecting us from "junk" faxes, SPAM, and electronic surveillance, for example, but each law is separate and in no way related to the other. There is a law that guards the privacy of student records (known as FERPA), another that protects your medical records (HIPAA), and one that provides some assurance that your financial records are kept secret (Gramm-Leach-Bliley). There also is one dedicated to protecting children (COPPA).

At the same time we now have laws that allow government to tap your telephone and intercept your electronic communications if officials think you might be a terrorist. In other words, this is a complicated and sometimes confusing area of law (Curran & Richards, 2004a). It is, however, an area of growing concern among consumers and, therefore, among advertising professionals.

## "They" Know Who You Are and What You're Doing

Recently, the Internet search engine company Google announced plans to buy the leading online advertising company, DoubleClick, for $3.1 billion. This set off alarm bells at the Federal Trade Commission (FTC), which quickly began a preliminary investigation based on antitrust law. The real concern, though, was not a typical antitrust issue, but the collecting and compiling of information about you and your neighbors.

Google tracks and records users' search histories. If you happened to search for "mountain bikes," or "chrome dishwasher," or "sex with mutant chickens," Google made a note of it. The amount of data on what people search, when they search, search trends, and much, much, more are all recorded. DoubleClick is a leader in delivering display ads to a huge variety of websites, and it also is compiling data on what websites people actually visit. The privacy fears arise from the fact that combining these two collections would give Google an unparalleled mountain of information about consumers' Internet activities (Lohr, 2007). This one company could know what you want and where you go in that virtual world. It would know a lot about you, and much of that you might prefer no company knew.

Of course, Google does not know your name. That is, unless you've registered for its Gmail service. Or Google Calendar. Or Google Desktop. Or Google Earth. Or some other service offered by the company. Oh, and not long ago Google bought YouTube, so if you registered there it knows your name and e-mail address and what sort of videos you like to watch. So maybe Google does know who you are, after all. And it knows a lot of your kinky personal interests. Then, an even bigger concern is that Google might share some of this information with its "marketing partners."

Suppose Google then shares your personal file with Amazon, which knows your book and movie buying habits. After all, marketing partnerships like this happen all the time. Then again, Google might share that information with eBay, which also owns PayPal, so all of your auction habits, and even your banking information, might be added to the pile of data already held about you. Or it could share with MasterCard. The possible combinations of data are endless. And Google is far from the only company doing this. Almost everyone is doing it.

Many years ago American Express was said to keep 410 attributes regarding each one of its customers, updated weekly (Jones, 1991). That is just a single company, and that was before the Internet made it so easy to collect information about consumers. The FTC did a study in 2000 that found nearly 100% of commercial websites collect this sort of information (Henderson, 2005).

Direct marketing companies have kept extensive databases of such information for decades so they can more efficiently target consumers with direct mail and other selective media. But today advertisers, ad agencies, media companies, and virtually everybody involved in the advertising process seems to have a computer full of information about thousands, or even millions, of consumers. And Google isn't the only big company with immense amounts of information. Yahoo and Microsoft, for example, are trying to compete with Google to be the biggest in data collection (Freedman, 2006).

If you go on the Internet with any regularity at all, you probably have run into a website that asks you to register, giving several pieces of important information about yourself. And if you buy something on the website, you add a lot more information to what that company already knows about you. Even your credit card number. Frankly, any advertiser who doesn't try to gather information about consumers is a fool. That information is valuable. It helps the advertiser to know your needs and to persuade you that a given product will serve those needs.

That information can help you, too, by assisting the advertiser in providing the information you really want and not information that wastes your time. If you go to the Amazon website and generally want to look for rock music, you don't want to wade through page after page of information about cooking utensils and romance novels. Since you've let Amazon know your interests, when you turn to that website it generally makes recommendations about new rock albums and other things that are likely to interest you. And if you get e-mail newsletters from an advertiser, by letting them know something about you, you're less likely to get news about items that don't interest you.

So providing Amazon with information can be of direct benefit to you. And signing up for one of those frequent-shopper cards at your neighborhood grocery can qualify you for a lower price on many of the products you buy at the store. But once you've given that information to the advertiser, it's out of your control.

*Web sites like Amazon.com offer suggestions based on past behavior.*

## Who Is in Control?

Consumers usually cede control of their private information once they hand it to the advertiser. The advertiser may use it to target you with a barrage of e-mails, or send junk mail to your house, or may even sell it to other companies. If they have your cell phone number, you may start getting text messages. And in the service of fighting terrorism, the government, too, has begun demanding access to that private information (Mohammed & O'Hara, 2006).

Technology is improving, too. Imagine using your cell phone to take a picture of a friend, then sending it to all of your other friends. Now suppose the computer in your phone is able to identify the person in that picture based on your contact list in the phone and the location where you take the photo. Oh, yes, the phone has a GPS unit built-in, so it knows precisely where you are, within a few feet. If your phone service is, for example, AT&T, that company not only knows to whom you sent the photo, but knows who you are with and where you are. So, with its records showing that both of you are coffee drinkers and that you're near a Starbucks, with which the phone company has a marketing arrangement, it instantly sends you a coupon for a free Cappuccino via text message. This may soon be reality (Freedman, 2006).

A new technology that already exists is Radio Frequency Identification (RFID). These are tiny little chips, some as small as a grain of rice, that carry information that can be accessed via radiowaves from several yards away. An RFID with all your demographic information and other personal data might be placed in that free key fob you received from your favorite department store, or in the "membership" card from a video rental store. Sensors then might "read" that information when you pass a store or a kiosk, causing an electronic billboard in front of you to say something like, "Hi, Jef. Have I got a deal for you! You just passed Sam's Video Rental, and Sam has a special on adult videos." You may have seen something like this in some recent science fiction movies, like *Minority Report*. Guess what! It's not science fiction.

Well, besides the fact that you don't know exactly how much or what information is being collected about you, or how it will be used by the advertiser, there is the concern that it might be used by someone you'd rather not have it. Even beyond the fact that the advertiser might give it to virtually anyone, what if a thief is able to scan your RFID tag simply by walking past you, is able to decrypt it, and uses it to steal your identity?

You might be a private person who doesn't like anyone to have personal information, or you could be an open book, caring little about what people know about your private life. Regardless, you should be concerned about the sheer volume of data, the potentially dangerous nature of some of it, and the lack of control surrounding it. It is as if you invited anyone who wants to rummage through your desk and underwear drawers. And if these companies discover that you normally don't shop for bargains but pay full price, there is nothing to keep them from having their web page show you a higher price than it shows someone else (Henderson, 2005). So the next question is how to avoid this happening to you. Well, it depends whether you need to opt-in or opt-out of this process.

## The Opt-In and Opt-Out Debate

There are two basic approaches to collecting personal information when a consumer visits a website. One approach is for the website to ask your permission to use that information for other purposes. For example, it may ask you to click on a box next to a statement like, "Yes, I would like to receive e-mail offers from other companies." This is known as the "opt-in" approach, since you must take some action to allow your information to be entered into this pool of shared data. The opt-in approach is one aspect of what's commonly called "permission marketing"—you've given the sponsor permission to share your information.

The more common method is just the opposite. Instead of the default being that your information will *not* be shared or used in other ways unless you specifically give permission, the "opt-out" approach assumes the advertisers *do* have your permission to use your information in any way they please unless you take action to withdraw that permission. In 2002 one of the big telephone companies sent out letters to about two million customers in Arizona telling them that they had 30 days to opt-out, then the company would start sharing phone bill information with other companies (Curran & Richards, 2004b). Usually businesses don't give you 30 days advance notice.

Many advertisers argue that opt-out is the cheapest, most efficient, approach and that it allows them to provide more and better service to consumers. So they have fought any attempt to legally force them to switch to the opt-in alternative. Of course, the reality is that the opt-out method results in the advertisers having more consumer information to use and sell, since opt-in requires the consumer to take some action. And the opt-out system presents obstacles for any consumer who does object to the information being open to the world.

One problem is that companies' privacy policies, explaining what they will and won't do with your private information, often are published on

Store Locator | About Us | Track My Order | Shipping | Returns | Help
Use of this site signifies your acceptance of Toys"R"Us Website Terms and Conditions and Privacy Policy.

*Notice the small "Privacy Policy" link at the bottom of this web page.*

their websites but frequently consist of pages of fine-print legal language. Chances are slim that a consumer will read it, let alone understand it. In fact, many consumers don't even find those pages.

But an even bigger problem is that your information can be shared with other companies instantly, meaning that by the time you are able to opt-out, the horse is already out of the barn. Then you need to go to all of those companies, separately, and opt-out from their use of your information. Of course, this is not easy because you probably will have a hard time finding out what companies have received your information. And, of course, by the time you find them, those companies may have shared your info with yet other companies (Henderson, 2005). But since this information can be collected in so many, often surreptitious ways, you may not even know the company has been collecting information in many cases. The so-called *spyware*, which invades a home computer to track users and report back to its owner, is but one example of this problem.

To date there is no law requiring companies to use one approach or the other. Since opt-out is far more attractive to advertisers, this tends to be the most common choice. The result, of course, is that many businesses at this very moment know who you are, your address, your phone number, your likes and dislikes, and a whole lot more, including things your best friends probably don't know.

## Conclusion

Do privacy issues affect you? At this very moment advertisers hold complete dossiers on you. They want to be your friend, and they are trying to learn all of your likes and dislikes so they can talk to you like a friend. On the plus side, the more they know you, the less annoying advertising becomes. They stop showing you ads for products you don't want and they stop telling you about one product feature when your interest is in another feature. And they start telling you about new products that do interest you. Imagine a world where advertising is actually interesting!

Then again, do you really want the guy at Bubba's Muffler and Bait Shop to know your preferences in underwear, or the fact that you're dating more than one person at the same time? There may come a time when no one will ever need to hire a private investigator, they'll simply go online to an information broker and buy all manner of private details about you.

Privacy, then, involves a trade-off. If you want it, you've got to give up a lot of convenience and put up with more annoying ads. If you really prefer the convenience, though, say goodbye to privacy. The real problem at this point is that it's not you who makes the decision whether or not you want that privacy. Because there are few laws, this is decided by the advertisers who stand to reap great profits from your secrets.

## Questions

1.      How important is the right of privacy? How dangerous are violations of privacy? Do you care about your own privacy?

2.      Should there be legal limitations on how much, and what, information advertisers can collect about consumers? What should those limits be?

3.      Should there be limits on how long advertisers can keep information about consumers? Does it depend on the type of information?

4.      Which makes the most sense, the opt-in or opt-out approach? Why?

5.      Should children be treated differently? If so, how?

6.      What is the difference between the sorts of information-gathering now conducted by advertisers, and the sort of surveillance done by a private detective? Would your opinion about such information-gathering be different if you knew it was the government gathering information on you?

# References and Recommended Reading

Curran, Catharine M., and Jef I. Richards (2004a). The complex web of regulation in the US: The case of privacy. *International Journal of Electronic Business*, 2 (2), 205-226.

Curran, Catharine M., and Jef I. Richards (2004b). Public privacy and politics. *Journal of Consumer Marketing*, 21 (1), 7-9.

Freedman, David H. (2006, April 3). Why privacy won't matter. *Newsweek*.

Henderson, Bethany Rubin (2005). Opt in or opt out: Are these the only options? *Journal of Internet Law*, 8 (11), 1.

Jones, Mary Gardiner (1991). Privacy: A significant marketing issue for the 1990s. *Journal of Public Policy & Marketing*, 10 (1), 133-148.

Lansing, Paul, and Mark D. Halter (2003). Internet advertising and right to privacy issues. *University of Detroit Mercy Law Review*, 80, 181-200.

Lohr, Steve (2007, May 29). Google deal said to bring US scrutiny. *New York Times*, 1.

Mohammed, Arshad, and Terence O'Hara (2006, May 13). NSA program further blurs line on privacy. *Washington Post*, D01.

## Online Resources

The following websites—both involving child audiences—illustrate the sort of privacy policies companies use today. The sites also show how lengthy these policies can be.

**Kellogg's Online Privacy Policy**
http://www.kelloggcompany.com/privacy.aspx

**Walt Disney Internet Group Privacy Policy**
http://disney.go.com/corporate/privacy/pp_wdig.html

The following two websites contain a lot of additional information related to privacy.

**Privacy Rights Clearinghouse**
http://www.privacyrights.org/

**Electronic Privacy Information Center**
http://www.epic.org/privacy/

# Sex, Drugs, and the Evening News:
## DTC (Direct-to-Consumer) Pharmaceutical Drug Advertising

## By Wendy Macias and Liza Stavchansky Lewis

THESE DAYS IT IS HARD TO MISS a direct-to-consumer (DTC) pharmaceutical drug advertisement. For many people, the first thoughts that come to mind about DTC drug advertising are Viagra—or other erectile dysfunction drugs—and the evening news because of the high number of drug ads placed there. Just tune into any of the networks' evening news programs and you will be glad you don't have an overactive bladder, reflux, or an STD.

DTC broadcast drug advertising took off around 1997 when the FDA lifted certain restrictions, and it has clearly been one of the most explosive growth areas of advertising in the past 10 years. Concerns about and support for DTC drug advertising have increased recently as the response of consumers has skyrocketed and the advertising spending continues to grow. The content and quality of DTC advertising is of great concern and interest to its many stakeholders—consumers, physicians, legislators, pharmaceutical marketers, advertising practitioners, and scholars.

## DTC vs. OTC

In most cases, a DTC drug ad is one that communicates information regarding a prescription (RX) drug, and is targeted toward consumers instead of physicians. In the United States, patients must have a prescription from their doctor to buy an RX drug. Depending on the medium in which it is placed (television, print, etc.), DTC ads contain elements of traditional advertising creative (essentially, benefits the consumer may receive) and detailed drug information about risks.

As evident in the Viagra and Nexium ads appearing in this chapter, risk information is usually included in both the first page of the ad (with the creative elements) and the second page (the fine print). The page of small type is often referred to as a *brief summary*.

DTC advertising is used most extensively for drugs that potentially have a large consumer base because of the high prevalence of the condition being treated (e.g., diabetes, heartburn, high cholesterol). Many of these drugs are considered maintenance drugs—patients need to use them the rest of their lives. For example, if you cannot control your high blood pressure with diet and exercise, a physician may prescribe medication to control your condition. If not, you may be at risk for developing heart disease, the leading cause of death in the US.

In addition, many DTC ads are for lifestyle drugs. A lifestyle drug treats a condition that is not considered life threatening, but can improve a patient's quality of life. For example, lifestyle drugs are used to treat everything from seasonal allergies to male sexual dysfunction. Certainly, men unable to complete sexual activity will not die, but Viagra and other erectile dysfunction drugs may be able to enhance one's quality of life.

The other type of advertising we see most often for drugs is referred to as over-the-counter (OTC) advertising. OTC drugs are ones that you can buy without a doctor's prescription (e.g., Tylenol, Robitussin). Be aware

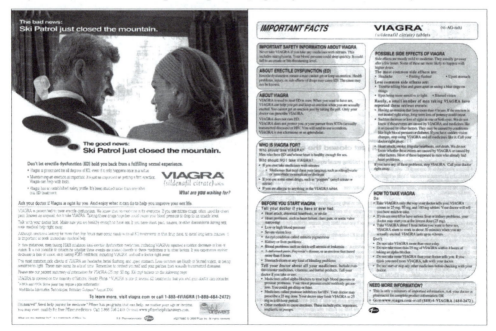

that some current OTC drugs were once RX medications that were advertised directly to the consumer before their patent expired (e.g., Claritin, Zantac, and recently Prilosec). Large advertising budgets usually accompany the rollout of both new DTC drugs and DTC drugs that transition to OTC. For example, Prilosec (heartburn drug) was once called the "purple pill," but now Nexium has spent millions to appropriate that moniker while $100 million was spent in 2007 to launch Prilosec as an OTC. Also, you may have noticed recent ads for Alli claiming that it is the first OTC diet drug approved by the Food and Drug Administration (FDA). It is, but that's because Alli was formally known as Xenical, an RX drug. Alli uses about 50% of the active ingredient found in Xenical.

## American History RX

Ads for drugs and medication are not a new phenomenon. In fact, one of the earliest sources of national advertising in the US was for *patent* medications. Despite the name, patent medicine had nothing to with the drug formula being protected by a patent. Instead, the products were called "patent" because the royal family liked them and endorsed them. Most of these formulations consisted of 20 to 40% ethyl alcohol. Floating in that alcohol could be anything from roots and herbs, to laudanum, to cocaine and opium. No wonder patients "felt good" after ingesting a swig of patent medicine.

With demand growing for these medicines, druggists and bottlers desired to run their ads in every community, which, in turn, caused the first advertising agents to find placements for such ads and create regular rates for advertising.

It's important to note that many of the claims made in the ads were outrageous. For example, ads for Lydia E. Pinkham's Vegetable Compound claimed that it cured—among other ailments—faintness, flatulency, bloating, headaches, nervous prostration, general debility, sleeplessness, depression and indigestion.

Obviously, most legitimate advertisers knew that some type of self-regulation was needed to enhance the credibility of all ads. Also, many of the ingredients in these medicines were harmful to people's health, and needed to be controlled.

By the end of the 19th Century, federal and state laws were enacted regarding truth-in-labeling and governmental pure food and drug inspection and control. Thus began a series of acts passed by Congress to control outrageous claims and to protect the health of Americans. It began with the Pure Food and Drug Act of 1906.

Most advertising in the US is regulated by the Federal Trade Commission (FTC). Not so, however, for RX drug ads which fall under the umbrella of the FDA. Under the mandate of the 1938 Food, Drug, and Cosmetic Act, the FDA is responsible for regulating RX drug advertising toward both doctors and consumers. Both then and now it is the belief of lawmakers that the FDA has the obligation to regulate RX ads because it deals with goods that the public consumes and can affect public health.

It was rare to see DTC drug ads after the demise of the patent medicine era. And, under the 1938 legislation, the same regulations applied to both print and broadcast advertising. Can you imagine today a TV commercial that contains a full verbal description of the brief summary you see in print ads? It would be both impractical and ineffective. So, on August 8, 1997, the FDA lifted this ban for broadcast advertising. Almost overnight, the DTC RX ad spending revolution, as we know it now, was born.

## Growth of DTC Advertising

DTC advertising is clearly having an impact on the advertising, healthcare, and pharmaceutical industries. For one, DTC drug ad spending continues to grow (up 28% in 2004) despite decreasing advertising spending in other industries in recent years (Dickinson, 2002; Thomaselli, 2005). Spending has steadily increased—$4.2 billion in 2005, $4.0 billion in 2004, and $3.18 billion in 2003, which was a 24.5% increase over the $2.55 billion in 2002 and the $2.5 billion in 2001 ("DTC Advertising Gets the Green Light," 2004; Thomaselli, 2005; USGAO, 2006).

Perhaps just as important, pharmaceutical marketers' messages are getting through to consumers. For example, an FDA survey found that "92% of patients had asked about an advertised prescription drug, with 86% identifying the brand and 59% requesting a prescription for that drug" ("FDA Study Supports DTC Ads," 2003, p. 19).

Traditionally, the bulk of media placement was in network television, but recently this has changed. Industry sources indicate that some companies are rethinking their TV media allocation because of the "return on the money spent as well as increasing public and regulatory backlash against TV ads for prescription medicines" (Hensley, 2005b, p. B1). In 2005, network TV spending was down 5% to $400 million, while cable TV rose 35% to $335 million, Internet spending was up 13% to $56 million, and print spending rose 3% to $719 million (Thomaselli, 2005).

Within the overall category, individual brands of prescription drugs have substantial advertising budgets. In 2005, for instance, the most heavily promoted drugs included Sepracor's sleep aid Lunesta ($227.3 million), AstraZeneca's gastrointestinal drug Nexium ($204.9 million) and Merck/ Schering-Plough's cholesterol lowering drug Vytorin ($161.5 million; Staff, 2006). DTC TV ads often receive more attention because of their high visibility. However, more than twice as many DTC dollars are spent

in print media. In addition, consumers are most likely to get more information from the Internet and magazines after seeing a DTC ad.

Although pharmaceutical companies have increased their spending on DTC RX drug advertising, it's important not to overlook how much the companies spend on other marketing activities. In fact DTC ads account for a small portion of their overall marketing budgets. For example, of the industry's total marketing expenditures in 2005, only 14% was spent on DTC ads. Most marketing was directed toward physicians (24%) and free drug samples (62%; Donohue, Ceasco, & Rosenthal, 2007). With all the controversy surrounding DTC ads, remember that in reality pharmaceutical companies spend most of their money leaving samples of their drugs with doctors so that patients can sample free medication.

## Key Issues of DTC Advertising

DTC advertising has inspired both supporters and detractors. Supporters contend that DTC advertising educates consumers about common, yet, serious conditions that often go untreated even when effective treatment is available. In addition, the ads also make consumers aware of the treatment options available to them. For example, someone may not be aware that they have diabetes until they see drug ads for a diabetes medication that lists symptoms.

Alternately, people may learn about drugs that can treat their urinary incontinence whereas they were previously unaware of any means of treatment. Although it is somewhat uncommon, some DTC ads list alternative, non-drug treatment options that further inform the consumer. For example, some ads mention "exercise" as a remedy for certain bodily aches and pains as opposed to pain medications.

Detractors challenge that advertising, with its overtly persuasive intent, is a form of communication ill-suited to educate consumers. In 1991, the US General Accounting Office (GAO) prepared a list of hypothesized outcomes of DTC advertising (USGAO, 1991). The possible negative outcomes identified by the GAO included the "misleading nature of promotional materials" and "inability of consumers to understand technical information."

Health communication researcher Barbara Mintzes (2001) expanded on the GAO's list to include concerns that DTC ads (1) may confuse patients into believing that inconsequential differences represent major therapeutic advances; and (2) create unrealistic expectations of drugs. Other researchers are concerned about the lack of information in ads and potential for miscomprehension by consumers. They also contend that DTC advertising rarely includes suggestions about lifestyle changes or other nonpharmacological interventions. In addition, erectile dysfunction drugs, like Viagra, have been criticized for promoting recreational drug use instead of use solely for medical conditions. How drugs are used, however, is essentially out of the advertiser's control.

As previously mentioned, physicians in the US have the authority to prescribe drugs. Traditionally, before the DTC RX ad spending revolution, the pharmaceutical companies targeted doctors with drug ads and other marketing efforts.

The American Medical Association (AMA) is a grassroots organization which represents many doctors in the US. AMA has always been against DTC RX drug advertising. The organization has called for research to be conducted concerning the advertising's effects on patients, on doctors, and the important relationship that exists between doctors and their patients. Despite the AMA's tough stand, it has recognized some benefits of DTC RX advertising, such as making patients aware of different diseases.

Many doctors, especially older ones, don't particularly care for DTC advertising because they feel it reflects a larger trend in medicine today. Patients used to get sick, go see their trusted doctor, get a diagnosis, take a medication, and, hopefully, get better. Today, the information age has created too many pseudo-physicians: patients using the Internet to self-diagnose. Despite the trouble patient information-seeking causes, most physicians do prefer patients that are knowledgeable regarding personal health and treatment options. Younger doctors who have grown up with DTC advertising appear to be more tolerant of it.

On the other side of the debate, individuals supportive of the information-value of DTC ads includes former FDA chief, Mark McClellan. His arguments, and those of others, are that DTC ads help patients become more knowledgeable about illnesses and drugs. As important, DTC ads appear to increase compliance—the chance that patients will take their medicine as prescribed—which, in turn, lessens long-term problems and health-care costs. In addition, some proponents believe that DTC advertising helps to expose the public to side effects that were previously not publicized.

## FDA and DTC Drug Advertising

Unlike most advertising, DTC drug advertising is regulated by the FDA as opposed to the FTC. The FDA has created "guidelines" for the industry about how to advertise pharmaceutical drugs directly to consumers. Although these are guidelines or suggestions, the FDA has been active in issuing warning letters to pharmaceutical companies using ads that fail to adhere to the guidelines. These warnings can be viewed at www.fda.gov/cder/warn/.

As previously mentioned, in August 1997, the FDA issued a Draft Guidance for consumer-directed broadcast advertising related to drugs. The new guidelines made it much easier for pharmaceutical companies to run DTC ads on television. Advertisers were no longer required to provide the somewhat misleadingly named "brief summary," described as "a true statement of information in brief summary relating to side effects, contraindications and effectiveness" of the drug (FDA, 1999). Before 1997, only two types of prescription drug ads were exempt from the FDA's brief summary requirement. These exceptions were (1) reminder ads that mentioned the drug's brand name but did not say anything about the condition to be treated, and (2) disease ads that mentioned the specific conditions that could be treated but did not mention the drug by name.

*Adequate provision* is the only item in the guidelines that does not apply to print because print ads do include the brief summary. However, the FDA still recommends that print ads include a toll-free number or website address so that additional information can be obtained. The FDA's 1999 Final Guidance set forth the following requirements for DTC broadcast ads:

1. Adequate provision for the dissemination of approved or permitted package labeling in connection with the broadcast presentation (e.g., toll-free number, website, print advertisements, publicly accessible brochures, or pharmacists and physicians).
2. "Are not false or misleading in any respect."
3. "Present a fair balance between information about effectiveness and information about risk."
4. "Include a thorough *major statement* conveying all the product's most important risk information in consumer-friendly language."
5. "Communicate all information relevant to the product's indication (including limitations to use) in consumer-friendly language." (p. 2; Note that italics were in original document but the underlining was added.)

In the 2004 Guidance for Industry, which focused on DTC magazine advertising, the FDA further defined consumer-friendly language as that which is fully understandable to the lay reader. Copy should not contain technical, scientific terms, or jargon. For example, a consumer may not know the term "contraindications" but is more likely to understand the phrase, "You should not take this drug if…" The latter is considered "consumer-friendly language."

In this guidance, the FDA also recommended that the traditional brief summary be replaced with a more comprehensible, consumer-targeting format. This change finally came about after years of criticism that "the volume of material, coupled with the format in which it is presented (i.e., very small print and sophisticated medical terminology) discourages its use and makes the information less comprehensible to consumers" (FDA, 2004, p. 2). The main change for print ads is that the brief summary should use consumer-friendly language and "highlights" of the key risk information. The brief summary for the Viagra ad shown in this chapter is an example of the FDA's recommended highlights.

The presentation of side effects—part of the risk information—has also been criticized for potentially scaring consumers so much that they do not want to talk to their doctor about taking the drug. Although many drugs have potentially mild side effects like dizziness, diarrhea, and dry mouth, others may have more serious side effects. One example is the Ortho Evra birth control patch and the possibility of serious cardiovascular side effects if the woman smokes while taking the drug (as discussed more later).

DTC advertising's presentation of side effects has often been spoofed because some seem ludicrous and more serious than the condition itself. For example, a popular rap song describes a man taking dozens of pills for ailments such as "soft eyeballs" and flatulence, who is told by his doctor that he must now take another pill for his mood swings. The lyrics then state: "side effects include headache, runny nose, drowsiness and a rash / a sugar high, bloating, and an absence of cash / vomiting, abdominal cramps and diarrhea / and an overwhelming urge to buy a couch from Ikea."

Fair balance is not specifically defined by the FDA. The following are qualities of fair balance that have been suggested or used in previous research—both content and format are important, physical features (e.g., color) helps distinguish text and leads to increased learning, quality and quantity of risk information is important, and risk information needs to be presented in the same scope, depth, and detail as benefit information. These recommendations may have been instrumental in the changes we are now seeing in DTC advertising that emphasize risk information more prominently in the ad as opposed to being obscured with small print.

## How DTC Drug Advertising Is Changing

Recently, there have been changes in how the pharmaceutical industry markets its drugs directly to consumers, how consumers perceive these ads, and how these communications are regulated. Self-regulation is becoming important as the government continues to threaten intervention and consumer confidence continues to decrease. Specifically, consumer polls have documented a 24% drop in approval ratings of pharmaceutical companies in the past seven years (from 73% in 1998 to 49% in 2005; Edwards, 2005).

Amidst criticism about DTC, in 2005 Johnson & Johnson tried a new DTC advertising format for one of its brands, Ortho Evra birth control patch. The approach increases the prominence of drug risk information (Hensley, 2005a; see examples at www.orthoevra.com and the accompanying Ortho Evra ad). One of the ads shows a split-screen image of a New York gynecologist on one side and a young woman in the other. The doctor says "Let's talk," and proceeds to caution the woman about blood clots, strokes, and the risks of smoking while on the medication. This ad is a prime example of a more safety-oriented approach that appears to be a new trend in some DTC ads.

Johnson & Johnson is urging other DTC companies to follow suit and place risks in a more prominent position as opposed to obscuring "safety information by showing such things as a 'swirling castanet show' as risks are being discussed" (Hensley, 2005a, p. B1). Johnson & Johnson is hoping this will not only be a better way to educate and counsel consumers, but also to improve relations with patients, doctors, and regulatory agencies.

There has been a change in DTC drug ads as a result of Johnson & Johnson's call. Print ads are including more consumer-friendly versions of the brief summary, and both print and TV ads are highlighting risk information to a greater degree. In addition, the Pharmaceutical Research and Manufacturers of America recently released a "DTC code of conduct" in an organized attempt to stave off government regulation (Thomaselli & Teinowitz, 2005).

The three key recommendations include: more focus on risks, more disease-awareness campaigns, and narrower targeting of specific patients (Thomaselli & Teinowitz, 2005). Pfizer has already responded to these recommendations by revamping their approach to DTC advertising by reducing spending on television and "redirect[ing] ad messaging to focus almost exclusively on encouraging dialogue between patients and physicians and includ[ing] more comprehensive risk information" (Thomaselli & Sanders, 2005, p. 1).

The reason drug marketers wish to avoid external regulation is similar to the reasons the advertising industry has historically sought to avoid legal directives (e.g., tobacco and alcohol advertising). The pharmaceutical and advertising industries generally believe that they will fare better creating their own solution as opposed to having a regulatory solution forced on them.

## Research Directions

Much of the early DTC research focused on print advertising with topics ranging from the content of the ads, to whether or not DTC print ads met FDA "fair balance" criteria, to consumers' attention to the brief summary and its effect on patient/physician discussions. More recently research has focused on other media, including TV and the Web, as well as how and whether or not DTC ads communicate effectively.

Although spending is increasing in other media, television advertising budgets are extensive enough that researchers are focusing on commercial content and how it affects consumers. The goal of this research is to better understand if consumers are receiving the information they need to make informed decisions about their healthcare.

The growth of DTC advertising has resulted in great interest among marketers, medical practitioners, and scholars alike. Marketers have been concerned with the question of how to measure the effectiveness of DTC advertising, an especially interesting problem in light of the fact that consumers cannot directly purchase the advertised brands. Although effects can also be measured using variables like memory, learning, attitudes, and intentions, marketers are often most interested with sales.

Medical practitioners and scholars in various disciplines are more concerned with the impact of DTC advertising on the individual and public health in general, the appropriateness (or lack thereof) of pharmaceutical use resulting from DTC advertising, and the impact of DTC advertising on the doctor/patient relationship, as well as the economic impact of such ads on overall health care costs (Mintzes, 2001).

## Future of RX Advertising

DTC RX advertising will likely continue to experience growing pains as it changes. In addition, there are many questions that research is still attempting to both answer and discover. There is even the possibility that government regulators may take more of an active role or even abolish DTC advertising completely. Although possible, this is unlikely given the increased interest in self-regulation that the industry has taken.

Since Ortho Evra utilized the new consumer-friendly format in 2005, the industry has seen similar changes for other drugs (e.g., Lipitor). These changes will likely continue because of regulatory pressure, and the consumers' desire for more information as they take a more active role in their healthcare. More people are utilizing information from sources such as the Internet and DTC ads to change the relationship they have with their healthcare providers by taking a more active, partnership-type role.

Last, allotment of advertising budgets will likely continue to shift from the broad audiences of network television to more targeted cable, print, and online venues. The Internet, in particular, offers very targeted advertising with search related DTC ads on sites like WebMD. If you search WebMD to find out more about heartburn, for example, you are likely to see banner ads for heartburn remedies. More targeted messages lead to lower advertising costs, but a downside is consumer confusion as the lines may become blurred between paid advertising for a DTC drug and objective, third-party medical information.

## Questions

1.      Why do you think there is so much controversy surrounding DTC RX advertising?

2.      How do DTC ads help or harm the doctor/patient relationship?

3.      In your opinion, do DTC ads increase or decrease the cost of RX drugs (not copays)?

4.      What's the difference between consumer advertising for over-the-counter drugs vs. prescription drugs?

5.      Since more American consumers are paying for a larger percentage of their healthcare costs, do you think DTC advertising will help them better understand their options?

6.      How do you think the Internet will influence future DTC advertising (e.g., format, targeting, budgets)?

## References and Recommended Reading

Dickinson, J. G. (2002). DTC report: FDA survey data supports DTC. *MM&M*, 32 & 34.

Donohue, J. M., M. Cevasco, and M. B. Rosenthal (2007). A decade of direct-to-consumer advertising of prescription drugs. *New England Journal of Medicine*, 357 (7), 673-681.

DTC advertising gets the green light. (2004). MM&M, 36-40.

Edwards, J. (2005). FDA: Quality of DTC ads is in noticeable decline. *Brandweek*, 46 (18), 12.

FDA. (1999). Final guidance for industry; Consumer directed broadcast advertisements. Retrieved July 30, 2007 from: http://www.fda.gov/cder/guidance/1804fnl.pdf

FDA. (2004). Guidance for industry; Brief summary: Disclosing risk information in consumer-directed print advertisements. Retrieved July 30, 2007 from http://www.fda.gov/cder/guidance/5669dft.pdf

FDA study supports DTC ads. (2003). *Broadcasting & Cable*, 19.

Hensley, S. (2005a). In switch, J&J gives straight talk on drug risks in new ads. *Wall Street Journal*, p. B1.

Hensley, S. (2005b). Some drug makers are starting to curtail TV ad spending. *Wall Street Journal*, p. B1.

Mintzes, B. (2001). An assessment of the health system impacts of direct-to-consumer advertising of prescription medications, volume II: Literature review. Retrieved December 2002 from: http://www.chspr.ubc.ca//hpru/pdf/dtca-v2-litreview.pdf

Staff, M. A. N. (2006). DTC takes a back seat [Electronic Version]. *Med Ad News*, May. Retrieved July 30, 2007 from: http://www.pharmalive.com/magazines/medad/view.cfm?articleID=3522

Thomaselli, R. (2005). The side effects of DTC change. *Advertising Age*, 76 (33), 1.

Thomaselli, R., and Ira Teinowitz (2005). DTC lobby scrambles to head off FDA guidelines. *Advertising Age*, 76 (20), 3.

Thomaselli, R., and L. Sanders (2005). Pfizer rips up DTC rule book. *Advertising Age*, 76 (30), 1, 53.

USGAO. (2006). Prescription drugs: Improvements needed in FDA's oversight of direct-to-consumer advertising. GAO report Number GAO-07-54 (December 14).

USGAO. (1991). Prescription drugs: Little is known about the effects of direct-to-consumer advertising. Retrieved August 2004 from: http://161.203.16.4/d19t9/144561.pdf

# Online Resources

### FDA Warning Letters to Pharmaceutical Companies
http://www.fda.gov/cder/warn/

This site includes warning letters to pharmaceutical companies for DTC advertising, including websites, when they violate FDA regulations, such as being false or misleading. For example, in May 2005 a Zoloft print DTC advertisement was found to be "false or misleading." You can view both the letter and the print ad found in violation.

### FDA Division of Drug Marketing, Advertising, and Communications
http://www.fda.gov/cder/ddmac/

"Research" and "Presentations" links on this site list a wealth of government research and information about DTC advertising. A related area of the site (www.fda.gov/cder/guidance/#Advertising) lists all the FDA guidances related to DTC advertising. Also, a search of DTC advertising on the FDA site (link at bottom of site) reveals even more information.

### DTC Drug Websites
http://www.lunesta.com
http://www.purplepill.com
http://orthoevra.com

Visit any of these DTC sites to better understand how the drugs are marketed online. Many of these sites include links to print and broadcast advertising.

# Alcohol Advertising:
## The Effectiveness and Future of Self Regulation

## by Stacey J. T. Hust

IN 2006, ANHEUSER-BUSCH revealed its "Budweiser Surfing" bill-board campaign. The outdoor ads showed an individual surfing and em-phasized the Budweiser brand. A complaint was soon filed with the Beer Institute's Code Compliance Review Board (CCRB) arguing that the ads associated drinking alcohol with a risky activity (e.g. surfing). The CCRB eventually ruled that the billboard ads were not in violation because they did not depict the actual consumption of alcohol. Further, the CCRB said the ad focused more on general brand identity since no specific alcohol product was identified.

As this example illustrates, the advertising of alcoholic beverages is challenging given that the advertised product has been shown to impair decision making and cause negative health effects, and yet is consumed by the majority of Americans. Unlike similar products such as tobacco, however, the federal government has not required alcohol companies to place a mandatory health warning on their products, and it has not required federal oversight of alcohol advertising. Instead, in an attempt to not limit free speech, the federal government has allowed the alcohol industry to oversee the regulation of its products through advertising codes developed by associations representing the three sectors of the industry (beer, wine, and distilled spirits). In fact, the Federal Trade Commission only regulates alcohol advertising that is unfair or uses deceptive acts of practice.

One of the main issues facing alcohol advertising in the coming years will be the effectiveness of its self-regulatory practices. This chapter con-siders the industry's self-regulation efforts as well as the nature and preva-lence of alcohol advertising. Four specific concerns about the industry's regulation efforts are discussed: the positive reinforcement of consuming alcohol, youth's overexposure to alcohol advertisements, the use of promotional items and websites, and the production of safety messages. Finally, the future of the self regulation of alcoholic beverage advertising is considered.

## Prevalence of Alcohol Advertising

The alcohol industry spends about $2 billion each year producing and placing ads in measured media such as television, magazines, and other media vehicles. For some brands, advertising accounts for a third to one-half of their marketing expenditures (Hurtz et al., 2007). For example, Anheuser-Busch annually spends about $633 million on measured media advertising, according to *Advertising Age*. Alcoholic beverage ads are so popular that they outnumber nonalcoholic beverage ads by four to one in mainstream magazines and two to one on popular television networks (Austin & Hust, 2005).

The remainder of the industry's annual marketing expenditures funds merchandising, such as retail advertising materials and promotional items. For example, many brewers and distillers place their brands on usable items such as toys, sports gear, and clothes, and almost all alcohol brands have websites complete with alcohol-related games, videos, and downloads. The majority of the leading brands have stores (both physical and on-line) where fans can purchase brand-related memorabilia. For example, an individual can visit Budweiser's "BudShop" to purchase trendy and well-designed branded tee-shirts, drink coolers, and "Budweiser barbeque sauces." They can also purchase die-cast cars and sports gear.

## Self Regulation

Alcohol advertising remains self-regulated, at least in part, because commercial speech enjoys some free speech protections under the First Amendment of the U.S. Constitution. As Jon Nelson (2005) pointed out in a recent article, the Supreme Court's case of Central Hudson established that these free speech rights are "not trumped by the restrictions on alcohol distribution contained in the 21st Amendment" (p. 40).

To avoid violating this right of free speech, the federal government encourages the alcohol industry to self-regulate its advertising. Advertising self-regulation requires an organization to have set guidelines for its advertising practices and an identified process to review potential violations of the guidelines.

In the United States, three trade associations, corresponding to the three sectors of the industry, oversee the regulation of its advertising. The Beer Institute, the Wine Institute, and the Distilled Spirits Council of the United States (DISCUS) have established advertising and marketing guidelines for their members and review complaints regarding potential violations. Overall, the advertising codes strongly discourage alcohol advertising that promotes underage drinking or over consumption.

In the past decades, the three associations have continued to strengthen the regulation of alcoholic beverage ads. In one notable exception, DISCUS repealed its regulation that banned the airing of liquor ads on television. Although this repeal was more consistent with the advertising codes for both beer and wine, it was hotly contested and many networks simply refused to air liquor ads. In 2001, NBC voluntarily lifted its ban and briefly aired hard liquor ads. Although the network reported that it was committed to promoting safety by requiring companies to also run social-responsibility ads for four months, it stopped airing liquor ads due to pressure from Congress, advocacy groups, and other networks, according to media coverage of its decision.

## Concerns with Self Regulation
### Positive Reinforcement of Consuming Alcohol

The alcohol industry is faced with the challenge of promoting a product that should primarily be used in moderation. Many of the industry's own standards, such as the Beer Institute's Advertising and Marketing Code, suggest that ads should "strongly oppose" alcohol abuse or inappropriate consumption of alcohol. Yet, studies have found that alcohol ads positively reinforce drinking and rarely, if ever, mention the potential negative effects of consuming alcohol.

An analysis in 1982 of alcohol ads found that they overwhelmingly emphasized the relationship between drinking and positive outcomes such as relaxation, romance, and adventure (Strickland, Finn & Lambert, 1982). For example, people in the ads were often shown enjoying a beer while relaxing outdoors. Four years later, mass communication researcher Charles Atkin and colleagues (1986) reported that people in alcohol ads portrayed as product users (those who appeared to be drinking) were depicted as successful, adventurous, young, and happy.

More recent studies indicate that these portrayals have not changed. For example, Austin and Hust (2005) found that alcohol ads continue to emphasize relaxation and sexual appeals. Models in the ads were often shown outdoors or in bars, and male and female characters were often shown relaxing or flirting. Further, within the ads models are rewarded with social approval, relaxation, and sexual encounters when consuming alcoholic beverages.

For the most part, the marketing codes governing the industry's advertising strategies do not specifically state themes and appeals that should be avoided. Yet all three codes specify that alcohol ads should avoid depicting alcohol use with activities that require alertness or coordination or that emphasize sexual situations. Despite these suggestions, content analyses have found that these themes are still included in a portion of ads. This content is especially concerning given that alcohol use is associated with impaired coordination and decision making, and that it is an addictive drug.

Studies of alcohol advertising in the early 1990s found that one-third of them included depictions of risky activities such as driving, boating, or recreational activities. More recent analyses have found that these "at-risk" depictions are not as prevalent. In their more recent analysis, Austin and Hust (2005) found that such activities were present in 15% of televised ads and were largely absent from magazine ads. Yet, the researchers also found that the majority of alcohol ads were set in the outdoors, largely removed from the safety of a public setting or the privacy of one's home. Further, consumption of alcohol was rarely depicted in association with dining. They also found that alcohol ads were often published in magazines that promoted sports and recreational activity (i.e. *Sports Illustrated*), so it may be that the placement of ads in these magazines further associates drinking with sports and recreational activities (Hust, 2006).

Last, alcohol ads are also more likely to emphasize sexual connotations than ads promoting nonalcoholic drinks. Relaxing, flirting, and romantic or sexual behaviors are the most frequently portrayed actions in alcohol advertising. Further, the majority of women in alcohol ads are portrayed as sexual objects, even though the Codes of Advertising Conduct discourage lewdness, vulgarity, and nudity. In fact, given the large amount of sexual content (including flirtations or romantic situations) present in ads, it appears the Codes narrowly define such offensive content. For example, a woman's body is used simultaneously to emphasize sex and product use in a Budweiser ad appearing in the *Sports Illustrated* 2006 Swimsuit Issue. Although the model is not nude per se, she actually appears to be unclothed. Many scholars and critics have argued that alcohol's connection to sexual content is distressing considering that its use has been linked to unsafe sexual practices.

## Youth's Overexposure to Alcohol Advertising

In December 2006, the American Academy of Pediatrics published a policy statement raising concern about the health effects of the great amounts of advertising that children see. In particular, the Academy identified alcohol advertising as one of five specific health-related areas of concern, citing its potential to reinforce alcohol use among young people.

The reason for concern is clear when one considers the numbers. Approximately 18% of young people aged 12 to 17 have used alcohol (SAMHSA, 2005). Further, close to 10 million underage youth (between the ages of 12 and 20) reported drinking alcohol in recent months, according to the 2000 National Household Survey on Drug Abuse. The majority of these youth (7 million) reported heavy, episodic drinking. In addition, six out of ten underage drinkers identified themselves as binge drinkers who consumed at least five or more drinks on the same occasion.

In the United States, minors are prohibited from purchasing and possessing alcohol in public. In 1984, the US set the highest drinking age limit in the world when it passed the National Minimum Drinking Age Act that set the minimum purchase and public possession of alcohol to age

21. It is important to note, however, that young Americans legally and illegally drink alcohol in a number of different circumstances. For example, some states allow minors to consume alcohol if a family member provides consent and some states provide exceptions for consumption on private property.

Underage drinking is disconcerting not only because it is illegal, however, but because of the number of health risks associated with adolescents' frequent alcohol use. Adolescents who drink alcohol regularly are more likely to engage in risky activities such as using illicit drugs and cigarettes, driving under the influence of alcohol, and engaging in unprotected sexual behavior (Valois et al, 1999). Adolescent drinkers may also exhibit higher levels of physical and psychological impairment when drinking and may develop alcohol dependency, especially those youth who begin drinking in preadolescence (prior to age 14; NIAAA, 2004/5).

Many scholars point to youth's overexposure to alcohol advertisements as a potential influence on their drinking behaviors. Each year the average underage drinker has an opportunity to see one thousand beer, wine, and liquor ads (Atkin et al., 1986), which, surprisingly, is more than people who are 21 years old or older. A recent study revealed that underage males saw 29% more beer advertising than men who can drink legally, and underage females saw 68% more beer advertising that women who drink legally (Jernigan et al., 2004).

Although all three councils discourage alcohol advertising directed toward underage drinkers, studies have found that some alcohol brands heavily place ads in youth-oriented magazines and TV networks with substantial viewership among underage drinkers. Further, content analyses have found that alcohol advertising contains themes, settings, and characters that appeal to youth. Austin and Hust found that one of every six magazine alcoholic beverage ads and one of every 14 commercials appeared to target underage drinkers. For example, in the 1990s Budweiser developed a widely successful advertising campaign based on three frogs that sang out "Budweiser." This approach was particularly appealing to youth, as a 1996 survey of children found that they were more familiar with Budweiser's frogs than with the Mighty Morphin Power Rangers or Smokey Bear (Laber, 1996).

Alcohol ads use themes and appeals that are similar to those used to promote nonalcoholic beverages. Both types of ads included outdoor settings and emphasized relaxation, according to the analysis by Austin and Hust (2005). Several brands of alcoholic and nonalcoholic beverages used cartoon characters to promote their products. For example, the Captain Morgan brand's icon is an illustrated pirate who often interacts with human models. This approach is similar to nonalcoholic beverage ads that use cartoon characters to grab young peoples' attention.

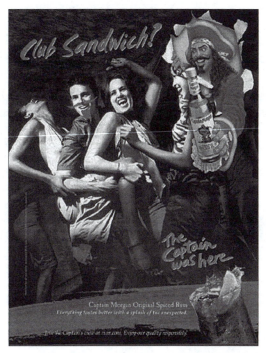

Some people have argued that youth may be more comfortable responding to and considering alcohol ads because of their similarity to nonalcoholic beverage ads.

Alcohol advertising is a stronger predictor for teenagers' beer and liquor drinking than other factors, including parental influences, age, gender, and social economic status of the teenagers' family (Atkin et al., 1986). Overexposure to such advertising has been found to increase individuals' reported tendencies to drink alcohol, and viewing television and magazine alcohol advertising predicted teenagers' alcohol consumption, especially consumption of hard liquor (Atkin et al., 1986). Middle school students, for example, who were heavily exposed to a variety of alcohol ads (both traditional advertising and promotional items) were subsequently 50% more likely to drink alcohol than those were not so heavily exposed to the advertising (Collins et al., 2007).

Even youth who did not consume alcohol, but who were exposed to alcohol ads, reported stronger intentions to drink than their counterparts who did not see the ads. Further, there is some indication that alcohol advertising reaches children under 12 years of age, and that this exposure may encourage children to have more favorable attitudes about drinking alcohol. Children exposed to alcohol ads were more likely to remember the ads and their slogans and were more likely to report that they intended to drink alcohol as adults (Grube & Wallack, 1994).

Last, it has been shown that the alcohol industry profits from underage drinking. In a ground breaking study, Foster and her colleagues (2006) estimated that underage drinking accounted for 17.5% of the total consumer expenditures for alcohol. "The short term cash value of underage drinking to the alcohol industry was $22.5 billion in 2001," noted the investigators (p. 473). These financial considerations likely result in a strong financial motive for the alcohol industry to continue selling its products to youth, yet it is also faced with continued pressure (both financial and social) to discourage underage use of alcohol.

## Promotional Items and Websites

Both the Codes for beer and liquor advertising state that, "no beer (or liquor) identification, including logos, trademarks, or names should be used or licensed for use on clothing, toys, games or game equipment, or other materials intended for use primarily by persons below the legal drinking age." Certainly, many of the industry's stores, such as the "Bud-Shop," restrict minors' access to the website and sells products that would appeal to adults. Some of these products do appeal to youth (e.g. footballs, coolers, jackets, and toy cars). In fact, existing research indicates youth do gain access to these promotional items, and that they may be especially appealing to underage drinkers (Austin & Knaus, 2000). One-fifth of middle school students reported owning at least one alcohol-related promotional item, and these students were more likely to report currently drinking alcohol than students who did not own a promotional item (Hurtz et al., 2007). In fact, students who owned an alcohol-related item were three times more likely than non-owners to report having tried drinking alcohol.

Almost every alcohol company has its own website complete with alcohol-related games and video clips. Visitors can peruse the on-line store for their favorite promotional items or can download pictures, songs, or icons. They can play their favorite commercials and revisit their favorite print ads. Visitors can download product inspired ring tones or graphics for mobile phones or PDAs. At Budweiser.com, visitors can even register for a free e-mail account.

The majority of these websites and venues require visitors to enter their date of birth prior to visiting the site. Even so, research has shown that underage individuals can still access them (The Center on Alcohol Marketing and Youth, 2006). These websites are likely to appeal to younger individuals and appear to positively reinforce drinking much like alcohol ads, although research focused on these sites is rare. Many of the sites promote sporting events, action movies, and outdoor activities. On some sites, visitors can view pictures of scantily clad women. Whether it's Budweiser's promotion of the *Sports Illustrated* swimsuit models or Captain Morgan's Morganettes, these women typically pose seductively in clothing to promote the brand. Given the shear number of alcohol ads, it is possible that these alternative promotions are less likely to be viewed by the advertising councils.

## Moderation and Safety Messages

Alcohol marketers often include moderation messages in their ads, such as "please drink responsibly," or "enjoy in moderation." As previously mentioned, the Beer Institute's Code encourages advertisers to be socially responsible by encouraging drinking in moderation. Unlike tobacco products, however, alcohol ads are not required to include such safety messages. In fact, these moderation messages were rare in alcohol ads (Madden & Grube, 1993). Austin and Hust found moderation messages to be more prevalent in recent years. For example, over two-thirds of magazine alcohol ads contain one, although the moderation messages are primarily in the background. Moderation messages were far less common in the commercials Austin and Hust analyzed, with less than 10% including one.

The alcohol industry also produces public service announcements (PSAs) that discourage underage drinking. In recent years, however, the industry's investment in such messages has declined. Between 2001 and 2005, alcohol companies spent close to $5 billion on televised advertisements, but less than $104 million of this went toward responsibility advertising (CAMY, 2007). Further, in 2005 only six alcohol companies, out of a total of 56 that aired televised ads, accounted for all of the responsibility ads.

## The Future of Alcohol Advertising

Although the alcohol industry should be commended for setting strict guidelines for its advertisers to follow, adherence to these standards, at the very least, is not consistent for all marketers or ads. Given that underage drinking is such an important concern, the U.S. Surgeon General issued a call to action in 2007 for alcohol marketers to take more responsibility for the prevention and reduction of underage drinking by insuring that youth are not overexposed to alcohol ads.

In December 2006, the U.S. Congress passed the Sober Truth on Preventing Underage Drinking Act, which requires the Secretary of Health and Human Services to provide an annual report to Congress about underage drinking, including the role of alcohol advertising and its potential appeal to youth. These recent developments have signified to some scholars that the federal government may choose to become more involved in the regulation of alcohol advertising if the evidence justifies it.

In response, some observers have argued that alcohol companies have set even stricter guidelines in an attempt to ward off federal involvement. The Sazerac Company, an independent, privately held producer of spirits and wine, for instance, announced that it voluntarily agreed to not use "Spring Break" references in its advertising. Further, the company will voluntarily restrict brand images in video games and will not publish ads near playgrounds. Shortly after Sazerac's statement, Beam Global Wine and Spirits, makers of Jim Beam, Sauza, and Courvoisier, followed suit by increasing the standards of its advertising guidelines.

Perhaps the real future of alcohol advertising lies not in whether it continues to be self-regulated, but in whether the industry can conceptualize marketing strategies that are even more "protected" than advertisements. One brand's most innovative marketing strategy turns the promotion of alcoholic beverages into mass media content. Budweiser recently introduced Bud TV, a series of television channels available to Internet users. Viewers can tune in to see movie trailers, original content, or can create amateur ads for their favorite beer. Although still in its infancy, Bud TV members can view videos that parody reality TV or news programs. New visitors are asked to virtually "join others at the bar" to view the alcohol related content (http://www.bud.tv/).

## Conclusion

The alcohol industry faces perhaps one of the most pressing ethical dilemmas in advertising—balancing financial interests with social responsibility. The very advertising techniques that make alcohol products household names also promote the use of a product that has the potential to be harmful and addictive. Further, although the industry has set standards for ethical and responsible advertising, it's clear that adherence to these codes may be inconsistent among both companies and marketing efforts. For example, ads are not reviewed and sanctioned by the conduct boards until after they have been published, which may be too late to prevent the concerns presented by self-regulation. Finally, although the industry has attempted to use advertising to promote responsible drinking, such as moderation and responsibility messages, these techniques may be overshadowed by the abundance of techniques that reinforce the positive aspects of consuming alcohol.

## Questions

1. Is the alcohol industry responsible for discouraging underage individuals from drinking its products? Why or why not?

2. What is the alcohol industry's possible rationale for using advertising techniques that are similar to those used in nonalcoholic beverage advertising?

3. Is the current process for reviewing alcohol advertisements that violate the industry's standards effective? Why or why not?

4.      Are age restriction mechanisms on alcohol-related websites worth-
        while? Do they deter underage visitors?

5.      Will the entertainment media on Bud TV be protected more under
        the First Amendment than traditional advertising content? Why or
        why not?

## References and Recommended Reading

Atkin, C., Hocking, J., & Block, M. (1984). Media effects on the young
        teenage drinking: Does advertising make a difference? *Journal of
        Communication*, 34 (2), 157-167.

Atkin, C., Hocking, J., & Block, M. (1986). Teenage drinking: Does ad-
        vertising make adifference?, in C. M. Felsted (ed.), *Youth and Al-
        cohol Abuse: Readings and Resources* (pp. 63-74). Montreal: Oryx
        Press.

Austin, E. W. & Hust, S. J. T., (2005). Targeting adolescents? The con-
        tent and frequency of alcoholic and nonalcoholic beverage ads in
        magazine and video formats November 1999-April 2000, *Journal
        of Health Communication*, 10 (8), 769-785.

Austin, E. W. & Knaus, C. S. (2000). Predicting the potential for risky be-
        havior among those "too young" to drink, as the result of appealing
        advertising. *Journal of Health Communication*, 5, 13-27.

The Center on Alcohol Marketing and Youth. (2002) Overexposed: Youth
        a target of alcohol advertising in magazines. Retrieved February
        23, 2005, from: http://camy.org/research/mag0902/

The Center on Alcohol Marketing and Youth (2007). Drowned out: Al-
        cohol industry 'responsibility' advertising on television, 2001 to
        2005. Retrieved July 15, 2007, from: http://camy.org/research
        /responsibility2007/responsibility2007.pdf.

Collins, R. L., Ellickson, P. L., McCaffrey, D., & Hambarsoomians, K.
        (2007). Early adolescent exposure to alcohol advertising and its

relationship to underage drinking. *Journal of Adolescent Health*, 40, 527-534.

Foster, S. E., Vaughan, R. D., Foster, W. H., & Califano, J. A., Jr. (2006). Estimate of the commercial value of underage drinking and adult abusive and dependent drinking to the alcohol industry. *Pediatrics & Adolescent Medicine*, 160, 473-478.

Grube, J. W. & Wallack, L. (1994) Television beer advertising and drinking knowledge, beliefs, and intentions among schoolchildren. *American Journal of Public Health*, 84 (2), 254-259.

Hurtz, S. Q., Henriksen, L., Wang, Y., Feighery, E. C., & Fortmann, S. P., (2007). The relationship between exposure to alcohol advertising in stores, owning promotional items, and adolescent alcohol use. *Alcohol & Alcoholism*, 42 (2), 143-149.

Jernigan, D. H., Ostroff, J., Ross, C., & O'Hara, J. A. (2004). Sex differences in adolescent exposure to alcohol advertising in magazines. *Archives of Pediatrics and Adolescent Medicine*, 158, 629-634.

Leiber, L. (1996). *Commercial and Character Slogan Recall by Children Aged Nine to 11 Years*. Berkeley, CA: Center on Alcohol Advertising.

National Institute on Alcohol Abuse and Alcoholism (NIAAA) 2004/2005. Alcohol and development in youth: A multidisciplinary overview. *Alcohol Research & Health*, 28 (3), 107-175.

Nelson, J. (2005). Advertising, alcohol and youth. *Regulation*, 5 (2). 40-47.

Strickland, D. E., Finn, T.A., & Lambert, M. D. (1982) A content analysis of beverage alcohol advertising: I, Magazine advertising. *Journal of Studies on Alcohol*, 43 (7), 655-682.

Substance Abuse and Mental Health Services Administration (SAMHSA). (2005), 2004 National survey on drug use and health. Retrieved November 7, 2005, from: http://www.drugabusestatistics.samhsa.gov/NSDUH/2k4NSDUH/2k4results/2k4results.htm#ch3

Valois, R. F., Oeltmann, J. E., Waller, J., & Hussey, J. R. (1999). Relationship between number of sexual intercourse partners and selected health risk behaviors among public high school adolescents. *Journal of Adolescent Health*, 25 (5), 328-335.

## Online Resources

### Center on Alcohol Marketing and Youth
http://camy.org/

This site represents CAMY, an organization housed at Georgetown University that monitors the alcohol industry's marketing to underage drinkers. The site contains reports and fact sheets about youths' exposure to alcohol advertising as well as coverage of the latest research in the area. The site also includes a gallery of recent alcohol advertisements.

### Beer Institute
http://www.beerinstitute.org/

This organization represents the beer industry before national, state, and local governments. The organization establishes the code of conduct for beer advertising and includes the Code Compliance Review Board.

### Distilled Spirits Council of the United States (DISCUS)
http://www.discus.org/

Similar to the Beer Institute, DISCUS represents the liquor industry before national, state, and local governments. The organization also established a code of conduct for liquor advertising and oversees the Code Review Board. Visit the link that describes advertising guidelines.

### Bud TV
http://www.bud.tv/

This site is Budweiser's new Internet-based television network. As mentioned, the site contains a variety of entertainment content, much of it related to Budweiser products. Visitors must be 21 to enter.

# The Two Faces of Tobacco Advertising:
## Marketing Triumph or Social Evil?

## by Hye-Jin Paek

IMAGES AND ICONS FROM TOBACCO ADVERTISING have become embedded in the consumer psyche. The Marlboro Man, Joe Camel, and the Torch of Freedom represent some of the most successful—and controversial—cigarette campaigns in marketing history.

The days of memorable pro-smoking ads, however, appear to be over. As the Virginia Slims campaign so aptly puts it, tobacco advertising "has come a long way." To be sure, cigarette advertising at its zenith saturated the media environment with ubiquitous ads and program sponsorships. Today, tobacco companies essentially fund "antismoking" efforts. Far from being vanquished, tobacco continues to mean big business. In 2003, for instance, tobacco companies spent a record $15.15 billion on advertising and promotion (Bosman, 2006).

Because of its powerful impact on individual consumers, as well as the unhealthy nature of its products, tobacco advertising has come to be seen as an enemy of public health. For this reason, it is a prime target for the regulatory efforts of governments, health professionals, and consumer groups. This chapter discusses the major issues regarding tobacco advertising, including its origins and development, its most successful marketing campaigns, its state of crisis during the antismoking era, and its future directions.

## Origin and Growth of Tobacco Advertising

Tobacco advertising in America first appeared in 1789, when the Lorillard brothers promoted their tobacco products in the *New York Daily Advertiser* (Petrone, 1996). From the beginning, tobacco companies employed various promotional techniques such as point of purchase displays, tobacco tins, cigarette package art, and both outdoor and print ads. America's first cigarette ads appeared on trading cards in the late 19th century, sponsored by tobacco brands such as Kimball, Kinney, Marburg, and Allen & Ginter. The cards employed broadly appealing advertising themes such as portrayals of children and young maidens.

Formed in 1890, the American Tobacco Company (a.k.a., the Tobacco Trust) played a significant role in stimulating demand for tobacco and building brand loyalty. American Tobacco soon became so powerful and dominant that in 1910 the U.S. Supreme Court divided it into smaller companies, most of which still exist today. During these years, according to Gerard S. Petrone (1996), author of a book on the early days of tobacco advertising, ad professionals were already creating memorable tobacco advertising slogans that expressed unique selling propositions. The slogans addressed quality ("Quality Superb" – Helmar), flavor ("Mild as May" – Marlboro), taste ("A Taste for Grays is a Taste that Stays" – Grays), and exoticism and luxury ("A Breath of Oriental Luxury" – Haidee).

By the early 1920s, tobacco had become a billion-dollar industry. The marketplace was dominated by ads for the "Big Four" (Camel by R. J. Reynolds, Lucky Strike and Chesterfield by Liggett & Myers, and Old Gold by Lorillard). By 1927, cigarette companies had become the third largest advertiser in American newspapers. At the advent of the TV era, cigarette manufacturers were one of the first industries to advertise widely on the new medium. Tobacco companies sponsored popular TV shows such as "I Love Lucy," "The Flintstones," and "The Addams Family." In addition to the customary commercial spots, the sponsoring cigarette brands even appeared within the shows and became part of their narratives. It was common to see 1960s TV dramas and sitcoms in which father and mother smoke at the dinner table and in front of their children.

After cigarette ads were eventually banned from broadcast media, the tobacco media buys moved more heavily into magazines and billboards. The images in many of these magazine ads portrayed images of adventure, recreation, romance, youthfulness, and sociability (King et al., 2001).

# Cigarette Advertising:
# Building Powerful Brand Images

Cigarette advertising has successfully built strong brand images for its products. Four of the most successful and memorable advertising campaigns include: Marlboro's Marlboro Man, Lucky Strike's Torch of Freedom, Virginia Slims' "You've come a long way, baby" slogan, and Camel's Joe Camel. Through their sustained campaigns, these brands have consistently promoted their unique images of American machismo, female independence and freedom, and youthfulness and sociability.

The cowboy Marlboro man was created by the Leo Burnett agency in the late 1950s. Phillip Morris's Marlboro brand had long been targeted toward women, but Leo Burnett repositioned it as a "real" man's cigarette by featuring tattooed cowboys smoking Marlboros. Depicting a rugged and independent cowboy riding his horse into a wild western landscape, the campaign successfully awakened male smokers' desire to project an overtly masculine persona. This campaign has remained relatively consistent over the years, with only a slight change from the tattooed "Marlboro Man" to "Welcome to Marlboro Country."

The Marlboro Man helped make the brand a best seller in the US, representing up to 21% of domestic market share in 1993. In addition, according to *Businessweek* (2006), the Marlboro man image contributed

substantially to the brand being ranked in 2005 among the top ten global brands, with a brand value of over $21 billion.

While Marlboro cigarette ads were appealing to male audiences, Virginia Slims' slogan "You've come a long way, baby" was successfully appealing to female audiences. But decades before the Virginia Slims campaign, Lucky Strike (also owned by Phillip Morris) was targeting female audiences in the early 20th century. It used female celebrity testimonials to promote smoking among women, and it used the slogan "Reach for a Lucky—instead of a sweet" to encourage women to smoke instead of eating candy (Petrone, 1996). The brand's strategy to empower female smoking rights peaked when its publicists staged the "Torch of Freedom" parade in 1929 on Easter Sunday. In the parade, women lit cigarettes and marched through New York City. The event drew much attention from the media and contributed to the perception of smoking as a symbol of women's freedom, equality, and liberation. One of the first modern-day "pseudo-events," the parade was orchestrated by Edward L. Bernays, an early pioneer in public relations. The event is reputed to be one of the most successful public relations campaigns in US history.

Similar to Lucky Strike, Virginia Slims, introduced in 1968, used feminist appeals. The early campaigns employed a comparison appeal, juxtaposing traditional women wearing dreary clothing and laboring at tedious household chores with modern, professional women wearing sleek outfits and "lighting up." In one of the ads, the copy reads, "Back then, every man gave his wife at least one day a week out of the house. You've come a long way, baby. Virginia Slims – Slimmer than the fat cigarettes men smoke." Along the same lines, their campaigns have used such slogans as "It's a woman thing" and "Find your voice."

Socializing and youth are two common images projected in cigarette advertising. Taking the lead in associating sociability with smoking was Camel's cartoonish Joe Camel. The "Old Joe" character was employed in 1988, when Camel's parent company R. J. Reynolds tried to refresh its brand image by launching the "Smooth Character" multimedia advertising campaign. Pictured hanging out with friends at bars and parties, lighting up in a sports car, and playing billiards, Joe Camel symbolized sociability and friendliness.

Another ad featured him in a tuxedo and introduced him as "The Character of the Year." Joe Camel brought stunning success to the RJR company. In three years during the time Joe Camel served as its "spokesperson," RJR quickly grew to become the sixth largest brand in a $40 billion market (Bird, 1991).

## Crisis and Controversy: Cigarette Advertising as a Social Evil

Ever since the early beginnings of tobacco promotion, some people have recognized the harmful effects of smoking. The tobacco scare emerged in the 1950s and smoking became a salient social issue in 1964 when US Surgeon General C. Everett Koop reported the first definitive conclusions about the links between smoking and lung cancer. These reports stimulated educational and legislative efforts to reduce smoking. To cite one notable legislative effort, in 1965 Congress began requiring health-risk warning labels to appear on all cigarette packs and tobacco advertisements. Facing fierce counterattacks and powerful lobbying by the tobacco industry, the Surgeon General reignited the tobacco control movement by calling for a smoke-free society by the year 2000. The smoke-free society plan spawned statewide and national antismoking movements (Paek, 2005).

In this antismoking social movement, cigarette advertising was an early and prominent target. In 1967, the Fairness Doctrine established by the Federal Communications Commission (FCC) required that all TV stations broadcast one antismoking public service announcement (PSA) for every three cigarette ads that aired. Congress went even further by banning cigarette ads from broadcasting media altogether, beginning in 1971.

Scholars have asserted that cigarette advertising improperly influences people's perceptions, beliefs, attitudes, and behavior about smoking. In particular, cigarette advertising has been blamed for the following: (1) it promotes smoking to children; (2) it makes audiences misperceive social images and norms associated with smoking; and (3) it provides falsely healthful images of smoking.

Related to the first point, for example, Fischer and his associates (1991) found that a majority of the studied 3- to 6-year-old children recognized the "Old Joe" character as much as they did Mickey Mouse, and that they were able to link the character with cigarettes. DiFranza et al. (1991) also found that the Joe Camel campaigns appealed more strongly to adolescents under 18 than to adults. As evidence for that finding, Camel's share of the adolescent cigarette market increased from less than 1% before 1988 to more than 13% in 1993 (Calfee, 2000). After fierce attacks from scholars, health officials, and consumer activists, in 1999 the Joe Camel campaign was finally discontinued. Similarly, Virginia Slims' campaign has been condemned for promoting smoking among teenage girls, and the Marlboro man has been criticized for associating a masculine American ideal with smoking. The Surgeon General's Report (1994) also noted that cigarette advertising of various brands has made pseudoscientific health claims by promoting filter effectiveness and mildness, and by depicting healthy and attractive models enjoying life in pure and natural settings.

## Antismoking Social Movements and the Birth of "Truth"

The antismoking social climate brought forth various legal battles between tobacco companies and either state governments or private individuals. Perhaps one of the biggest legal battles came in 1998 when the tobacco industry approved a 46-state Master Settlement Agreement, totaling a landmark sum of $246 billion to be paid. From that sum, tobacco companies agreed to spend $1.5 billion over five years to fund antismoking campaigns, including the Phillip Morris Youth Smoking Prevention campaign.

In April 1999, as part of the Master Settlement Agreement, the major US tobacco companies agreed to remove all advertising from outdoor and transit billboards across the nation. The remaining time on at least 3,000 billboard leases, valued at $100 million, was turned over to the states for posting anti-tobacco messages. Alongside statewide smoking prevention programs, antismoking media campaigns have flourished.

The "truth" campaign has proven to be one of the most successful antismoking campaigns in US history. It originated in Florida in 1997 after the state won a legal battle against the tobacco industry. The legal settlement earmarked $200 million for a state-run pilot program to prevent youth smoking. The "truth" campaign targeted 12- to 17-year-olds, and it aimed to create unfavorable attitudes toward the tobacco industry. It also adopted the following social marketing techniques: focusing on narrowly defined target audiences; setting realistic goals and objectives; employing top advertising professionals; and collaborating with Hollywood celebrities, government policy makers, and teen opinion leaders.

The campaign contributed to a decline in the smoking rate from 18.6 to 11.1% among middle-schoolers and from 27.4% to 22.6% among high-schoolers (Kotler et al., 2002). After its stunning success in Florida, the campaign expanded into a nationwide campaign sponsored by the American Legacy Foundation and funded from the Master Settlement Agreement.

Most importantly, the success of the "truth" campaign stems from its sustained and consistent efforts to build brand images around the concept of "truth." The campaign also vilifies the tobacco industry by associating it with an antithetical concept—"lies." By revealing the tobacco industry's unethical and manipulative business practices, the campaign theme appealed to adolescents' rebellious tendencies against anything that represents "the establishment." The campaign also employed brilliant creative and media strategies. When the campaign was launched, it used curiosity appeals by not revealing that it was an antismoking ad. All it initially said was, "Knowledge is infectious. Truth." Its TV ads also used various shocking visuals like body bags symbolizing smoking victims, an image that a wide audience still remembers.

The campaign also mocked cigarette advertising by parodying their techniques. One example parodies the classic Marlboro ads in which two macho-looking western men ride horses side-by-side into the wilderness. In the "truth" magazine ads, one rider and his horse are accompanied by a saddled but riderless mount. The headline asks, *What if cigarette ads told the Truth?* Instead of cigarette warning labels, the copy within the warning label box reads, *YEE HAW! You Too Can Be An Independent, Rugged, Macho-looking Dead Guy.*

Another TV spot parodied Virginia Slims's "Find Your Voice" campaign by showing a "truth" spokesperson asking through an artificial voicebox, *"Was this the voice you wanted us to find?"* In conjunction with this successful antismoking campaign, active antismoking movements reduced smoking rates among adults from 41.9% in 1965 to 20.8% in 2004 (NCHS, 2006).

## Continued Criticism, Social Dilemmas, and Future Directions

Tobacco advertising will continue to draw criticism and condemnation. Ever since it has been targeted for criticism and regulation by governments, scholars, and antismoking activists, tobacco companies have resorted to other promotional techniques such as in-store signage, event promotions, product placements, and sport sponsorships. For example, University of Georgia professor Dean Krugman and colleagues (2005) report that about 91% of the total cigarette advertising and promotional spending in 2001 was for sales promotion, which included retail value-added, promotional allowances, and coupons. Also, according to *Advertising Age*, in 2006 Phillip Morris did not spend any money on advertising for the Marlboro brand. Instead, it spent its money on direct marketing and in-store promotions. Even with the redirected funds, Marlboro still leads the tobacco market with its 40.5% market share.

The new promotions are far from immune to criticism, however. For example, research has found that smoking scenes in popular movies are creating social images of smoking and influencing underage people to smoke (Distefan et al., 1999). In response to recent advocacy and Congressional calls for Hollywood to participate in the antismoking movement, the Motion Picture Association of America announced that it would consider smoking as a factor in rating movies. Accordingly, several movie companies such as Walt Disney and Universal Studios have promised to remove smoking from some of their films (Fixmer, 2007).

In this new phase of the antismoking era, tobacco companies are finding other ways to survive. For example, Altria, the newly renamed parent company of Philip Morris, is increasingly relying on international tobacco sales, partly because of the transnational appeal of Marlboro's brand image. Virginia Slims advertising has maintained its campaign theme with the slogan of "Find your voice," but it has expanded its target audiences to Asian, African American, and

Hispanic females. Camel is even developing new products that have candy-like flavors such as Kaui Kolada, Twista Lime, Margarita Mixer, and

Beach Breezer. In addition, the tobacco companies are now relying on "stealth," "viral," and "buzz" marketing techniques.

Last, smokeless tobacco promotion has recently come under increased scrutiny. In 2005, the five largest tobacco companies spent about $261 million to promote smokeless tobacco products like Skoal and Copenhagen (FTC, 2007). In the future, increased attention to smokeless tobacco will broaden the scope of public concern and initiate movements toward regulation.

## Conclusion

Despite intense and widespread criticism, tobacco advertising has been an undeniable marketing triumph, and it has set milestones in the development of modern advertising. Tobacco campaigns have successfully associated cigarette brands with rugged outdoorsmen, independent and modern women, and sociable and youthful hipsters. Facing continued regulations and controversies, tobacco companies will aggressively try to find ways to survive. Whether they flourish or perish depends on how they respond to changing marketing and social environments. Ultimately, from a broad social and ethical perspective, the question of whether tobacco advertising should be banned or permitted continues to pose complex dilemmas.

## Questions

1.  Which tobacco ads do you think are most effective and memorable? Why?

2.  Do you think tobacco ads are to blame for youth smoking?

3.  Do you think tobacco ads should be banned or permitted? Why?

4.  If you were working for one of the tobacco companies, how would you promote your tobacco products?

5.  Is there any way tobacco companies can both practice social responsibility and achieve their marketing goals?

## References and Recommended Reading

Marlboro man rides into the sunset (2007, June 25). *Advertising Age*. pp. S-1, 50.

Bird, L. (1991, May 20). Joe Smooth for president. *Adweek's Marketing Week*, 20-22.

Bosman, J. (2006, March 10). For tobacco, stealth marketing is the norm. *The New York Times*, p. C4.

The 100 top brands: 2006 (2006). *Businessweek*. Retrieved July 25, 2007, from http://bwnt.businessweek.com/brand/2006/

Calfee, J. (2000). The historical significance of Joe Camel. *Journal of Public Policy & Marketing*, 19, 168-182.

Cohen, J. B. (2000). Playing to win: Marketing and public policy at odds over Joe Camel. *Journal of Public Policy & Marketing*, 19, 155-167.

DiFranza, J.R., J.W. Richards, et al. (1991). RJR Nabisco's cartoon camel promotes Camel cigarettes to children. *Journal of American Medical Association*, 266, 3149-3153.

Distefan, J. M., Gilpin, E. A., Sargent, J. D., & Pierce, J. P. (1999). Do movie stars encourage adolescents to start smoking? Evidence from California. *Preventive Medicine*, 28(1), 1-11.

Federal Trade Commission (2007). Smokeless tobacco report for the years 2002-2005. Washington, DC: Federal Trade Commission. Retrieved July 29, 2007, from http://www.ftc.gov/reports/tobacco/02-05smokeless0623105.pdf

Fischer, P.M., Schwartz, M.P., Richards, J.W. Jr, Goldstein, A.O., & Rojas, T.H. (1991). Brand logo recognition by 3- to 6-year-old children: Mickey Mouse and Old Joe the Camel. *Journal of American Medical Association*, 266, 3145-3148.

Fixmer, Andy. (2007, July 26). Walt Disney to snuff smoking in some films. *Washington Post*, Retrieved July 30, 2007, from http://www.washingtonpost.com/wp-dyn/content/article/2007/07/25/AR2007072502103.html

King, K. W., Reid, L. N., Moon, Y. S., & Ringold, D. (1991). Changes in the visual imagery of print cigarette ads, 1954-1986: The years of major smoking and health events. *Journal of Public Policy and Marketing*, 10(1), 63-80.

Kotler, P., Roberto, N., & Lee, N. (2002). *Social marketing: Improving the quality of life* (2nd Ed). Thousand Oaks, CA: Sage.

Krugman, D. M., Quinn, W. H., Sung, Y., & Morrison, M. (2005). Understanding the role of cigarette promotion and youth smoking in a changing marketing environment. *Journal of Health Communication*, 10, 261-278.

National Center for Health Statistics (NCHS) (2006). *Health, United States, 2006 with chart book on trends in the health of Americans*, Hyattsville, MD: NCHS.

Paek, H.-J. (2005). *Perceived peer influences in the effects of antismoking media messages: An exploration of mediating and moderating mechanisms*. Unpublished Dissertation, University of Wisconsin, Madison.

Petrone, G. S. (1996). *Tobacco advertising: The great seduction*. Atglen, PA: Schiffer.

Surgeon General. (1994). Preventing tobacco use among young people: A report of the Surgeon General (pp. 175-184). Washington, DC: U.S. Department of Health and Human Services.

## Online Resources

**Tobacco Advertising Gallery**
http://tobaccofreekids.org/adgallery/
The website provides a large collection of cigarette advertisements searchable by country, company, brand, or type of advertising. It is sponsored by the non-profit antismoking organization, Tobacco-Free Kids.

**The Richard W. Pollay 20th Century Tobacco Advertising Collection**
http://www.tobacco.org/ads/index.php?tdo_code=pollay_ads
The website presents a catalogue of tobacco advertising examples collected by prominent cigarette advertising scholar, Richard Pollay. The site also provides the latest tobacco-related news.

**Tobacco TV advertising collection:**
http://www.tvparty.com/vaultcomcig.html
The website presents historical examples of portrayals of cigarette products advertised on television.

## Media Literacy Clearing House

http://www.frankwbaker.com/smokingintroduction.htm

The website includes various antismoking and smoking ads so that students learn how both types of ads target audiences, the types of communication techniques they use, and how the ads can affect audiences. The purpose of this media literacy website is to educate students to critically read and understand media presentations.

# Sweet Innocents or Savvy Consumers?
## Exploring the Controversial Practice of Advertising to Children

## By Catharine M. Curran & Joël Bree

"IS SPONGE BOB THE NEW JOE CAMEL?"

This provocative question was posed in response to a promotional campaign for Pop Tarts featuring SpongeBob SquarePants. The campaign, and others like it, have prompted an increasing number of calls by parents, advocacy groups, and concerned others to ban the use of popular children's cartoon characters in advertisements for products these groups consider "junk food."

Not only are these groups asking questions, they are filing lawsuits. The Pop Tarts campaign, for example, led to a recent lawsuit in Massachusetts filed against Viacom, the owner of Sponge Bob, and Kellogg's, the manufacturer of Pop Tarts. The lawsuit claimed that children are unfairly influenced by such popular characters promoting unhealthy products. This argument is similar to claims made in the 1980s and 1990s about the use of the cartoon spokes-animal Joe Camel in cigarette advertising having unfair influence on children.[1]

Because of the lawsuits and efforts of various advocacy groups, many food marketers are now foregoing the use of cartoon characters in their advertising. Globally, some countries are now banning the use of cartoon characters and other popular children's icons in advertising for many food products.

Food advertising is only one of many issues surrounding the promotion of products to children who, for the purposes of this chapter, are defined as youth under the age of 15. In this chapter we will briefly review the history of children's advertising in the United States, we will examine children's understanding of advertising, and we will examine some of the current issues in children's advertising. Finally, we will describe how children's advertising is regulated in the US.

## From Cherubs to Barbie Dolls

Images of children have been used throughout the history of U.S. advertising. Originally images of children were used to sell products to adults. Also, in these early ads children often were depicted in an idealized form or as cherubs. Even many children's products, such as toys and clothing, were marketed to adults instead of children. Beginning in 1955, all of that was about to change with the proliferation of television.

With television came children's programming that provided an opportunity for advertisers to speak directly to children and to shape their preferences for a variety of products. One of the first marketers to realize the potential of television as an advertising vehicle to children was Ruth Handler, a founder of the Mattel toy company.

In 1955 Handler bought advertising for a full year on the *Mickey Mouse Show*. The cost was roughly equal to the value of Mattel at the time. She believed television would allow children to no longer be dependent on their parents for information, thus empowering children to make their own consumer choices. The first product Mattel advertised on television was a toy gun, followed by the "Betsy Wetsy" doll. Fortunately for Mattel, Handler's gamble paid off. The ads were so successful that the factory could not keep up with demand for either toy (Evans, 2004).

In 1959, Handler also used television advertising to introduce her most daring new product, the Barbie doll. Handler realized that girls would be interested in a sophisticated toy with lots of options and accessories. Although Barbie was a flop at the International Toy Fair, the doll quickly became Mattel's best-selling toy not just in the US but globally. Even today they are sold at the incredible rate of two dolls per second (Evans, 2004).

Much has changed since 1955. Children are now a fully realized market sector in the US and internationally. In 2000, children under 12 in the United States accounted for $28 billion of direct spending and influenced $250 billion in family spending (Gunter, Oates, & Blades, 2005). There has been an increase in all forms of marketing communications targeted at children with the aim of encouraging children to spend their own money, or to get them to encourage their moms and dads to make purchases for them.

## Children's Exposure to Media

It's obvious that today's children live in a saturated media environment. From the youngest ages children are placed in front of screens displaying many types of media: television screens, computer screens, and video game screens. In a typical day, for instance, roughly 83% of children ages zero to six use media with a screen (Rideout, et al, 2003). In other words, for children there is no avoiding advertising and other forms of brand communication.

### Print Media

There are a wide variety of print media targeted at children today. Children, especially young boys, often read comic books that feature fantastic characters and risqué images. But it wasn't just the stories inside the pages that were notorious. The ads in the back of the comics promised incredible items such as the World's Smallest Monkey, X-ray glasses, and a Monster Sized Skelton (see Figure 1). These ads were often at best misleading and at worst deceptive. Often children were required to sell products or perform

some other task to get the advertised item. Once the product was delivered it often was not exactly as described. For example the infamous "Sea Monkeys" of comic book fame are actually a form of brine shrimp.

In addition to comic books, during the 20th Century the number and variety of print media targeted to children steadily increased. Some adult magazines are now producing a version for teens. Examples of these more popular magazines include: *Sports Illustrated Kids* (1.2 million readers, average age 14.2), *Teen Vogue* (2.3 million readers, average age 15.5) and *Cosmo Girl* (8.7 million readers, median age 15.4). Just like their adult counterparts these titles all rely on advertising revenue, and there is no shortage of advertisers trying to reach this demographic. For example, between 2004 and 2005

*Cosmo Girl* generated over $88 million in advertising revenue. The most frequently advertised categories, in order of prevalence are: cosmetics, clothing, footwear, media (i.e., movie and television show promotions), hair products, personal care products, sporting goods, audio/visual equipment, government/organizations, and medicine.

## Radio

In the early part of the 20th Century, radio advertising was used to encourage children to ask for certain products and encourage their parents to purchase certain items. Radio ads often used the characters in popular children's radio programs such as the *Lone Ranger*, *Dick Tracy*, or *Little Orphan Annie*. Children were enticed with premiums that involved collecting labels from the products, or getting prizes that were used to decode secret messages to show their membership in a secret club.

Today, radio is still an important medium for reaching children. On average, children listen to 5.4 hours of radio per week. Interestingly, radio is used by both boys and girls. However, as children age, girls tend to listen to more hours of radio than boys, primarily listening to music (OfCom, 2006).

## New Media

The Internet is now a popular medium that reaches children. Branded websites now feature what have been termed "advergames" which encourage children to play a game set in a branded environment with branded characters (Winkler & Buckner, 2006). For example, the website for Kraft Macaroni and Cheese (www.thecheesiest.com) offers children a variety of games and activities.

Branded websites are not the only ways in which advertisers are using the web to reach children. Advertisers have also been embedding advertising messages in popular children's websites such as Neopets.com. On this site the user can take their virtual pet to McDonald's or buy them branded products. Social networking sites such as MySpace and Facebook have also become popular with advertisers looking to reach a younger market.

Mobile marketing, via short message service (SMS), and downloads for either MP3 players or portable gaming systems such as the Nintendo DS or Sony's PSP, also are becoming a more common way to reach children with advertising messages as more and more children now have access to these media players.

## Television

As previously mentioned, children spend a good deal of their conscious lives in front of the television screen. From Saturday morning cartoons, to after-school specials, to programming on the Cartoon Network, the CW, Disney Channel, and Nickelodeon, there in no dearth of content designed to attract children. On average, children spend 3.5 hours per day watching television. The result is exposure to a good deal of commercial messages. The most popular categories of products advertised to children in descending order are: toys (including video games), CDs and DVDs, and cereals and breakfast foods. Snacks are actually one of the products least advertised to children.

Television advertising now often includes website addresses for the product or service that effectively links the two advertising media. One interesting fact about television advertising to children is that children don't mind repetition. This allows advertisers to keep the same commercial airing for longer periods than can be done with adults. For example, Life Cereal's "Mikey" campaign first aired in the 1970s with a finicky four year-old who hated everything but, to his brother's surprise, Life Cereal. The famous tag line "He won't eat it, he hates everything. Hey Mikey! He likes it," is one of the most recognizable lines in television advertising. The Mikey ad is still occasionally shown today even though the actor who played Mikey is now in his mid-thirties.

# How Children Process Advertising

Overall, younger children tend to have a globally positive attitude toward TV advertising (Bree, 1993). However, those attitudes tend to become less positive as they get older. Even if their global view of advertising becomes less positive, children can still possess a positive attitude toward individual ads.

89

## Table 1: Factors Influencing Children's Attitudes Towards Ads

| Appreciated Criteria | Rejected Criteria |
|---|---|
| • humor<br>• animated cartoons<br>• pleasant music or catchy song<br>• easily recognized/memorized slogans and jingles<br>• animals<br>• action<br>• favorite heroes or stars<br>• ads referring to cultural values like American myths<br>• older people<br>• children (facilitates identification) | • ads considered "stupid" (subjective judgment)<br>• ads perceived as lies: actions too spectacular to be true, exaggerated effects of product qualities<br>• ads that are too long or have slow rhythm<br>• lack of original argumentation<br>• confusing the links between the images and the product<br>• scary ads<br>• serious testimonials that resemble school<br>• unfamiliar references (e.g., literary) |

Table 1 summarizes the factors identified by previous studies as the main elements influencing children's attitude toward ads (Guichard & Pecheux, 2007). Advertising designed for children often combines several of these criteria, such as action with bright colors and animation. In addition, commercials directed toward children generally employ music and memorable slogans. Children often can easily recall specific ads or identify advertising characters since they find the commercials so appealing.

The ability of even young children to recall ads or to identify ad characters has led to charges that advertising exerts undue influence—or manipulates—children. In addition, children's ability to critically analyze advertising is also at the crux of why groups call for bans on all advertising targeting children. These groups maintain that children are unable to understand the persuasive intent of advertising, so they can only be victims of it. However, nearly 40 years of research shows that reality is more complex than these simplistic generalizations.

By and large, children's understanding of the persuasive intent of advertising increases with age. This improvement is correlated with the child's ability to take into account the point of view of other people and, more generally, to understand that others can have a different perspective. Though observed in children as young as six years, the consensus among researchers is that this ability generally appears between the ages of 8 to 12. Over time there is a gradual change in the child's comprehension of advertising's objectives, as being either to inform or persuade. The informative objective is understood even by very young children ("is to inform us about new products"), whereas the comprehension of the persuasive intention is, again, generally gained between 8- to 10-years of age.

Therefore, many people argue that advertising takes unfair advantage of children since they do not have the cognitive abilities to protect against the persuasive nature of advertising (to be able to counter-argue, to criticize advertisers and messages). Think of how often you find yourself saying, "Yeah, right," to a statement made in an ad. You were involved in counter-argumentation. You know—now that you are an adult—that ad claims can be exaggerations, but when did you develop that knowledge? Obviously, education and accumulated experience are essential to a child's ability to counter argue.

For many of you reading this chapter, you can probably recall buying an advertised toy only to become disappointed once you got it home. Yo-Yo's are a great example. TV commercials show individuals doing all sorts of cool tricks with a Yo-Yo. To perform those tricks, however, one must practice, practice, practice. Thus for many children, the Yo-Yo was a huge disappointment since kids lacked the skill to make it do much of anything beyond going up and down, and even that took a lot of practice.

Disappointing buying experiences can, over time, lead to increased skepticism of advertised claims. Researchers are continuing to determine when and how children develop and use their abilities to counter-argue advertising claims rather than demonstrating passive acceptance. The ability to counter-argue claims and to decrease one's susceptibility to the persuasive nature of advertising lies at the heart of three important issues discussed in the next section.

## Critical Issues in Advertising to Children

Throughout the modern history there have been a variety of social and public health issues that have in part been blamed on advertising to children. Generally, the claims are that advertising poses a threat to children's moral or physical development. The following issues—two current, and one enduring—relate directly to these threats.

### Global Increases in Levels of Childhood Obesity

Obesity, specifically childhood obesity, became a true global, social and medical crisis in the early 21st Century. The origin of this epidemic is complex and it involves various genetic, social, and economic factors. In spite of the multifaceted nature of this problem, food marketing, and especially advertising, has received the most virulent criticism. In 2004 the American Psychological Association convened a task force on children's advertising. The task force reviewed the relevant research and found that advertisers were spending more than $12 billion annually on advertising targeted at children, which resulted in the average child seeing over 40,000 commercials per year.

According to the task force "… the most common products marketed to children are sugared cereals, candies, sweets, sodas and snack foods. Such advertising of unhealthy food products to young children contributes to poor nutritional habits that may last a lifetime and be a variable in the current epidemic of obesity among kids" (APA, 2004).

Many studies were initiated in order to understand the link between advertising—particularly television advertising—and childhood obesity. The conclusion drawn from this research is that there is no absolute, causal link between advertising and childhood obesity.

Moreover, when we consider that several European countries prohibit or severely limit advertising to children, we should expect to see much lower childhood obesity rates in those countries compared to surrounding countries. However, that is not the case. In 1991, Sweden enacted strict laws prohibiting television advertising targeted at children less than 12 years old. Yet, the percentage of older children between 7 and 11 years classified as obese or overweight is 22% compared to other countries where there is no such prohibition such as Greece (22%), France (18%) and Germany (16%). In Italy, where cartoons cannot be interrupted by commercials and where advertising to children is prohibited, the rate of overweight children between 7 and 11 years is 31%.

In the US the Federal Trade Commission's (FTC) own research found that over the last decade television food advertising to children had actually declined an astounding 65%. However, food (especially breakfast cereal) still remained one of the top categories of products advertised to children. Regardless, the link between advertising and childhood obesity remains anecdotal.

## Marketing in Schools

Advertisers realized that one way to reach children with their messages was to advertise in schools. This controversial practice allows marketers to deliver a message that can be narrowly targeted to specific ages in very specific locations. Two practices have been discussed in detail.

One practice is exclusivity agreements between schools and corporations, particularly beverage companies. These exclusivity agreements allowed usually either Coca-Cola or Pepsi to install vending machines in schools and to exclusively distribute their products at school functions (Curran, 1999). In exchange the schools received necessary funding for, ironically, equipment for physical education and playground activities. Both marketers are now keenly aware of the pressure on schools to eliminate vending machines. Thus, each has promised to set rules for selling certain products and is only now stocking certain brands that the firms have deemed to be part of a "healthy" lifestyle such as baked chips, low fat snacks, diet sodas, waters, and sports drinks in school vending machines, and limiting when items can be purchased from the machines.

The second practice is related to exploiting school children as a captive audience for advertisers by using ad-supported programming in schools. For example, Channel One (www.channelone.com), a 12-minute news and entertainment show seen by over seven million middle and high school students in the US, is often criticized as exploiting children.

Despite winning two Peabody Awards, Channel One continues to be criticized for the advertising that accompanies the content. Critics contend that students are not able to avoid the ads since the commercials are delivered as part of a school requirement. In exchange for showing the program, schools are given video equipment that can include satellite dishes, VCRs and television sets for every 23 students. Because the equipment can be used for other purposes, the schools often claim the benefits of Channel One far outweigh the drawbacks.

## Pester Power

Since the 1980s, children have been increasingly involved in family purchase decisions (MacNeal, 1998). Today, the children's sphere of influence is no longer limited to products that directly target them. Thus, in addition to intervening directly in the purchases concerning child products (cereals, toys…) children play an increasingly active role—at all the stages—in buying decisions for family products (food, cars, vacations, computers, electronics…), and even for products used by their parents (cosmetics, appliances…; Guichard, 1995).

Children's appetite for new and novel products can be a proverbial "Trojan Horse": Firms can use the child's interest to introduce new products and brands to the family; a phenomenon referred to as reverse socialization.

Sometimes the information provided in advertising is contrary with the parents' values. As a result, "parent/child advertising" can introduce conflict. Parents often report feeling overwhelmed by the number of advertised products demanded by their children. In reality, these requests are often triggered by other sources of influence such as friends or seeing the product in use, not just in advertising. The mechanisms of influence in the formation of consumer choice are too numerous to blame advertising for all children's product desires and the conflicts that stem from them, even if advertising's weight in the equation is substantial.

Researchers have found that there can be a benefit from these conflicts in that they help the child to better decode advertising. For example, parents may point out that to have an advertised product perform as demonstrated requires practice and patience (e.g., the Yo-Yo example). Such discussion can help the child to understand that advertised claims may not always tell the whole story.

## Regulation of Children's Advertising

At various times different groups have called for regulation—ranging from bans to limits—on certain forms of advertising, or advertising of certain products, to children. People are often surprised to learn that there are only two federal regulations of children's advertising in the US.

The first is the Children's Television Act of 1990 (CTA). The CTA includes time limits on children's advertising during their peak viewing hours to 10.5 minutes per hour on weekends and 12 minutes per hour on weekdays, as well as requiring separation of the advertising content from the programming. The CTA also prohibits the practice of host selling which was common in the early days of children's programming on both radio and television (Curran and Richards, 2000).

Host selling is when the program's host—or characters from the program—are used to promote products during the program. Doing so blends the entertainment content with the advertising content and is thought to confuse children. Also under the CTA, no ads adjacent to the program can contain that program's characters.

In 2006, the CTA was expanded to include websites that are included in television programming. Therefore, a website that a program refers children to cannot contain advertising and can only be for entertainment or educational purposes. Enforcement of this act rests with the FCC and the Federal Trade Commission (FTC).

The second Federal regulation is the Children's Online Privacy Protection Act. This legislation regulates the collection of personal information from children. It requires website operators to get parental permission before collecting personal information, as well as disclosing how that information will be used and how parents can access that information. Enforcement of this act rests with the FTC.

As noted, there have been calls for bans on various forms of advertising to children beginning with comic book ads and continuing today with calls to regulate ads for "junk" food. The primary impediment to bans such as these is the U.S. Constitution's First Amendment. Although advertising is not fully protected speech under the First Amendment, it is a form of protected commercial speech. This means that advertisers of lawful products have a right to deliver their message to the marketplace (Beales, 2004). For example, products such as cigarettes, alcohol, and junk foods, that are considered either dangerous or at least harmful to children, are lawful products. In order for the federal government to limit advertising for these products to children, it must prove that limiting advertising will prevent the harm. In other words, in the case of junk food advertising, the government must prove that banning it will positively affect the problem of childhood obesity. If not, the government is reluctant to enact restrictions.

Despite an all-out ban, other means can be used to regulate advertising to children. For example, in the US the primary means of control is through industry self-regulation, primarily through the Children's Advertising Review Unit (CARU) of the Better Business Bureau. This group monitors all forms of advertising to children and can ask an advertiser to make changes to any ad it believes violates its guidelines. Advertisers even send ads to CARU for review prior to airing the commercials.

CARU employees attempt to view the advertising from the child's point of view. For example, in a recent case the advertising for Mattel's "Shonen Jump Naruto" toys was first thought to be misleading since the toys are shown destroying a target made from rice paper—though it was labeled as such in the ad. Initially it was thought that children might believe the toys could destroy all targets, but after review CARU determined that the disclosures in the ad about the type of target were adequate to prevent confusion. Obviously, CARU's guidelines prohibit showing a toy doing something it does not do.

At various times through the history of advertising regulation other groups such as various State's Attorneys General or legislative bodies have imposed regulation on advertising practices or content to children. For example, the removal of all tobacco advertising was accomplished through the 1999 Tobacco Settlement which was an agreement between the tobacco companies and a group of State's Attorneys General.

## Summary

In response to lawsuits such as the Massachusetts "Sponge Bob/Viacom" suit, as well as increasing pressure from advocacy groups, we are now seeing marketers and various parts of the regulatory system address concerns over food advertising and childhood obesity.

As discussed, beverage marketers have announced a voluntary change in their policy about the type of products sold in schools. Recently, Kraft Foods announced that it would voluntarily stop advertising certain foods to young kids. In addition, the FTC has held a series of workshops for marketers and advertisers to discuss how to best address these concerns.

Other groups have gotten involved such as the Center for Science in the Public Interest which has issued a list of junk foods that should not be advertised to children, and the grocery manufacturers association has begun to highlight the efforts of its members at identifying healthy alternatives. Last but not least, CARU has begun a reorganization and review of these issues. The ultimate outcome of these collective efforts is not yet known, nor is it known if efforts to reduce food advertising will influence the incidence of childhood obesity. But the concern is there and action is taking place.

If we can learn one thing from the history of children's advertising, it is that at some point in the not-to-distant future, there will once again be a social issue that will involve calls for limits on advertising in the name of protecting children.

## Questions

1. In your opinion would banning food advertising to children decrease the incidence of childhood obesity? Why or why not?

2. What are the main issues in the controversy over children's advertising?

3. Recall an incident in your past involving a negative experience with an advertised product? Did that experience impact your faith in advertised claims?

4.      What do you believe is the influence of advertising on children's purchase decisions? Are there other influences that are stronger? What are they?

## References and Recommended Readings

American Psychological Association (2004). Television advertising leads to unhealthy habits in children. Retrieved November 21, 2007, from: http://www.apa.org/releases/childrenads.html

Beales, J. Howard III (2004). Advertising to kids and the FTC: A regulatory retrospective that advises the present. *George Mason Law Review*, 12, 873.

Brée, Joël (1993). *Les enfants, la consommation et le marketing*. Paris, P.U.F.

Curran, Catharine M. (1999). A best buy in advertising: Schools selling students as media audiences. *Journal of Consumer Marketing*, 16 (6), 534-536.

Curran, Catharine M., and Jef I. Richards (2000). The regulation of children's advertising in the U.S. *International Journal of Marketing and Advertising to Children*, 2 (2), 139-154.

Derbaix Christian & Joël Brée (1997). The impact of children's affective reactions elicited by commercials on attitude toward the advertisement and the brand. *International Journal of Research in Marketing*, 14, 207-229

Evans, Harold (2004). *They made America*. London: Little, Brown.

Greenberg, Bradley S., and Jeffrey E. Brand (1993). Television news and advertising in schools: The "Channel One" controversy. *Journal of Communication*, 43 (1), 143-151.

Guichard, Nathalie (1995). *L'influence de la publicité télévisée sur le comportement de l'enfant dans les décisions d'achat de la famille: Essai et expérimentation*. Thèse de Doctorat ès Sciences de Gestion, Université de Paris I – Panthéon-Sorbonne.

Guichard, Nathalie, and Claude Pecheux (2007). Les enfants et la publicité, in Joel Bree (Ed.), *Kids Marketing* (233-273). E.M.S.

Gunter, Barrie, Caroline Oates, and Mark Blades (2005). *Advertising to children on TV: Content, impact and regulation.* Mahwah, NJ: LEA.

McNeal, James U. (1998, April 20). Exploring the three kids' market. *American Demographics*, p. 37-41.

Mediamark Internet Reporter (2007, Spring). Magazine circulation report for teens. Retrieved June 12, 2007, from MRI Plus database: http://www.mriplus.com.

Moore-Shay, Elisabeth S., and Richard J. Lutz (2000). Children, advertising and product experiences: A multimethod inquiry. *Journal of Consumer Research*, 27 (1), 31-48.

Pecheux, Claude (2001). *Children's reactions to advertising communication: The moderating effect of involvement and mood on advertising processing and effectiveness.* Thèse de doctorat, Labacc, Facultés Universitaires Catholiques de Mons.

Rideout, Victoria J., Elizabeth A. Vandewater, and Ellen A. Wartella (2003). Zero to six: Electronic media in the lives of infants, toddlers and preschoolers. Kaiser Family Foundation. Retrieved November 21, 2007, from: http://www.kff.org/entmedia/3378.cfm

Winkler, Tina, and Kathy Buckner (2006). Receptiveness of gamers to embedded brand messages in advergames: Attitudes towards product placement. *Journal of Interactive Advertising*, 7 (1), 37-46.

## Online Resources

### Children's Advertising Review Unit
http://www.caru.org

This is the website for CARU, the primary self-regulatory body for children's advertising. The site contains the CARU guidelines and well as information about recent CARU actions.

## Center for Science in the Public Interest
http://www.cspinet.org

This is the website for the Center for Science in the Public Interest which traditionally has been one of the most virulent critics of advertising to children. They were instrumental in a number of regulatory attempts and prior calls for bans of advertising to children.

## Federal Trade Commission
http://www.ftc.gov

This is the website for the Federal Trade Commission which is the primary federal agency in charge of regulating most advertising.

# Notes

[1] In the infamous *Journal of the American Medical Association* study that found that the vast majority of preschool aged children recognized Joe Camel, many drew the conclusion that children would hold favorable views of the brand Camel or of cigarette smoking in general. Subsequent research revealed, however, that this was not the case. In fact, the majority of children held strong negative beliefs about cigarettes and about the Camel brand. Further, the children did not consider cigarettes to be an appropriate product for them nor did they demonstrate any interest in smoking. The only exception was children whose parents were smokers; these children still held negative views of smoking but were conflicted about some aspects of smoking behavior.

# Section 2

# Media:
## New Media Tools,
## Product Placement, and Saturation

# From Viral Videos to the Third Screen:
## Welcome to the New Media Ad Game

## by Tom Reichert

VIRAL VIDEOS, BLOGS, PODCASTS, DVRs and mobile downloads are just a few of the new and in-vogue media phenomena influencing today's marketers and consumers.

It seems as if each issue of *Advertising Age* or *Adweek* heralds a technological breakthrough—primarily through digital technology—that allows marketers to reach millions of potential customers in new and inventive ways.

Who knows? By the time you read this chapter some or all of these emerging means of communication may be passé or obsolete.

### A Media Revolution

The media world is in the midst of a revolution. More content choices and delivery options are available than ever before. "It is truly an exciting time in our industry," notes David Cohen, Director of Digital Communication for Universal McCann, a global media agency.

"We are facing a period of unprecedented change. Change in consumer expectations. Change in marketplace dynamics, and a change in the way we conduct business" ("The New 'Digital Divide'," 2006, p. 2).

As a consequence of these changes, media specialists, often looked upon as representing the least glamorous role in the advertising business, are evolving as strategists who are directing today's campaigns.

Creativity now is in the hands of these specialists who have a grasp of the media landscape and how innovations can be tapped to target consumers when and where they want to hear a brand message—while watching videos on iPods, searching the web on cell phones, or downloading TV shows on laptops.

This chapter touches on some of the more notable emerging new-media developments that are impacting advertising, as well as to show how today's media professionals are really where it's at.

# Trends Influencing Advertising

Several trends are influencing the traditional delivery of advertising to consumers. Many of these changes are due to emerging media and new technologies.

## Online Advertising

After taking a beating from 2001 to 2004, online advertising is back on its feet and accelerating.

Consider, for example, that online advertising is up 34% from 2005. It hit $16.8 billion in 2006 which puts it on par with radio advertising. In 2007, growth is expected to reach $21 billion. Anticipated 20% annual increases mean that online is expected to surpass both cable TV and magazine advertising by 2009.

Online ads make sense when one considers that, as Universal McCann's report indicates, 90% of heavy Internet users (about one-third of Americans) shop online and use the web to research future purchases.

## Differences in Usage

But not everyone is using the Internet to the same degree and for the same purposes. For instance, not only are young people more likely to use the web, but they are more likely to use it for socializing and downloading content.

David Cohen's agency recently released a study on what it calls "The New 'Digital Divide'" (2006).

Looking only at frequent Internet users, they found that 40% of 16- to 34-year-olds belong to a social-networking site, 75% regularly instant message, 71% participate in blogging, and 33% participate in peer-to-peer file sharing.

Advertisers who need to reach this audience can use these online usage patterns to develop more effective campaigns because it's obvious that limiting efforts to traditional media simply won't cut it.

## New Media Influencing Major Media

Also, consider that new media is definitely influencing major media.

Classified advertising, a long-time source of newspaper revenue, is making a mass migration to the web. People are selling their items on eBay and Craigslist, or posting jobs on Monster.com, instead of placing pricey classified ads in local newspapers.

Publishers are adapting, but the hemorrhaging is substantial and doesn't look to abate anytime soon. Partly as a result, newspaper circulation is trending downward. Recently, the *Dallas Morning News*, a major metropolitan daily, reported a 14% circulation decline. Newspaper circulation across the nation was down 2% in the first half of 2007.

Similarly, some magazines are finding it difficult to survive. *Premiere*, a movie and entertainment magazine, closed its print edition after 20 years amid drop offs in circulation and ad pages. The magazine is expected to continue as an online publication (Ives, 2007).

But not all magazines are going the way of *Premiere* or classified advertising. *Playboy* is altering its marketing strategy as it recognizes the impact of the web on advertising and readership. In an unconventional move, the publisher is intentionally cutting circulation by 13%. "We have a very strong print product," noted Bob Meyers, media group president at *Playboy*, "but there is a revolution that is taking place around us" (Ives, 1997, p. 3). Reporter Nat Ives observes that print advertising still commands higher revenues but the future lies in the fast growth of web audiences. *Playboy*'s current plan is to increase its total audience with more free content on its website. That way the company will be positioned to potentially make more money with bigger audiences as online advertising gains more respect.

In what looks like good news for television, Nielsen recently reported that the average US household now watches 8 hours and 14 minutes of television each day which is up slightly from 2005.

And despite what many analysts have considered a long downslide, more people are watching television. Just consider the first lines of a recent front-page story in *Advertising Age*:

**Cancel The Funeral:** Broadcast TV is alive and kicking harder than it has in years. Audiences have shown up in droves for the start of the fall season; 30-second-spot prices are reaching some of the highest levels of all time [and] marketers are throwing more money at the medium (Atkinson, 2005, p. 1).

In addition, Universal McCann's study shows that 85% of heavy Internet users report that when online they use other media such as television and radio.

Even telecommunications professor Michael Castengera (2006a) notes that during major events people overwhelmingly turn to and trust traditional media such as television, radio, and newspapers compared to "emerging media."

## Fragmentation

However, fragmentation is still a concern.

Since it is more difficult to reach consumers with traditional advertising, there is increasing interest in marketing services, also referred to as "below-the-line" advertising.

These nontraditional means of reaching consumers include event marketing, sponsorship, public relations, direct marketing, and sales promotion. These areas of marketing communication are experiencing rapid growth.

In fact, a recent report revealed that in 2005, for the first time, US agencies earned more revenue from marketing services than from traditional advertising and media (Johnson, 2007). One reason often cited for the shift is the measurability of marketing services. That's the view of industry observer and *Advertising Age* reporter Brad Johnson (2007, p. 1): "...what marketers need isn't just measured media; it's measurable results."

According to Castengera (2006b), however, marketing services are expanding because "it is becoming harder to reach the audience and marketers are looking at different ways to do that. That's the fragmentation."

Marketing guru Al Ries set forth a similar hypothesis in his recent book, *The Death of Advertising and the Rise of PR.*

## New Challenges

Several new challenges have advertisers and industry watchers guessing the impact new technologies will have on traditional advertising.

Most of these challenges pertain to the new ways many people are watching television such as DVRs, downloading, and mobile viewing.

### Digital Video Recording (DVR)

Digital video recording (DVR) is quickly gaining ground in the US. It's estimated that up to 15 million homes contain a DVR, which is at least a 65% increase over 2005.

DVRs are essentially VHS devices on steroids as they allow recording and playback of hours of programming.

TiVo is one of the leading DVR services.

Advertisers are especially wary of DVRs because they offer viewers the ability to fast forward or skip commercial pods. Television commercials have long been the gold standard of advertising, and any technology that threatens the 30-second spot moves marketers to wring their hands.

The move toward product placement is seen as one reaction to the perceived threat of the DVR.

Interestingly, however, some industry research suggests that DVRs are not having the negative impact on advertising effectiveness as expected.

It seems that people with DVRs not only watch more television, but they watch most of it live and they don't use the ad-skipping option as often as predicted.

In fact, ratings for prime-time programs actually increase—up to 5%—in homes with DVRs (Littleton, 2006).

Overall, that means more ad exposure, or at least as much as in non-DVR homes, which debunks media prognosticators' death knell for the 30-second spot. "Broadcast TV has always shown an ability to adapt to technological change," states media researcher Alan Wurtzel (2006). "It adapted to the remote control, the VCR, and even to competition from hundreds of cable and satellite channels. It will adapt now to the DVR."

Despite the ability to adapt, more recent research released by TiVo reveals that DVRs do influence TV ad viewing and receptivity. For example, one study reported a 12% sales drop for an established advertiser in DVR homes. Researcher Sunnil Garga summarized the findings in this way: "In every household that has a DVR... sales of all products are down, and sales of new products are down even further" (Neff, 2007a, p. 8). The study indicated that DVR effects are most pronounced for price-sensitive packaged goods and products advertised during dayparts more likely to be recorded; such as daytime television. Also affected are new products that depend on massive awareness to generate consideration.

In addition, DVR research can indicate which commercials are most likely to get "fast-forwarded." A separate report from the one previously mentioned indicated that creative approaches garnering the highest viewership ratings include (1) low-budget direct response ads and (2) high-budget ads previewing movies. These two types of commercials represent both ends of the budget spectrum.

Regardless of which study you reference, it appears that DVRs are influencing the media experience. They are contributing to more overall viewing of programming, which means that people have more opportunity to see the commercials. But digital recording also influences advertising effectiveness based on the type of product, placement, and creative approach.

## Downloaded Programming

Another challenge facing networks is the heightened interest in downloaded programming.

Recent findings from the summer 2006 Motion digital video study indicated that 10 million Americans have downloaded TV shows from the Internet, with over seven million downloading in the last month alone.

ABC has capitalized on this trend by selling its shows on iTunes since 2005.

More recently, ABC is making many of its programs such as *Cavemen*, *Lost*, and *Desperate Housewives* available for viewing on its website.

Viewers can watch for free but each show contains ads that can't be deleted or skipped. If you don't want to watch the ads, just download the show for a fee.

## The Third Screen

The screen on mobile phones—often referred to as the "third screen," TV and computer screens are the first and second screens—also is gaining momentum as another channel for advertisers to reach consumers.

Advertising on mobile phones has been limited thus far, primarily because service providers fear consumer annoyance and frustration.

With the sharp increase in interactivity and downloads on cell phones, however, marketers have figured out that ads placed within video-on-demand products are acceptable to consumers, as are banner ads on web pages.

According to *Times* reporter Amanda Andrews (2006, p. 61),

You don't have to be a rocket scientist to understand why advertisers value the potential of mobile phones. Not only do mobile operators have huge databases that contain the age and sex of their customers—giving them the ability to target advertising—but the introduction of entertainment on mobile phones, from video games to music videos and mobile television, has transformed the humble mobile phone into a personal entertainment centre.

Today, 70% of mobile advertising is in the form of text messages. But by 2007, it is predicted that 60% of all mobile advertising will be browser-based banner ads, followed by text-message advertising at 25%.

The key, says Enpocket CEO Mike Baker, is to frame the advertising so that "it doesn't even look like an ad to the end user, but a service" (Bruno, 2006).

Mobile advertising is expected to grow from $871 million in 2006 to over $11.3 billion in 2011.

Content sponsorship is expected to be an advertising catalyst, especially for stock quotes, sports scores, and weather forecasts which have been available on mobile phones for some time.

Despite the rosy outlook, some in the industry are warning that mobile advertising is a potential landmine. A recent editorial warned marketers to tread lightly as they figure out how to reach consumers on mobile phones: "Note to marketers: The mobile phone is not a toy. And it isn't a TV or a computer. So you should… quit trying to shove advertising—often irrelevant, often unwanted—into consumers' handsets" ("Rush to Mobile," 2007, p. 10).

The editorial writers also predict that crossing the intrusion line will result in irate users and potential legislation. Mobile advertisers, if they're not careful, might inadvertently trigger regulation similar to the telemarketing "Do Not Call" registry.

## Net Effect

As you can see, many options are available for viewing entertainment content.

What's the net effect?

Disney CEO Robert Iger told the *Calgary Herald* that because viewers will be able to get the content they want in multiple ways, television viewing will increase 10% in the next several years: "The more you make content available to buy, the more people will consume and the bigger the market will become" ("Disney seeks big bucks," 2006, p. D9).

## Measuring Exposure

How those bigger audiences are tallied is a major issue facing the advertising industry. Audience measurement, especially of television advertising, remains a contentious challenge given the penetration of DVRs and online viewing at network sites.

For many years, the Nielsen program ratings have served as proxies for exposure to TV commercials. It makes sense. If someone is viewing a program, they are probably viewing the commercials. For the most part that is true, but the current system doesn't accurately reflect the natural drop in ad viewing due to channel surfing, bathroom breaks, the usual zipping and zapping with VCRs and DVRs, and, well, bad creative.

With the growth of DVRs and media fragmentation, the calls for commercial viewing precision have grown louder. As a result, Nielsen, TiVo, and TNS Media Research have been working toward a solution and they are just beginning to offer ratings for the commercials themselves. Not only can these new ratings track ad exposure, but measurement options can include second-by-second, minute-by-minute, or average commercial minutes. "What this all means," says reporter Brian Sternberg (2007), "is that ads will be put under the microscope as never before" (p. 33).

Programming viewing is being scrutinized as well. According to Jon Nesvig, president of sales at Fox, "the biggest issue [in 2007] is measurement" of television audiences (Atkinson, 2007, p. S-6). He was talking about how program ratings are going to be calculated.

As mentioned, for many years Nielsen measured "live" viewing; how many people are watching the program when it airs. With DVRs and network downloads, many people now watch a program within 24 hours. So networks are arguing for "live-plus-one," which includes people who watch the program the day after it airs. Other options now include "live-plus-same day," "live-plus-three," and "live-plus-seven." The weekly metric obviously is the highest because it includes the most viewers, but playback quickly diminishes over time.

Referring to "live" or "live-plus-time-shifted" viewing, John Swift, VP-managing partner, PHD, New York, said, "The elephant in the room—

whatever the measurement system—is if less people are watching TV than a year ago is the advertiser going to pay more or is the network going to take less money" (p. S-6). At this point, Swift's question is yet to be answered.

## New Tools for Marketers

Blogging, podcasting, sponsored search, and other innovative emerging new-media means are creating opportunities for marketers.

Gwendolyn Bounds (2006) of the *Wall Street Journal* recently told the story of a Minnesota taxi driver who tried and failed to use traditional advertising to promote his business. He didn't have the budget to compete with larger cab companies, and other forms of promotion—yellow pages, airport ads—weren't generating business.

As a last option, he tried Google's Adwords, a cost-per-click keywords program. Potential customers are able to find him through sponsored links on Google searches for "taxi" and "airport" in his local area: "People with cell-phones on planes can find me… Almost every time I ask someone, they tell me it was on the Internet. And 9 times out of 10 it's from Google" (p. R1).

Using sponsored search terms, the taxi entrepreneur went from virtually broke to a fleet of three dozen cabs.

### Search

Indeed, predictions for search marketing foresee unlimited potential. In 2007, PC-based online ad search is predicted to surpass $8 billion. At 41%, search is the largest category of online advertising.

Similar to the Adwords example, search primarily consists of the sponsored ads at the top or sides of web pages that link to websites. Google is the dominant player in this arena because it is the most commonly used search engine. For example, Google was used for 53% of the 61 billion searches worldwide in September 2007. For comparison, 20% of searches were conducted on Yahoo. The average person conducts about 80 searches per month (Burns, 2007).

In the third quarter of 2007, Google generated over $4.2 billion, much of that coming from paid search in which companies and individuals bid for keywords. Those sponsors pay Google each time a person clicks on their ads.

Google and other search engines are vying for the opportunity to offer the lion's share of mobile search. Searches via cell phones are anticipated to represent tremendous growth in the next few years. For example, mobile search is expected to grow from $7 million in 2006 to over $1 billion by 2011 (Cuneo, 2007). Worldwide, revenue in 2011 is expected to reach $2.4 billion with 850 million mobile-search users.

Whether PC or mobile, search ads are expected to encompass more than words as technology is enhanced. Bill Gates recently predicted that media-rich images will be the norm for search ads. All a surfer will need to do is to move his/her cursor over the ad and images will appear; displaying anything from video to brochures to print ads (Klassen, 2007).

## Online Display and Video Ads

After search, at 21% banners and buttons represent the second largest type of online advertising. Most of these "display" ads are static or animated but offer the direct response feature of a simple click to connect advertiser and consumer. Whereas many in the business consider "behavioral response" or click-throughs as the ultimate measure of banner-ad success, display ads also contribute to brand recall and brand identity.

According to the Interactive Advertising Bureau, online video ads are the fastest growing advertising format on the Internet. These rich-media ads often contain moving images and sound as well as a variety of interactive features.

Consider a recent triumph for an innovative use of video embedded in banner ads. The marketers of Zapzyt, an acne medication, are seeing success from media-rich ads on social networking sites such as MySpace. According to one

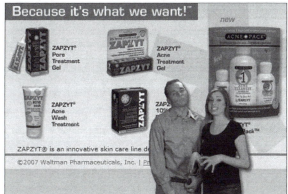

113

description, "actress Kate James and former MTV 'Real World' star Derrick Kosinski pop in to chat when MySpace users listed as ages 13 to 17 roll over a banner ad" (Neff, 2007, p. 8).

Results thus far show an 11% click-through rate compared to Zapzyt's standard banner ads. Not only are the ads getting noticed, but they are reaching a tough-to-target demographic; teens. Whitney Burns, an executive for the company that makes Zapzyt, says that, compared to traditional media, the Internet is where it's at: "We decided to go with the premier networking site and just reach teenagers where they are today" (Neff, 2007b, p. 8).

## Online Video

People like to be entertained, so it is no surprise that online video is having an impact on the marketing world.

A recent AP-AOL survey found that video viewing is growing, with 54% of all US Internet users saying that they have watched video online ("New AP-AOL Video Survey," 2006). In 2007, the percentage of Internet users watching video approached 80%. The study also found that news (72%), TV and movie clips (48%), and music videos (48%) were the most popular downloads. In addition, over 43% of viewers reported that they had watched an amateur video.

People are creating their own videos and sending them to friends or posting them on video-sharing sites like YouTube, Revver, and MySpace. Most of the videos on these sites are created by amateurs, so the videos are often referred to as user-generated content (UGC).

The popularity of these videos is obvious when you consider that in one month MySpace generated 37.4 million unique visitors who viewed 1.4 billion videos (Castengera, 2006c).

## Viral Video

If these videos are funny, intriguing, or just plain weird they get forwarded to friends, who watch them and forward them to their friends, who…. Before you know it you have a video that has gone viral.

Carol Ellison (2006) describes viral as a form of "word-of-mouth buzz" that gets passed from friend to friend. "Now many consumers have digital communications at their fingertips, and information travels rapidly via e-mail, blogs, Internet links, and cell phone text messages" (p. 26).

Ellison noted that a recent study showed that 89% of respondents have forwarded jokes and other content to friends and that 63% did so on a weekly basis.

Savvy marketers are not ones to let the viral video phenom pass without a try. "Viral marketing and its ability to generate buzz around brands can turn relatively unknowns into celebrities and put the names of their products on the tongues and in the e-mail boxes of millions overnight," notes Ellison (2006, p. 26).

You may remember Burger King's Subservient Chicken. Created by Crispin Porter + Bogusky, the video has generated over 400 million hits. Similarly, JibJab Media's spoof of Bush and Kerry in 2004 also made the rounds.

In the summer of 2006, another video made the circuit; this one featured rapping yuppies in a short clip called "Tea Partay." The video was produced by Bartle Bogle Hegarty for Smirnoff. In 2006, online video advertising represented about $385 million, which was up 71% from the previous year.

*Business Week*'s Catherine Holahan (2006) tells the story of Ed Robinson, an advertising executive who in 2000 produced his own creative video, a 12-second clip of a guy inflating a raft, for $10,000. The end of the video featured Robinson's website. He then sent it to five of his friends.

Within the first week the video was viewed 60,000 times, and within three months his company's website had received over 500,000 hits. Robinson's company, The Viral Factory, now charges up to half a million dollars to produce a viral video.

According to Competitrack, an ad tracking service, Nike, Anheuser-Busch, and Microsoft are three of the largest viral brands—marketers that use viral web content as part of their promotion strategy. Other top online viral marketers include Volkswagen, Axe, and Apple.

Inventive online video can also result in success for small niche brands with limited promotion budgets. For instance, paper manufacturer Kimberly-Clark has seen a 30% sales increase for its do-it-yourself product line—Duckbill—because of the viral success of its surgical masks.

The masks are not marketed as surgical supplies but as dust masks for people needing to protect their lungs from sawdust, spray paint, and airborne grime. The videos are essentially product demonstrations: people getting "blasted" with black paint. Those wearing Duckbill masks fair much better than those wearing the competitors' masks (www.duckbill.tv).

"We needed to come up with some nontraditional marketing approaches to introduce our dust mask," commented Brad Herron, a Kimberly-Clark executive (Neff, 2007c, p. 8). By summer 2007 the viral effort had generated 115,000 mentions on blogs and 65,000 visits to the website.

## Consumer-Generated Ads

In addition to producing their own online videos, marketers are taking advantage of the UGC explosion by creating contests and asking amateurs to produce videos about their brands. Doritos sponsored a very successful contest when it aired two winning 30-second spots during the 2007 Super Bowl.

According to *USA Today*'s Laura Petrecca (2007), the strategy appears to be working. "In theory, consumer-generated advertising seems like a no-brainer. Just ask people to upload favorable videos about a brand, offer a modest reward, and watch the funny/clever/touching entries roll in" (p. 1B).

Heinz, one of the world's leading condiment marketers, hosted a contest in which it offered $57,000 to the creator of the best spot. Noted David Ciesinski, a manager for Heinz ketchup: "[The contestants] buy the (ketchup) bottles, take the time to shoot the ad... and then send it to 10 friends... We're getting exactly what we want" (Petrecca, 2007, 5B).

## Advertising on Video-Sharing Sites

YouTube and other video-sharing sites are working to capitalize on their popularity. Currently, these sites are seeking to determine how best to generate revenue from advertising. Some of the sites are developing advertising supported models where short commercials are shown either pre- or post-viewing. Currently, most sites simply offer banner advertising.

According to the AP-AOL survey, 71% of respondents said that they would be willing to watch an ad before a video in order to view it for free, compared to 23% who said that they would pay a fee to watch ad-free videos.

## Widgets

A widget was a generic term for nameless manufactured products; a moniker for "X product" in business classes. Today, widget has an entirely new meaning. By the time you read this, many of you will be very familiar with the "new" widget. Yahoo defines it as a "live, at-a-glance view of… Internet information and services on the desktop."

Widgets can display time, weather, sports scores, stock quotes, television listings, and just about anything else one can imagine. It's easy to imagine a *New York Times* Sudoku right on your desktop. What about the most popular YouTube videos, breaking headlines from *USA Today*, or game scores from ESPN? These branding opportunities can be embedded on desktops, websites, blogs, and social networking microsites.

Marketers are just now realizing the potential widgets offer by having their branded content constantly in front of consumers. Steve Rubel (2007), a columnist for *Advertising Age*, offers marketers the following advice: "Make everything portable. The next version of the Macintosh operating system… has a small feature called Web Clip that turns any part of a site into a widget that lives on the consumer's desktop. This is a big sign of things to come… Don't wait. Start now to make everything on your website embeddable."

How marketers use widgets remains to be seen, but you can bet they are working to find a way.

## Podcasting

Podcasting represents yet another emerging media tool, although marketers are still figuring out how best to utilize it. A podcast is a program in audio or video format that can be downloaded from the Internet to a computer or digital music player like an iPod. A key to podcasting is "time-shifting," which means listening to content offline at a time after the initial broadcast.

According to one report, podcasting is growing 100% annually. By 2010, predictions are that 56.8 million Americans will be using podcasts (Gibson, 2006).

Although many podcasts have not included advertising, many are be-ginning to do so. For example, sponsorship of podcasts is growing: "This program brought to you by…" Think Paul Harvey and his long-time rela-tionship with Bose.

In addition, marketers are both creating entertaining and informative podcasts and making them available to consumers.

For example, a Nike videocast (or vodcast) about Brazilian football hit number four on the iTunes chart of Top 20 podcasts. According to Neil Christie, managing director for the agency that created the Nike podcast, "Our view is we have to stop interrupting the stuff that people want to watch and start to become the stuff that people want to watch" ("Why it pays," 2006, p. 24).

From a production standpoint, podcasting has a very low barrier of entry. All that one needs to create a podcast is a microphone, a computer, and an Internet connection.

## Diesel Does It Online

What do you get when you combine MySpace, streaming video, and underwear-clad young women? Would you believe me if I told you, "a top international advertising award?"

That's what happened when Diesel, the Swedish clothing brand, staged its "15 Megabytes of Fame" campaign to promote its intimate collection. The five-day event earned the marketers a Gold Lion in the Cyber category at the 2007 Cannes Lions International Advertising Festival.

Reporter Emma Hall (2007) described the approach thusly: "Two gorgeous, crazy girls steal an underwear collection, kidnap a sales manager and lock themselves in a hotel room with their victim for five days" (p. 86).

Sounds like a "can't-miss" event, right? It was for many in the target audience (or just plain voyeurs) as evidenced by a 500% increase in the website's traffic over the five days.

The women "hijacked" the Diesel website. Accordingly, they were after fame and notoriety; mimicking the personal hype and sensationalism spawned by the social networking sites.

Engagement was a central theme of the campaign. The two women tried to get as many MySpace "friends" as possible. Viewers sending a "friend request" would have their names streamed on the Diesel site. Also, viewers could e-mail requests such as "have a pillow fight," and the women would accommodate—within reason.

Diesel's campaign is notable because it demonstrates that today's marketers don't have to rely on traditional media to sell their brands. They can successfully raise awareness and engage prospects entirely online using some of the tools discussed in this chapter. Two marketers at the forefront of this trend are described in the next section.

## The (New) Media Specialists

As previously mentioned, media professionals are the newest stars in the advertising world.

According to Joe Cappo (2003), author of *The Future of Advertising*, the media revolution will "make the media-buying function even more important in the years to come as the range of new media continues to expand" (p. 242).

Each year, *Advertising Age* names its list of Media Mavens—people in the industry who are successfully reinventing the rules when it comes to reaching consumers.

### Creative Career Paths

A member of the 2006 list, Kim Kadlec exemplifies maverick advertising approaches as well as the creative career paths being taken by media professionals.

At 42, Kadlec currently reigns as VP of Worldwide Media for the eighth largest US advertiser; packaged-goods conglomerate Johnson & Johnson (Neff, 2006).

She started her career in 1985 as a media planner for a Madison Avenue agency. She then moved to two media agencies, one being Zenith, the other Universal McCann where she was a lead buyer for Verizon and Coca-Cola.

Kadlec was then hired to sell media at Fox before putting together product placement deals as the VP for Branded Entertainment at NBC Universal.

Kadlec is raising eyebrows because she's scaling back the traditionally large television buys Johnson & Johnson makes each year and is shifting the budget toward new media.

She's also focusing on implementing an integrated communications plan—above- and below-the-line advertising—and including consumer involvement measures as a form of media accountability.

One of the reasons for Kadlec's success is that through her experiences as both a media buyer and seller, she came to have a good grasp of (1) how the media are structured, and (2) how to creatively combine traditional and new media to reach today's consumers.

Kadlec also demonstrates how a smart, confident person can get an entry-level job in media and advance to the top of the heap.

## Viral Internet-Generated Phone Calls

Remember the hype over *Snakes on a Plane*? The author does. He even recalls receiving a personalized phone call from Samuel L. Jackson.

It went something like, "Hey Tom, this is Samuel L. Jackson. Skip your next class so you can see my new movie, *Snakes on a Plane*."

Amy Powell, a senior VP for interactive marketing at Paramount Studios—and another one of *Advertising Age*'s Media Mavens, was responsible for that call and millions of others like it.

There is some debate about whether the movie hit number one opening weekend, but the viral Internet-generated phone calls and associated hype certainly got more people to the theaters than would have gone otherwise. The author was there opening weekend.

### Interactive and Inventive

Powell's job is to use interactive media to find new and inventive ways to promote her studio's movies. For example, the highly popular iTunes podcast, "Jack Black's Confessional," was one of the ideas she developed to promote *Nacho Libre* (Stanley, 2006).

Similarly, she put teasers and trailers for *The Longest Yard* on Sony's PSP.

Powell has said that if her job was just about buying online media, she'd be bored. "She'd rather create original content to hype Paramount's films and find ways to embed that material into new media places and devices," noted *Ad Age*'s T. L. Stanley (2006, p. S10).

Kadlec and Powell are just two examples spotlighted by *Advertising Age* of people who are making the most of recent media trends by inventively applying new media tools.

Others include researchers Greg Johnson and Steve Sternberg, and executives Craig Woerz and Meredith Jamim.

These people are excited about the evolving media landscape and they are actively looking for opportunities to give their clients a competitive edge.

## Questions

1.  Consider again the quote by Neil Christie, Wieden & Kennedy managing director: "Our view is we have to stop interrupting the stuff that people want to watch and start to become the stuff that people want to watch." What does his approach mean for traditional advertising?

2.  Have you recently viewed any amateur videos? Did any of them include a brand-name product? What was your reaction to the presence of that product?

3.  Are you cynical of advertising that accompanies your downloaded content?

4.    What aspect of emerging media intrigues you the most? What activities—blogging, video viewing (or creating), podcasting—are you engaging in? Is it all that its cracked up to be?

5.    If you were marketing director for a big studio and needed to create a successful campaign for a new romantic comedy, how would you do it? What new media tools might you use?

## References and Recommended Reading

Andrews, Amanda (2006, September 15). Operators relish future of mobile advertising. *Times* (London), p. 61.

Atkinson, Claire (2006, October 2). Comeback trail: Broadcast TV storms into fall. *Advertising Age*, p. 1.

Atkinson, Claire (2007, May 14). Measurement remains the key sticking point. *Advertising Age*, p. S-6, S-15.

Bounds, Gwendolyn (2006, September 25). How to get attention in a new-media world. *Wall Street Journal*. Retrieved September 29, 2006, from: http://online.wsj.com

Bruno, Antony (2006, September 30). *Ads go mobile*. Billboard.com. Retrieved October 18, 2006, from LexisNexis.

Burns, Enid (2007, October 17). *Worldwide Internet: Now serving 61 billion searches per month*. Retrieved October 24, 2007, from http://searchenginewatch.com/showPage.html?page=3627304

Cappo, Joe (2003). *The Future of Advertising*. New York: McGraw-Hill.

Castengera, Michael (2006a, October 16). Message from Michael [e-mail newsletter]. Contact: newsconsultant@aol.com

Castengera, Michael (2006b, September 18). Message from Michael [e-mail newsletter]. Contact: newsconsultant@aol.com

Castengera, Michael (2006, October 3). Message from Michael [e-mail newsletter]. Contact: newsconsultant@aol.com

Cuneo, Alice (2007, July 30). Mobile still up for grabs. *Advertising Age*, p. S-2.

"Disney sees big bucks in iTunes sales: Movie, TV downloading on the rise" (2006, September 20). *Calgary Herald*, p. D9. Retrieved September 18, 2006, from LexisNexis.

Hall, Emma (2007, May 14). Diesel underwear viral sends web surfers into tizzy. *Advertising Age*, p. 86.

"Heard on the street" (2006, April 22). *Economist* (US edition). Retrieved October 18, 2006, from LexisNexis.

Ives, Nat (2007a, March 12). 'Premiere' death stands out in era of mag closings. *Advertising Age*, p. 10.

Ives, Nat (2007b, October 1). Playboy freer online, more restrained in print. *Advertising Age*, p. 3, 44.

Johnson, Brad (2007, June 11). Where's the money moving? Out of media. *Advertising Age*, p. 1, 43.

Klassen, Abbey (2007, May 14). MSN's online-ad plan: Let the web evolve. *Advertising Age*, p. 12.

Littleton, Cynthia (2006, may 26). Less fear factor over DVR growth. HollywoodReporter.com. Retrieved October 18, 2006, from LexisNexis.

Neff, Jack (2006, September 18). Kim Kadlec. *Advertising Age*, p. S-12.

Neff, Jack (2007a, March 5). Skip this TiVo story at your peril, top marketers. *Advertising Age*, p. 8.

Neff, Jack (2007b, May 7). Zit cream targets teens with direct web effort. *Advertising Age*, p. 8.

Neff, Jack (2007c, August 13). Sales for K-C's Duckbill line get goosed by viral. *Advertising Age*, p. 8.

Petrecca, Laura (2007, June 21). Madison Avenue wants you! *USA Today*, p. 1B, 5B.

Rubel, Steve (2007, August 20). Three strategies for thriving on the decentralized web. *Advertising Age*. Retrieved October 25, 2007, from: http://adage.com/article?article_id=119926&search_phrase=rubel

"Rush to mobile marketing will lead only to fool's gold" (2007, August 20). *Advertising Age*, p. 10.

Sternberg, Brian (2007, July 16). How to stop them from skipping: TiVo tells all. *Advertising Age*, p. 1, 33.

"The new 'digital divide'" (2006, August). Universal McCann. Special Report.

"Why it pays to podcast" (2006, April 21). *Campaign*, p. 24. Retrieved October 18, 2006, from LexisNexis.

Wurtzel, Alan (2006, May 29). Pause on this. Mediaweek.com. Retrieved October 18, 2006, from LexisNexis.

## Online Resources

### Ad Media.org

http://admedia.org

This site is hosted by the Department of Advertising at Michigan State University. It contains recent news about advertising and media. It was created by Hairong Li, a professor in MSU's advertising program.

### Center for Media Research

http://mediapost.com/research

This site contains research briefs and links to media research and media organizations. Subscriptions and membership are free.

### Interactive Advertising Bureau

http://iab.net

The IAB is a tremendous resource for information, formats, and guidelines about online advertising. Explore the site and look for definitions and case studies about Internet advertising. You can find relevant research on just about any topic that involves the intersection of advertising and interactivity.

**Media Post**

http://mediapost.com

"Home on the web for media, marketing, and advertising professionals." The site is designed to help media planners and buyers make informed decisions. It contains links to data, reports, and relevant blogs.

# Pay to Place:
## Product Placement Comes on Strong

## by Tom Reichert

TODAY'S CONSUMERS REPORT that they are more cynical of advertising than ever before. They say that they hate being bombarded with pop-up ads, more minutes of commercials, and overstuffed mailboxes.

In addition, marketers are finding it more difficult to reach consumers with traditional media because viewers are spending time with an increasingly wide assortment of media choices.

One creative idea gaining momentum that addresses these issues is to put brands *into* programs instead of placing them *around* programs.

This rapidly growing practice is commonly referred to as product (or brand) placement.

## What Is Product Placement?

All of us have seen product placement at work.

Most movies and television programs include a shot—or mention—of a branded consumer product. What many people fail to realize is that these brand appearances are the result of a transaction between the studio and the marketer.

For example, many viewers were not aware of the behind-the-scenes activities at play when Tom Hanks' character in the movie *The Terminal* requested a specific brand of wine. Getting ready for a romantic dinner, Hanks ordered a bottle of Clos du Val's cabernet.

According to Jenny Turnbull, a product placement agent, the winery had been cultivating relationships with the studios for at least five years, and placement in the film was one of the major outcomes of those efforts (Locke, 2006).

### Several Definitions

Product placement can be defined several ways.

For example, Siva Balasubramanian and colleagues (2006) report that "brand appearances represent deliberate promotional efforts that are reinforced by formal agreements between marketers and the creators/managers of editorial content" (p. 115).

More simply, product placement has been defined as "the purposeful incorporation of a brand into an entertainment vehicle," (Russell and Belch, 2005, p. 74).

Scott Donaton, an editor for *Advertising Age*, uses a play on words to describe the interaction between studios and marketers. The title of his recent book about product placement, *Madison & Vine*, plays off references to the famous intersection "Hollywood and Vine."

"Madison" refers to the avenue in Manhattan that houses many of the world's leading advertising agencies. Vine—an infamous street running through Hollywood, California—symbolizes the heart of the entertainment industry.

Many people talk about product placement as a hybrid of traditional advertising. Both forms of promotion are placed and paid for by a representative for the brand.

But advertising is very distinct from editorial content while product placement is not. For this reason, marketing scholars Cristel Russell and Michael Belch (2005), argue that product placement "epitomizes the blurring of the lines between advertising and entertainment" (p. 74).

Wayne's World (1992)

127

## Important Differences

Advertising and product placement also differ in several important ways.

For one, advertising is a regulated practice, whereas product placement is not. Also, ads attempt to communicate product utility—how the product can help a consumer attain a goal or solve a problem.

Product placements overwhelmingly lack any informational value about the brand. Viewers see the product, sometimes in use, but that is about the extent of it.

# Yesterday and Today

Product placement is not a new concept. Marketers have been sponsoring media content for many decades.

In the 1930s, for instance, radio programs were sponsored by a single advertiser. In addition, the soap opera is a program genre that represents a very close link between scripts and brand integration by the big soap marketers.

Eventually, advertisers made the decision to reach consumers by advertising on several programs rather than affiliating with only one program. However, as consumers prove more difficult to locate because they are spending time with an assortment of media, marketers are discovering that product placements have value.

## The *E.T.* Success Story

Product placements have been rising since the success of Reese's Pieces in the 1982 movie *E.T.: The Extraterrestrial*. In the film, E.T., an alien from outer space, takes a liking to Reese's Pieces while hiding out with a bunch of kids in southern California.

According to Hershey's, sales of the candy increased 65% as a result of its prominent role in the movie.

You can imagine the reaction by marketers, in an era of intense competition, to any form of promotion that can generate a strapping sales increase and build strong brand favorability for millions of consumers around the globe.

## Exciting Growth

Today, product placement represents a promotion area with exciting growth. Russell and Belch report that "product placement is one of today's hottest new media" (2005, p. 73). In 2005, product placement was estimated to be a $3.4 billion business.

Over 1000 brands include it in their marketing mix, and there are over 42 specialized agencies that deal directly with product placement (Russell & Belch, 2005).

The number of product placements per program is especially surprising. Any branded product from cars, to air carriers, to storefronts can make a paid appearance.

According to one studio executive, "For a typical movie, there could be 100 to 150 placements in a production that the studio has to obtain to get production off the ground" (Russell and Belch, 2005, p. 76). A fully produced movie could contain up to 500 paid placements.

# Why Is It used?

Studios and other producers of content are favorable to product placements for several reasons.

For one, placement deals defray the costs of production which ultimately reduces financial risk. Why invest millions of dollars into production costs when companies eager to get exposure for their brands are willing to foot the bill?

Others have argued that well-placed brands can influence the quality of the narrative.

For example, a distinctive brand can lend a sense of reality to a set. In addition, a character's use of a certain brand can add additional insight into that character's personality.

As we know, brands say a lot about the people who use them. For example, what is the difference between someone who drives a Volvo and someone who drives a Tahoe? Someone who drinks Francis Ford Coppola's Shiraz or Carlo Rossi's Vin Rose? Sweetwater 420 or Miller High Life?

You get the picture. Brands contribute a great deal to character development.

## How Does It Work?

The consensus among professionals and scholars is that product placement is effective—to some degree.

Disagreement surfaces over the extent and measurement of that effectiveness. Research by two marketing professors at San Diego State revealed that while professionals talk highly of the effectiveness of product placement, they have a difficult time supporting their assertions:

"Currently, there are no bona fide companies offering valid and reliable measures, and most of those in the industry do not care or, for that matter, want to know if their placements work" (Russell & Belch, 2005, p. 90).

### Prominence

Generally, everyone agrees that the goal is to get the brand mentioned or shown on screen.

A key concept is prominence.

A *prominent* placement means that the product is an integral part of a scene. *Hero placement* means that the brand finds its way into an actor's hands. For example, one of the characters might drink a Pepsi. Even better, one of the characters might request a Pepsi by name after an intense car chase.

Another example of a highly prominent placement occurred during the first season of *The Apprentice*.

Two teams were assigned to create an advertising campaign for the Marquis Jet Card, a service for executives to secure rides on corporate jets.

The Thomas Crown Affair (1999)

The team with the best campaign was flown on a chartered jet from Manhattan to Boston for a special dinner. As a result, the Jet Card—how it works and its benefits—was discussed in great detail throughout the program as the two teams developed their campaigns.

A *low-prominent* placement means that the brand is visible somewhere in the scene, but not as part of the action.

## Effectiveness Increases with Prominence

Research generally shows that effectiveness of the placement increases as prominence increases. Industry folks usually measure effectiveness in terms of exposure. They might say, "Our brand was shown on an episode of *Smallville*, which has two million viewers. We generated two million impressions with that placement."

For most placements, any type of measurement, such as products sold, buzz, or increases in favorability ratings, are tough to measure and they are equally tough to attribute to product placement as opposed to other parts of the campaign.

Academic researchers, on the other hand, are more precise in their assessment of how product placement works.

One set of researchers proposed in the *Journal of Advertising* a model that says that how the product is displayed and the audience's perceptions and attitudes toward the placement will influence the degree to which the exposure is consciously processed (Balasubramanian et al., 2006).

That, in turn, should influence message outcomes, which include common indicators of success such as brand-name recall, feelings toward the brand, and intentions to purchase the brand.

## Perceived Popularity

However, Max Sutherland, an Australian scholar, thinks that product placement works on the premise of perceived popularity.

"People infer what is popular by what is prominent," says Sutherland (2006, p. 108). In other words, products that are able to enter into the public's awareness through brand placement will be viewed as what "everybody else is using," and people will want them.

On the other hand, Larry Percy (2006), a long-time marketing professor, is not too enthusiastic about the effects of product placement. He argues that most exposures are processed unconsciously and that information gleaned in that manner has very little influence on brand attitudes or choice.

## Prominence Plus Story Value

The key is to have a highly prominent placement that blends in well with the story. According to Turnbull, an effective placement is one in which the brand is "noticed yet not blatantly obvious" (Locke, 2006).

If that is achieved, people will remember the product, like it more, and go out and buy it.

Although researchers have only been studying product placement for about 10 years, the findings thus far generally support this pattern of results.

Cast Away (2000)

## Why Do We Care?

The growth of product placements is a critical issue in the area of advertising. It matters because its use suggests that traditional advertising isn't working like it used to.

Studies continue to show that consumers are increasingly cynical of traditional advertising, and that they are increasingly annoyed by the intrusiveness of today's marketing efforts. In addition, new technologies such as digital video recorders are allowing more consumers to watch their programs while skipping the commercials.

If people are paying less attention to the messages surrounding the program, it makes sense to get your brand in the program because viewers aren't going to zip or zap the show.

The Placement Agency's Turnbull says, "People aren't even watching commercials any more, so at least you know you have that audience who are watching the show" (Locke, 2006).

## No "Full Disclosure"

Another reason product placement causes concern is that audiences are not provided "full disclosure" when it is employed.

Some have likened placement to subversive manipulation because its success depends on a lack of audience awareness.

As you know, advertising is the paid placement of a message in the media by an identified sponsor. All audience members recognize that the ad is a persuasive message—that some company is trying to convince them to think or feel differently about its brand. Moreover, the audience is fully aware that the sponsor paid the media to broadcast its message.

With brand placements, however, audiences typically are not aware that a branded product has been intentionally inserted into the plot line.

According to Donaton (2004), product placement only works if the brand is seamlessly embedded within the narrative such that attention is not drawn to it—the "cardinal rule of product integration: make it seamless and subtle" (p. 12).

In other words, most product placement efforts by marketers are to intentionally hide the fact that they are paying studios to include the product on screen.

## brandhype.org

Matthew Soar, a communications professor at Concordia University in Montreal and creator of a website designed to identify product placement efforts (http://brandhype.org), takes issue with the "seamless" aspect of product placements.

He sees it as an "underhanded kind of advertising. It's one more area of culture that's started to become saturated in advertising" (Locke, 2006).

Sutherland (2006) likens product placement to "payola," record companies paying disc jockeys to play songs. Payola is an illegal practice but product placement is not.

He asks, "If it is acceptable for corporations to make undisclosed payments to push brands into the public awareness through product placement, why is it illegal when record companies do it?" (p. 108). Sutherland argues that regulation of product placement is needed.

## Proposal for Full Disclosure

Back in the days of "Texaco Star Theater," everyone was fully aware that Texaco was sponsoring some, if not all, of the costs of the program. If the name of the program didn't give it away, several "Texaco" promos within the program made the connection very clear.

At least one organization has recognized the connection between audience awareness and product placement.

According to *Congressional Quarterly*, Commercial Alert suggested to both the Federal Trade Commission and the Federal Communication Commission that onscreen pop-ups should be required every time a paid product placement appears in a program.

Imagine how annoying that would be.

But at least everyone would be fully informed.

Free markets are based on full disclosure—that all parties involved in a transaction are made aware of any conflicts of interest. Commercial Alert's proposal, while cumbersome, is a step in that direction.

# Branching Out

While most instances of product placement occur in television programs and motion pictures, marketers are getting inventive.

Deborah Vence (2006), a reporter for the Associated Press, recently noted that in 2005 over $385 million was invested in product placements within media other than television and film. These media include books, magazines, radio, and video games. Controversy is being generated as marketers venture into these non-traditional product placement areas.

## Booking New Opportunities

Recently, for instance, there was a commotion when the authors of a book written for teen girls, *Cathy's Girl*, intentionally included references to a brand-name product in exchange for help promoting their book (Rich, 2006).

Specifically, authors Jordan Weisman and Sean Stewart tailored the text to explicitly mention several shades of Cover Girl eyeliner and its "Lipsticks" line of lip gloss.

In exchange, the book received valuable exposure on Procter & Gamble's website beinggirl.com—Procter & Gamble owns Cover Girl.

Reactions to the partnership inside the book industry ranged from "a brilliant idea" to disapproval. One source questioned whether the book was a true novel or just part of a corporate marketing campaign directed toward unsuspecting teens.

Another instance of product placement within the publishing industry occurred in 2001 when leading British author Fay Weldon was commissioned to feature a watch in her book *The Bulgari Connection*. Bulgari, a high-fashion Italian jewelry maker, paid Weldon an undisclosed sum to write the book with their brand as a central element.

### Video Game Placement

Product placements are also very common in video games. In many instances companies pay gaming marketers to include billboards and other forms of signage within the game itself that can feature their brand.

According to an article in *Billboard*, companies also can get their products integrated into the action for a share of the production costs. For example, characters onscreen can drink a Coca-Cola or some other identifiable beverage. Or they might drive a certain make and model of automobile.

What does it mean when kids and young people, the majority of gamers in our society, are continuously exposed to marketing products that they are not necessarily aware of—but that they pay for? Understandably, there have been several calls, even within the gaming industry, to either limit product placement or to ensure some form of disclosure.

## Questions

1.  In your opinion, are product placements manipulative?

2.  Should consumers be informed of paid placements in each program? Perhaps if only in the credits?

3.  Imagine that a marketer offered you $1 million to include references to its brand in your latest book. Would you do it? Would you disclose that information to the reader?

4.      What is your reaction to product placements when they are "obvious" instead of "seamless"?

5.      Are you influenced by product placements? What about your friends?

## References and Recommended Reading

Balasubramanian, Siva K., James A. Karrh, and Hemant Patwardhan (2006). Audience response to product placements: An integrative framework and future research agenda. *Journal of Advertising*, 35, 3 (Fall), 115-141.

Bruno A. (2006, May 27) Gamers, this ad's for you. *Billboard*, 118, p. 14.

Donaton, Scott (2004). *Madison & Vine*. New York: McGraw-Hill.

Donaton, Scott (2004, June 28). Cautionary tales from Mad & Vine. *Advertising Age*, p. 12.

Galician, Mary-Lou (2004), Product placements in the mass media: Unholy marketing marriages or realistic story-Telling portrayals, unethical advertising messages or useful communication practices? *Journal of Promotion Management*, 10 (1/2), 1-8.

Locke, Michelle (2006, July 6). Wine product placement is ad message on a bottle. Retrieved September 28, 2006, from LexisNexis database.

Percy, Larry (2006). Are product placements effective? *International Journal of Advertising*, 25 (1), 112-114.

Petrecca, Laura (2006, September 11). Authors strike deal to squeeze in a few brand names. *USA Today*. Retrieved September 28, 2006, from LexisNexis database.

Rich, Motoko (2006, June 12). Product placement deals make leap from film to books. *New York Times*. Retrieved September 28, 2006, from LexisNexis database.

Russell, Cristel Antonia, and Michael Belch (2005). A managerial investigation into the product placement industry. *Journal of Advertising Research*, March, 73-92.

Sutherland, Max (2006). Product placement—regulators gone AWOL. *International Journal of Advertising*, 25 (1), 107-110.

Vence, Deborah L. (2006, September 15). The Bulgari precedent. *Marketing News*. Retrieved September 18, 2006, from LexisNexis database.

## Online Resources

**Brand Hype**

http://brandhype.org

A web resource designed to foster informed debate about product placement in the movies. The Brand Hype team is based in the Department of Communication Studies, Concordia University, Montreal, and is led by Dr. Matt Soar. Here you will find videos, commentary, and recent articles.

# How Advertisers Want to Cozy Up Between You and Your Friends:
## Word-of-Mouth and Social Networking in the Digital Age

### by Jacqueline Lambiase

WHEN ADVERTISING EXECUTIVES characterize the profession as dependent on creativity, it has always meant more than devising clever ads. Creative efforts have long included finding audiences in new ways and in new spaces, and this has never been so true as in electronic media. Using war metaphors such as *guerilla* or *stealth marketing*, advertisers seem literally to be fighting their ways into electronic social networks. The term viral marketing evokes the circumstances of epidemic, with advertisers urged to "plant germs" or ideas in the marketplace. For the epidemic to work, these germs are carried by a robust word-of-mouth network (Gladwell, 2000; Levine, 2002).

No matter what their strategies are called, advertisers strive to create a buzz by using technology to stimulate something organic, something as natural as conversation between friends. Using the oldest communication system in the world—the human voice—people have always exchanged information and recommendations about the things around them. Online, the human voice becomes text, images, and sounds, a merger of organic exchange and digital tools. Unlike the human voice, however, digital word of mouth stays in circulation, either adding to a brand's reputation or diminishing it. Finding ways to enhance the word of mouth about brands becomes for companies an important challenge in digital media. Advertisers face the difficult task of trying to cozy up between you and your friends.

## A Short History of Digital Social Networks

Engaging both people's eyes and fingers in online media makes sense, especially after the slow demise of the 30-second television ad in the age of couch potatoes. After the Internet interrupted the mainstream media scene in the 1990s, a few companies exploited its interactive features. Most did not. Older community-building sites (America Online, Geocities, the original Napster, and countless forum sites) featured banner advertising but few examples of corporate-initiated buzz marketing. Yet all of these sites demonstrated the potential of electronic word of mouth, coupled with people's passion for products, services, and ideas they loved to promote electronically to their friends. These real-life evangelists began to use social networks to tout products, prompting marketers and online retailers to capture their enthusiasm within rate-and-review sections on web sites.

Now, examples of *user-generated content*—from messages and photographs to videos and music—abound on blogs and peer-to-peer sharing sites. Content includes classifieds, contest videos, avatars, forums, stories, digital art, and more. Amazon features user-generated ratings and reviews. At StarbucksEverywhere.net, a fan of the stores posts photos and occasional comments about all the stores he has visited. At HackingNetflix.com, news about the online DVD rental industry is shared and discussed by self-described fan and journalist Michael Kaltschnee. And conversely, anti-fans create web sites, blogs, and messages within social networking sites that criticize companies and their products. Word of mouth cuts both ways.

## MySpace, Facebook, and YouTube

With the rise of social networking sites such as MySpace in 2003 and Facebook in 2004, and corresponding increases of millions of young participants, advertisers have naturally followed. Corporate advertisers have made advances within these social networks by setting up their own pages and becoming "friends" with others by sponsoring contests, creating online postcards, offering wallpaper or music downloads, and sending messages to friends about upcoming events and product launches. While corporate-sponsored pages in MySpace may have thousands of friends, these sites are also greeted with cynicism. Clayton Miller, author of a technology blog called No Substance/All Eloquence, writes that "host and guest here... are almost polar opposites; Apple on MySpace seems something akin to installing an [expensive designer] chair inside a McDonald's" (Miller, 26 October 2006, 2 pp). He also questions whether comments on Apple's MySpace wall are authentic user comments or spam from the company itself.

With YouTube's debut in 2005, web users could find spaces for their own creative video products, plus their *mashups* of video borrowed from other sources. A mashup or remixed video uses video and music from many sources, recombining it in different ways. Favorite videos, as rated by participants, receive prominent placement on YouTube's home page, while others are listed as "promoted videos." Again, corporate advertisers have entered into this file-sharing frenzy, uploading their own videos in formats similar to home video and with edgier content than mainstream ads. These efforts must compete with content from well-established users who have been elevated within the social network of YouTube and who are seen as especially entertaining, funny, or thought-provoking. At YouTube, AOL Video, and other video-sharing sites, professionally made videos serving commercial interests strive to look as though they are homemade.

Based on these developments, *Time* magazine named "you" as person of the year for 2006, placing a mirror on its cover, which was spoofed endlessly by comedians and bloggers. That year, however, seemed to be a watershed for the realization that *Advertising 2.0* wasn't a futuristic concept, but was happening, often without major media's participation. Paul Beelen calls *Advertising 2.0* an inversion of traditional advertising principles such as top-down content delivery and information asymmetry. He urges agencies to learn "how to communicate with a micro target, not just talk to a large target group. Future communication will be about conversations, and conversations have traditionally been more a public relations matter than an advertising agency's job" (Beelen, 2006, pp. 13-14).

To survive, then, corporations must turn from big-media advertising campaigns to relationships, from monologue to dialogue with their customers. When people no longer privilege official sources for information, when a Google or Technorati search becomes a starting place for gathering information, then the lines between consumers and producers begin to blur. When advertisers learn to inject themselves into these digital conversations, a cycle begins in which fans' values are sold back to themselves (Hills, 2002), with the Internet serving as a literal conduit for a "circuit of culture" (du Gay, Hall, Janes, Mackay, & Negus, 1997). While word-of-mouth advertising certainly fits nicely within the model of a circuit of culture, perhaps more relevant theories better explain its dependence on individual persuasion.

## How Word of Mouth Works

The trend known as *Advertising 2.0* suggests that something fundamental has changed about advertising. Yet really, the term encompasses interactivity and new digital technology in the service of an older word-of-mouth network. Just as orality preceded literacy, word of mouth preceded advertising, and so the profession is returning to its roots, but this time within an electronic network.

Before and during the rise of mass media in the last two centuries, interpersonal communication has always been seen as a powerful force for persuasion. Ethos, or credibility, is one of three types of appeals discussed by Aristotle, who lived at a time when literacy was on the rise and when interpersonal communication stretched itself to serve the needs of speech-making. Aristotle provided guidance for orators who could no longer rely on their audiences to know them personally, but who had to convey their authenticity and credibility in other ways.

More recent rhetoricians have discussed the evolution of orality and literacy into the electronic age, calling it *electracy* (Ulmer, 2003) or *secondary orality* (Ong, 1995). For Ulmer, electracy flows from and to an affective body, just as literacy is dependent on an analytical mind. Ong believes that a literate society engaged in secondary orality through electronic networks bears "striking resemblances to the old in its participatory mystique, its fostering of a communal sense, its concentration on the present moment" (p. 136). Personal credibility, fact, and feeling—or Aristotle's ethos, logos, pathos—still combine in these newer models of electronic communication to help persuasion do its work.

Interpersonal recommendations like those found on social networking and peer-to-peer sharing sites may be seen as electronic examples of ethos—or *source credibility*—at work. In communication theory, much research has focused on the dimensions of source credibility, in terms of defining it and testing its effects. Currently, following Hovland and Weiss' work on trustworthiness and expertness (1951), researchers are exploring relationship building, referral networks, service switching, and peer recommendations in the online environment (see Hennig-Thurau, & Walsh, 2003; Smith, Menon, & Sivakumar, 2005). One online community's linking patterns showed that news media sites still carried power, but the study also demonstrated the power of the community members themselves, since participants could communicate with many people at one time and could communicate with strangers, which is less likely in off-line word of mouth (Vilpponen, Winter, & Sundqvist, 2006). Credibility was extended to those who were official members in the community, and they were not seen as strangers.

## The Technology Behind Social Networks

Electronic word-of-mouth and advertising's use of online social networks to spread brand information have expanded in large part because of new software technology and its ease of use. Low-resolution streaming video, RSS capability, easy blogging templates, and other technologies have enabled people without advanced skills to create their own web sites and to post web content. RSS stands for Really Simple Syndication or Rich Site Summary, allowing people to receive updates to their own "feed sites" from web sites of their choosing.

RSS is the same technology that allows participants in social networks to choose to receive information about friends within that network, without having to go to all friends' sites individually. So, when a human friend (or corporate friend) uploads photos, video, or other information to his or her own pages, the user receives information about the new content and is given the choice to visit those web pages to see the extended content. By providing podcasts, blog messages, corporate news, and other content to these feeds, an advertiser "overcomes many of the shortcomings that traditional marketing channels encounter, including spam filters, delayed distribution, search engine rankings, and general 'in-box' noise" ("Feed 101," 2007). RSS technology is part of the reason advertisers can operate within the social networks, giving them access to existing and potential customers.

## Generating WOM Within Electronic Networks

For success, advertisers must rely on new strategies to appeal to audiences in electronic word-of-mouth networks. In general terms, advertising must not seem like advertising, at least not like old media advertising.

This includes shortened formats, compelling content, technological in-gredients (like video clips for mashups, icons, and wallpaper), and forms that seem native to online media. All of these strategies minimize the conscious presence of advertising while helping marketing messages be-come naturally integrated within the network and its users. Advertisers must listen to people within these online word-of-mouth networks, truly inviting "users to take control, to create their own messages and share them" (Evans, 2006).

## MySpace, Music, and Minisodes

Corporations create profiles on MySpace, ending up with hundreds, and sometimes thousands of friends. Musicians, and especially their fans, were first in understanding the power of promoting music within MySpace by offering concert schedules, reviews, gossip, photos, audio tracks, and video clips from live events. Examples include Fall Out Boy, with more than 30 million profile views and nearly 2 million friends (www.myspace. com/falloutboy); Heart, with more than 1.1 million profile views and 14,000 friends (www.myspace.com/heart); Usher, with 7.4 million profile views and 151,000 friends (www.myspace.com/usher); and Trisha Year-wood, with 1.3 million profile views and 36,000 friends (www.myspace. com/trishayearwood). All of these sites maintain daily activity, so clearly, staff members working for these musicians are responsible for updating pages and responding to friend requests. Most music sites are now labeled "official site of," rather than being maintained by fans, and most offer links to their artists' own web domain.

Marketing and corporate sites aside, MySpace is still dominated by in-dividual users, more than 100 million profiles worldwide in 2007, making it the No. 3 site in the United States and No. 6 globally (Alexa, 2007). With millions of daily visitors to the site—an average of five percent of global Internet users visited the site daily in July 2007 (Alexa, 2007)—MySpace has begun experimenting with economic models to exploit its high traffic. Online video stands at the center of this effort (Elliott, 2007). At MySpa-ceTV in June 2007, Honda began to sponsor "minisodes" of classic tele-vision series. An eight-second commercial or "pre-roll ad" played at the start of each four- to six-minute program. Featured in the commercials was Honda's small car, Fit, targeted to a demographic that remembers these classic TV shows, including *Who's the Boss*, *What's Happening*!, and *The Facts of Life*. Some of the minisodes, all starting with Honda's Fit commercials, have been played thousands and hundreds of thousands of times. MySpace users may subscribe to these shows as new minisodes are released, and they may rate, comment, and share links to the shows with friends in the MySpace community.

## YouTube, Mashups, and LonelyGirl15

At YouTube, the No. 5 site in the United States with double the global traffic of MySpace (Alexa, 2007), registered users upload more than 65,000 videos every day, with more than 100 million video views daily (YouTube press release, 2006). Video uploading across the web has become the Internet's current killer application. Content ranges from new, professionally produced videos to amateur video and mashups, in which users remix video clips already available online. One such effort includes Microsoft's Gears of War game. Microsoft produced a short ad, then posted it to YouTube and other sites, resulting in 5 million viewings and more than 700 different mashups created by fans of the game for Xbox 360 (LaMonica, 2007, May 2). Robert Bach of Microsoft said "the community took over and did the marketing for us" (qtd. in LaMonica, 2007, May 2). Gears of War became the top-selling game for Xbox 360.

LonelyGirl15 has produced some of the most popular videos at YouTube, with views for some of the episodes reaching more than 700,000 and more. This popularity prevailed, despite the fact that the "girl" of the user name was a paid actor for a professional production, rather than a "real" user posting video blogs from her bedroom (Associated Press, 2007; see www.lg15.com). Multiple characters join Bree, who is LonelyGirl15, in the approximately 250-episode series, posting from their own sites, and other non-paid YouTube users post video responses, mashups, ratings, and comments about the storyline. While the short-video series has used product placement in a traditional way, LonelyGirl15 also signed with Johnson & Johnson's Neutrogena brand to include a character who works for the company. One month after the character, Spencer Gilman, was introduced in dialogue, 11 out of 830 comments on episode 223 (Rockin' the Boat) refer to Neutrogena. These include "What does Neutrogena have to do with anything (besides a blatant plug)?" and "Neutrogena website? ... that

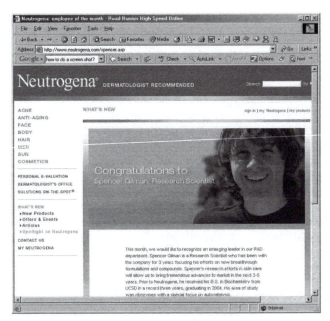

*Spencer Gilman appears on the Neutrogena Web site as a research scientist, and he's also a character in LonelyGirl15, a popular video series appearing on YouTube.*

is the lamest thing I've ever heard." At Neutrogena's web site, Gilman is nebulously identified as a research scientist and video blogger while featured as employee of the month for July 2007. His presence on the official brand site raises questions about whether he's an actor or a scientist, and about the brand's willingness to damage its credibility while pursuing product placement.

A campaign for Unilever's Axe body spray and deodorant launched in spring of 2007 used a microsite, or a small product-based web site, to offer downloads of its Bom Chicka Wah Wah commercials, ringtones, and theme song (see www.axebcww.com). Also released to video-sharing sites along with so-called audition tapes for the Bom Chicka Wah Wah band (that features scantily clad women), segments of the commercials began showing up in mashups. Even when the product, Axe, wasn't shown in these amateur mashups, often the name Axe was used in the titles. The microsite, along with downloadable music and video, was not an electronic add-on to a traditional off-line media campaign. Rather, the microsite and free downloads were at the center of the brand's effort to create buzz and to infect the video-sharing community with "Bom Chicka Wah Wah."

## Professionalized Buzz

In the past decade, companies have begun specializing in exploiting word-of-mouth networks and creating buzz. One example, Bzzagent (see www.bzzagent.com), shares information with several thousand "buzz agents," enticing them to try products and encouraging them to share samples and coupons within social networks. These friends then become evangelists, spreading the word about products to other people. One success story involves Dunkin' Donuts, in which 3,000 volunteer buzz agents were recruited and sent kits with coupons and information. These volunteers reached about 40,000 first-generation contacts, who then spread the word about the company to more than 100,000 people. Overall, these efforts generated higher sales, and presumably, more brand awareness.

In the viral video business, the U.K.-based Viral Factory creates video products that are completely different from traditional advertising. One example of its work is a documentary, news-style video for Axe body spray, in which a small town full of men is sprayed with a scent from a crop-dusting airplane, in order to attract women. The video was then uploaded or "seeded" to video-sharing sites, which were tracked by the company to determine reach and effectiveness.

Hundreds of brands have erected spaces in Second Life, a virtual environment created by millions of people and populated by their avatars. In order to have a presence in virtual space like Second Life or within social networks, corporate designers and other employees are charged with building and maintaining both virtual spaces and online conversation. Advertising and public relations agencies are also hiring researchers to scour networks for information and conversation about brands, and to track and to measure these networks' effects on their brands.

## Issues and Concerns

The problems of the Internet in general must also be addressed in electronic social networking sites, including privacy and identity issues, copyright infringement, and censorship and the regulation of hate speech. Members of networks, especially corporate entities, must respect guidelines for conduct within the community. *Cloaking*, a practice by a company to make a profile appear to be that of a real person, is discouraged by the Word of Mouth Marketing Association code of ethics. Equally unethical is a paid marketer disguising himself or herself as an unaffiliated community member, a practice known as *infiltration*. Wal-Mart, chief sponsor of a group called Working Families for Wal-Mart, paid for an RV, gas, and payment for blogging by a freelance writer. The writer also happened to be a member of Working Families and loves Wal-Mart. Her blog posts to "Wal-Marting Across America" and her interviews with employees are uniformly positive, but critics see the relationship between the writer and the company as disingenuous at best (Gogoi, 2006).

Advertisers who wish to participate in these networks should be aware of the dangers of offering brand images to Internet users who might use them to create potentially obscene, libelous, or threatening videos. If brand images are used for these purposes, and if those images or videos gain popularity, then damage to the brand might erase the benefits of a video-sharing campaign. Likewise, advertisers should be ready to weather disparaging comments that will appear in ratings sections or blog messages. Lastly, companies may be tempted to create marketing material for the Internet that is edgier than that produced for mainstream media, but this material will be shared across web spaces, since everything circulates with no boundaries and since children are present within these networks (Lambiase, 2003).

Other issues also concern a company's control of its brand, including the timing and dissemination rate of viral messages. For example, Dominoes Pizza produced a viral video titled "Spoiled Rich Girl" to promote a limited-time discount; however, by the time the viral video caught on and people tried to understand its ties to a brand and solve clues, the discount was no longer offered. In addition, copyright and control of intellectual property continue to be debated as file-sharing networks gain popularity. Once a company offers downloads to consumers, it should expect that relationship to continue, because the company has branded itself as digitally savvy and open to file sharing.

Lastly, some brands and products may be more suitable than others for generating buzz and for attracting attention within social networks, according to Nielsen BuzzMetrics (Neff, 2007). Despite its organic aspirations, the most successful word-of-mouth campaigns are often the result of substantial investment as part of a broader advertising campaign. People have grown wise about ways to keep advertising out of their lives, and when someone or something is seen as "shilling" or selling, often the audience tunes out those messages.

## Summary

No matter its name—word-of-mouth, viral advertising, buzz marketing, or guerilla public relations—the activity of placing brand information within online social networks is an important tool for companies when handled responsibly. It requires not only the convergence of old and new media, but also the merging of two distinct advertising activities: creative work and media planning. It is difficult to craft messages that are credible in online social network, or in other words, that are not identifiable with traditional advertising tactics. Moreover, truly organic word-of-mouth is often "volatile and inexplicable," in the words of Malcolm Gladwell. He believes these social epidemics, or tipping points, are an affirmation "of the potential for change and the power of intelligent action" (2000, p. 259). Companies trying to exploit word-of-mouth would be wise to remember the intelligent people within these networks, listening as much as communicating, improving brands as much as trying to sell them.

## Questions

1. Have you engaged in social networking recently? Were any marketers involved?

2. Why might a brand use a careful approach when considering whether to share its intellectual property online?

3. Why do video series like LonelyGirl15 become popular? What makes these ventures desirable to advertisers?

4. Do you remember someone "shilling" a product online? What was your reaction?

## References and Recommended Readings

Alexa (2007). Traffic rank and traffic graph. Retrieved July 31, 2007, from http://www.alexa.com/data/details/traffic_details

Beelen, P. (2006 February). Advertising 2.0: What everybody in advertising, marketing, and media should know about the technologies that are reshaping their business. Whitepaper. Retrieved July 13, 2007, from http://www.paulbeelen.com/whitepaper/Advertising20.pdf

du Gay, P., Hall, S., Janes, L., Mackay, H., & Negus, K. (1997). *Doing Cultural Studies*. London: Sage.

Elliott, S. (2007 June 15). MySpace mini-episodes, courtesy of Honda. *The New York Times*, C5.

Evans, D. (2006, January 4). Word of mouth: Advertising 2.0. Retrieved June 13, 2007, from http://www.clickz.com/showPage.html?page=clickz_print&id=3574721

"Feed 101." (2007). Feedburner. Retrieved July 31, 2007, from http://www.feedburner.com/fb/a/feed101

Gladwell, M. (2000). *The Tipping Point: How Little Things Can Make a Big Difference*. New York: Little, Brown & Co.

Gogoi, P. (2006, October 8). Wal-Mart's Jim and Laura: The real story. *Business Week*. Retrieved Aug. 15, 2007, from http://www.businessweek.com/bwdaily/dnflash/content/oct2006/db20061009_579137.htm

Hennig-Thurau, T., & Walsh, G. (2003). Electronic word-of-mouth: Motives for and consequences of reading customer articulations on the Internet. *International Journal of Electronic Commerce* 8(2), 51-74.

Hills, M. (2002). *Fan Cultures*. London: Routledge.

Hovland, C. I., and Weiss, W. (1951). The influence of source credibility on communication effectiveness. *Public Opinion Quarterly* (15), 635-650.

Lambiase, J. (2003). Sex—online and in Internet advertising. In T. Reichert & J. Lambiase (Eds.) *Sex In Advertising: Perspectives on the Erotic Appeal*, pp. 247-269. Mahwah, NJ: Erlbaum.

LaMonica, M. (2007, May 2). Microsoft's Bach pitches "user-driver marketing." CNET News com. Retrieved July 18, 2007, from http://news.com.com/2101-1012_3-6180742.html.

Levine, M. (2002). *Guerrilla PR Wired: Waging a Successful Publicity Campaign Online, Offline, and Everywhere in Between*. New York: McGraw-Hill.

Neff, J. (2007, May 21). The key to building buzz is ... advertising. *Advertising Age*, p. 12.

Ong, W. (1982). *Orality and Literacy: The Technologizing of the Word*. New York: Routledge.

Smith, D., Menon, S., and Sivakumar, K. (2005). Online peer and editorial recommendations, trust, and choice in virtual markets, *Journal of Interactive Marketing* 19(3), 15-37.

Ulmer, G. (2003). *Internet Invention: From Literacy to Electracy*. New York: Longman.

Vilpponen, A., Winter, S., and Sundqvist, S. (2006). Electronic word-of-mouth in online environments: Exploring the referral network structure and adoption behavior. *Journal of Interactive Advertising*, 6(2), 71-86.

YouTube press release. (2006, Sept. 18). Warner Music Group and YouTube announce landmark video distribution and revenue partnership. Retrieved July 31, 2007, http://www.youtube.com/press_room_entry?entry=vCfgHo5_Fb4

## Online Resources

### Word of Mouth Marketing Association
http://www.womma.org

This web site for the Word of Mouth Marketing Association offers support for generating and exploiting "genuine customer enthusiasm," through ethical guidelines and up-to-date strategies.

**BzzAgent Case Studies**

http://www.bzzagent.com/pages/Page.do?page=Case_Studies

This award-winning company shares word-of-mouth case studies for Lee Jeans, Dunkin' Donuts, and other brands.

# All Ads, All the Time:
## Are We at the Tipping Point of Advertising Saturation?

## by Jay Newell

*The ad business is crushing itself under the weight of its own messaging, squeezing the effectiveness out of its products as consumers get more and more inured to the commercialization of their culture and surroundings.*
—Matthew Creamer, *Advertising Age* (2007)

OVER THE LAST 50 YEARS there has been a vast increase in the exposure of individuals to mass media such as television and the Internet. Because mass media are primarily funded by advertisers, there has been a parallel increase in the amount of advertising individuals are exposed to. Simply, more media means more advertising.

In fact, there is so much advertising—ever creeping into people's previously private spaces—that some industry observers believe we may be nearing a point where advertising will lose its effectiveness. That point can be characterized as an environment of advertising saturation or "all ads, all the time."

This chapter explores the topic of advertising saturation and what it means to consumers and the advertising industry. Specifically, the following questions are addressed: Does clutter reduce the effectiveness of advertising? What happens when advertising enters formerly ad-free zones such as personal phone calls? What organizations, if any, regulate the amount of advertising to which people are exposed?

## More Ads, Please

Americans see a lot of ads. Estimates of the number of ads a person sees in a day vary widely, from 300 to over 6000 per day. In truth, there are no reliable estimates of advertising exposure. The definition of advertising is itself fluid, leading to varying tallies, depending on whether or not the researcher counts classified ads, product placements, and "branding messages" such as product packaging.

While the total number of ad exposure is conjecture, there is no disputing that people encounter more ads each day than they can see or remember. Advertising guru Al Ries recently complained about the seemingly endless commercial breaks on radio, terming the excess of spots "advertising obesity" (Ries, 2007). But, annoyance with excessive advertising is nothing new. Almost 200 years ago, the poet Thomas Carlyle built a soundproof room in his London townhouse in order to get away from street hawkers advertising their products.

While Carlyle could insulate himself from ads by retreating into his home, people today are far more exposed to mass media. The current and projected amounts of media exposure, and the advertising that accompanies it, is unprecedented in human history.

Media exposure occupies a larger portion of the day than any other activity. On average, 70% of waking time is accompanied by media consumption (Papper, Holmes, & Popovich, 2004). In fact, a media industry consulting company estimated that the average person will be exposed to 9.9 hours of media per day by the year 2010 (Veronis Suhler Stevenson, 2006).

Overall, media time and advertising time are converging. Advertising spending has risen, more than doubling over the last 50 years, to a current total of over $950 per person (Johnson, 2007). The single largest source of media exposure is television, with about one-third of each hour filled with commercials, and product placements in the programming between the commercials. Internet use is the fastest growing source of media exposure, and is accompanied by banner ads and more subtle placements, such as Google's paid listings, on nearly every web page.

## One Person's Clutter Is Another Person's Content

*Clutter consists of nothing but the sum of all prior attempts to break through the clutter.*

—Todd Gitlin, *Media Unlimited* (2001, p.68)

Clutter is one dimension of advertising saturation. There is no single definition of clutter, but media researcher Louisa Ha (1996) conceptualizes clutter as the (1) quantity of advertising as a proportion of the overall program or publication, (2) intrusiveness (the degree in which the ads interrupt the program), and (3) competitiveness (the degree of similarity between advertised products). An everyday example of Ha's clutter is a radio station that programs each hour with 30 minutes of music and 30 minutes of commercials (a high ratio of advertising to commercials), the DJ introduces the commercials while the music is playing (intrusiveness), and lots of spots for car dealers (competitiveness).

Individual perceptions play a role in determining what is perceived as clutter. Take, for example, *Bride's Magazine*, one of the most successful publications of the 20th century. Weighing in at over 600 pages per issue, more than half of the pages are advertising. To a non-reader, the abundance of ads appears to be clutter. To a reader, however, the ads are welcomed as an interesting and essential part of the magazine's value and reading experience.

A limitation when researching clutter is that most investigators only consider one medium (e.g., the number of ads in a newspaper). However, the current media environment is more complex because individuals often are exposed to several media at a time. People multitask, both viewing and surfing multiple media during a single time period. For example, an observational study in 2005 found that multiple media were in use for about one-third of the time that any media was in use (Holmes, Papper, Popovich, & Bloxham, 2006). Given the amount of commercial time in the media, this means that people who multitask are exposed to multiple commercial messages as well.

Overall, while the definition of clutter remains elusive, advertisers are deeply concerned that their messages might not be getting through, especially when the exposure of individuals to traditional media such as television and radio is concurrent with exposure to new media such as Internet. More media means more advertising, but is clutter undercutting the value of advertising?

## Why Advertisers Care about Clutter

In media such as television, radio, print, and Internet, advertisers typically don't pay for the number of people who actually see the ad, but for the number of people who have the "opportunity to see" the ad because they tuned in to the program, purchased the magazine or newspaper, or opened up the web page. The justification for "opportunity-to-see" pricing is that an individual's choice of the programming is assumed to indicate attention to the advertising as well. But to the extent that clutter incites individuals to switch their attention away from the program, the value of the advertising time and space is diminished.

There is some recent evidence that clutter decreases advertising response. Starcom Mediavest, a media planning company, conducted a study in which they varied the amount of advertising on web pages. Overall, more advertising was associated with fewer clicks as viewers followed links, as well as reduced interest in purchasing the advertised products.

In addition, academic research has shown that clutter diminishes an individual's memory for ads. In the case of magazines, more advertising leads to less recall for any single ad (Ha, 1996). Clutter may also drive audiences from the medium. In one study of consumer magazines, clutter was associated with a reduction in advertising revenue, as space in ad-saturated magazines was sold at a lower rate than magazines with less advertising (Ha & Litman, 1997).

In sum, clutter is an annoyance to some people in the audience, but a bigger problem for advertisers and advertising. Clutter undermines the assumption that an ad that is placed in front of people is an ad that is seen, which undercuts the perceived value of advertising to marketers.

## Expanding Venues For Advertising

As sociologist Todd Gitlin noted, advertisers typically respond to clutter with more advertising. One strategy has been to expand advertising to locations that had been free, or nearly free, of advertising.

One avenue that seems ripe for the injection of advertising are motion pictures and network programming. Product placement has played a small role in movies since the invention of motion picture projection in the late 1800s (Newell, Salmon, & Chang, 2006). But over the last 20 years, the innocent appearances of branded products as props have been transformed into brand integrations, in which the product plays an integral role in the on-screen action of both movies and television programs. Some network television programs, primarily reality shows, have 20 minutes or more of screen appearances of branded products (Goetzl, 2006). At least for now, it appears that television programming is plagued by ad clutter between commercial breaks.

The search for less cluttered environments is leading advertisers to depend more heavily on outdoor advertising, with its billboards, transit ads, and mall kiosks.

Outdoor advertising is second only to the Internet in its rate of growth. But the increasing popularity of outdoor advertising means that like television and other traditional media, billboards may become a victim of their own success. Too many outdoor ads competing for a limited amount of consumer attention will force advertisers to look to new—less cluttered—venues. For example, ads are now routinely integrated into video games, music (both videos and lyrics), and even novels.

156

Next up as new territory for advertising is the mobile phone. Advertising on cell phones is projected to be a $1.4 billion advertising marketplace in the next few years (Booth, 2007). Cell phone advertising is inherently intrusive, with ads fighting for attention with interpersonal communication. Cell phone advertising is also one place where the consumer can choose whether or not to receive ads. In the US, the 2003 CAN SPAM act requires advertisers to get each potential target's permission before sending out cell phone ads. As academic studies report, about half of cell phone users plan to reject incoming ads (Hanley & Becker, 2007). But as the size of the "third screen" increases with devices such as the iPhone, and content-rich advertising services such as Google become more available, cell phones are likely to join traditional media as advertising saturated environments.

## Origins of Advertising Saturation

To understand how we arrived at an advertising-saturated environment, it helps to understand how people incorporate new media formats into their lives. At one time, the popular theory was that a new medium, such as television, would displace the time spent with other media, such as radio and motion pictures. However, what happens is that when people add a new medium, they do not immediately disconnect from the old media. And so today, television has not displaced radio, and the Internet has not displaced television. People find time to use media, both new and old. And with the new media comes new advertising, on top of the advertising in the traditional media.

Increased media consumption means that marketers must continue to advertise in traditional media, or risk losing contact with their customers. Yet while the advertisers continue placing ads in traditional media, they also experiment with inserting advertising into new media, hoping to reach new and continuing customers.

This process is evidenced in the spending patterns of the top advertisers in the United States. Overall, they are maintaining their spending in traditional media such as television, radio, and magazines, while substantially increasing their spending in new media outlets such as Internet, product placement, and cell phone advertising. The end result is more ads in more places.

*Artists Burtonwood and Holmes combine military and marketing imagery to make statements about the interrelationships of war and commercialism. Sort of a real-life "Marketing Warfare." Burtonwood & Holmes, "Product Placement," site-specific installation, 2006. Courtesy of the artists.*

## Responses to Advertising Saturation

As exposure to advertising has increased, the response of government, the media industry, and consumers has varied. For the most part, the government has declined to regulate the amount of advertising people see, but there are a handful of laws in the US that aim to reduce the quantity of advertising.

- In 1965, the Highway Beautification Act cut the number of billboards on federally-funded roads. The stated goal was to open up scenic areas to the view of travelers. Currently, though, there are more billboards on roads than when the law was passed, and the average billboard is 50% larger.

- Health concerns about tobacco products have played a role in limiting the amount of cigarette advertising. The most significant reduction in advertising occurred when the Attorneys General of multiple states made an agreement with a number of cigarette companies that eliminated tobacco advertising on television, radio, and media vehicles with a substantial under-smoking-age audience. The tobacco companies discontinued TV and radio spots, but increased their budgets for sports sponsorships and events.

- The CAN SPAM Act of 2003 reduced the amount of product telemarketing by creating a do-not-call list of consumers. Additionally, the law requires cell phone users to "opt-in" to receive ads. The law also created the legal foundation to fight e-mail based spam. While not outlawing over-advertising, the CAN SPAM Act gave individuals the tools to reduce their own exposure to some types of advertising.

- Several public-interest groups have petitioned the Federal Trade Commission to regulate brand integration and product placements, but each time the FTC has declined. The chairman of the FCC has proposed that the commission review in 2008 the need for rules on product placement and brand integration on television and radio.

The overall rationale for the infrequent legal restrictions on the amount of advertising is that business can regulate itself by limiting advertising. However, anti-trust laws prohibit industry trade groups from mandating commercial reductions. In the 1950s, the major broadcast

television networks limited the minutes of advertising per hour, but that agreement was judged to be price fixing, as it limited the supply of ad time, thus increasing advertising rates.

While it is illegal for competitors to act together, individual companies have moved on their own to limit the amount of advertising in their programs. Clear Channel radio, the nation's largest operator of radio stations, has cut the number of commercials to under 10 minutes per hour, while trying to raise the price of each commercial. But Clear Channel's commercial reduction has been exceptional: For the most part, media companies are not willing to walk away from advertising revenue.

## Consumer and Industry Responses

If government regulation is not forthcoming, and industry self-regulation is either illegal (as in price fixing) or unrealistic (as in foregoing advertising revenues), are individuals helpless victims of advertising saturation?

To a large extent, individuals have trained themselves to avoid some advertising. For instance, eye tracking studies have shown that people are adept at avoiding ads on the top and sides of Internet pages (Drèze & Hussherr, 2003). Television viewers have always had the ability to flip channels during breaks. To track the flip-away behavior, Nielsen Media Research offers ratings for commercial breaks as well as program ratings. In prime-time programs, the audience for commercial breaks is up to 20% lower than the program itself (Dana & Kang, 2007). For example, a recent report in *Advertising Age* noted that MTV's commercial ratings were 15% below its program ratings. Afraid of losing advertisers, the music network is experimenting with inventive ways to keep viewers engaged during commercial breaks.

Digital video recorders, with TIVO as the leading brand name, provide viewers with the ability to fast-forward through television commercials. And while a majority of TIVO owners skip commercials, there is a still a substantial number that watch some or all of the commercial breaks. Additionally, TIVO offers the devices to advertisers as a direct commercial delivery machine, sending ads to subscribers on an individual basis. Thus a device designed to skip commercials is being repurposed into one that continues to contribute to the overall quantity of advertising.

But advertising avoidance is not absolute. If it were, more people would subscribe to commercial-free media. As it stands, that is not the case. Only about a third of cable or satellite television subscribers are willing to pay for commercial-free networks such as HBO or Showtime, and less than six percent of adult radio listeners pay to access the commercial-free channels on satellite services such as Sirius. There are a few advertising-free magazines, but their circulations tend to be small and subscription costs high. Overall, most people do not appear to be willing to pay more for fewer ads.

The media industry has its own response to advertising saturation: Find new places within existing media to place ads. On television programs, semi-transparent network logos, called "bugs," are now joined by ads that are similar to web page banner ads. NBC bannered the movie *American Gangster* within its top-rated episodes of *Heroes*. The search for new advertising locations within existing media is not limited to television. Magazines are now experimenting with fold-out ads that play music (Steinberg, 2007).

The search for new locations for advertising is taking ads out of cluttered media vehicles and into the conversations of consumers. One of the fastest growing segments of the advertising business is word-of-mouth, with estimated spending of over $1 billion per year to incite individuals to become brand ambassadors for favored products. Agencies such as Tremor specialize in word-of-mouth campaigns that identify opinion leaders, then send those people samples and coupons to pass along to their friends. The result is to move the ad out of media and into everyday conversations. It remains to be seen how much discussion between individuals becomes saturated with—what is in essence—sponsored brand messages.

## The Future of Advertising Saturation

As long as advertisers follow a "reach" strategy in which they set a goal of showing their ads to as many people as possible within their target market, it is unlikely that the overall quantity of advertising will be reduced. The problem is reach itself. While many media are used by almost every person, no media vehicle, such as a single magazine or specific television show, reaches everyone. So in order to generate the broadest possible reach, an advertiser must buy multiple ads and use multiple media.

Reaching light users means that moderate and heavy users will be exposed to the commercial an excessive number of times.

Addressable advertising, where viewers get ads only for products that they have an interest in, might be one solution. The integration of computers and television in the form of set-top digital video recorders makes addressable advertising a viable proposition (Marcus & Walpert, 2007). Addressable advertising gives marketers a tool to distribute ads only to likely prospects, thus avoiding over-distribution of ads. In theory, non-prospects are not forced to sit through personally irrelevant advertising. For example, households without children would probably see fewer commercials for sugary breakfast cereals.

However, the reality experienced by the recipients of direct mail, a printed form of addressable advertising, has differed from addressable advertising's utopian vision. Direct mailers pay by the piece, and thus have a powerful incentive to avoid wasting advertising impressions on non-prospects. Even so, an uncountable amount of direct mail, each piece costing the advertiser anywhere from 50 cents to several dollars, is treated as junk by the recipients. Addressable video, with its potential to have even lower per-piece costs than direct mail, would have even less incentive to limit the distribution of advertising material to only those who are interested.

Apart from resistance by public interest organizations, there have been few protests about the quantity of advertising or the spread of advertising into formerly non-commercial spaces (Klein, 1999). Perhaps the lack of consumer resistance to the oversupply of ads is related to the entertainment value of commercials and print ads. Humor, drama, and spectacle are built into ads to attract attention and communicate brand messages, and some people find the benefit of the entertainment outweighs the inconvenience of the interruption.

Another reason for the lack of consumer protest against advertising saturation may be that most advertising is for socially acceptable products. Product placement studies have shown negative reaction only to socially sanctioned products such as tobacco and firearms (Gupta & Gould, 1997). Overall, positive feelings toward the products and brands generally carry over to the advertising.

Perhaps, most importantly, individuals believe that they are in control of their media experience. If there are too many ads, individuals feel that they can move on to another channel or medium. However, given how media makes its money and the desire of marketers to continue to reach consumers, even new channels or media are soon cluttered with advertising.

*Attempts to beat clutter only end up yielding to more of it, a bitter irony bound to have dire consequences for a business already struggling with questions of relevance and effectiveness.*

—Matthew Creamer, *Advertising Age* (2007)

In the end, advertising saturation is only a source of irritation for consumers. But for marketers, advertising saturation may ultimately be a serious barrier to advertising effectiveness. In this chapter we've seen how the expansion of media exposure has brought with it a parallel increase in advertising exposure. Marketers are jumping into new media with ads—think of how many more ads are seen in video games and movies—without a comparable drop in advertising in traditional media. The end result is more ads seeking the attention of the same number of people, and less confidence that those ads are worth the investment.

## Questions

1. Are there locations where it would be unethical to advertise?

2. For many people, time is as important a resource as money. Do advertisers have an obligation not to waste people's time?

3. Are people aware of how many ads they encounter in a day?

4. Apart from a handful of interest groups, there have been few protests about the amount of advertising. Why?

5. The Internet was originally advertising-free. Would it have developed differently had it remained free of ads?

6.    Does government have a responsibility to protect individuals from too much advertising? Does government have a responsibility to protect the environment from too much advertising?

7.    To what extent should advertisers be permitted to buy ads in public spaces such as schools?

## References and Suggested Readings

Booth, M. (2007). U.S. mobile advertising forecast, 2007-2012. Retrieved September 5, 2007, from http://www.kelseygroup.com

Creamer, M. (2007, April 2). Caught in the crossfire: Your brand. *Advertising Age*, p. 1.

Dana, R., & Kang, S. (2007, October 17). Answer to Vexing Question: Who's Not Watching Ads. *Wall Street Journal*, p. B2.

Drèze, X., & Hussherr, F. X. (2003). Internet advertising: Is anybody watching? *Journal of Interactive Marketing*, 17(4), 8-23.

Gitlin, T. (2001). *Media Unlimited: How the Torrent of Images and Sounds Overwhelms Our Lives*. New York: Metropolitan.

Goetzl, D. (2006). Product placement fueling TV clutter, brand now present more than half the time. Retrieved June 7, 2006 from http://publications.mediapost.com

Gupta, P. B., & Gould, S. J. (1997). Consumers' perceptions of the ethics and acceptability of product placements in movies: Product category and individual differences. *Journal of Current Issues and Research in Advertising*, 19 (1), 37-50.

Ha, L. (1996). Advertising clutter in consumer magazines: Dimension and effects. *Journal of Advertising Research*, 36(July/August), 76-84.

Ha, L., & Litman, B. R. (1997). Does advertising clutter have diminishing and negative returns? *Journal of Advertising*, 26 (1), 31-42.

Holmes, M. E., Papper, R. A., Popovich, M. N., & Bloxham, M. (2006). *Engaging the Ad Supported Media*. Muncie, IN: Ball State University.

Johnson, B. (2007, June 25). Top 100 spending up 3.1% to $105 billion. *Advertising Age*, S-2.

Klein, N. (1999). *No Logo*. New York: Picador.

Marcus, C., & Walpert, T. (2007). Emerging Applications and Challenges of Addressable Television Advertising. *Journal of Integrated Marketing Communications*, Retrieved August 2, 2007, from http://jimc.medill.northwestern.edu/JIMCWebsite/site.htm

Newell, J., Salmon, C. T., & Chang, S. (2006). The hidden history of product placement. *Journal of Broadcasting & Electronic Media*, 50 (4), 30-48.

Papper, R. A., Holmes, M. E., & Popovich, M. N. (2004). Middletown media studies. *International Digital Media & Arts Journal*, 1 (1), 5-56.

Ries, A. (2007). How radio is becoming radiADo. *Advertising Age* Online, 2007. Retrieved March 4, 2007, from http://www.advertisingage.com.

Veronis Suhler Stevenson. (2006). Consumer industry forecast. New York.

## Online Resources

### Brand Channel
http://www.brandchannel.com/brandcameo_films.asp

Updated weekly by Omnicom's Interbrand agency, this website tracks appearances of branded products in major motion pictures. This website provides insights into the range of products in new movies.

### Commercial Alert
http://www.commercialalert.org/

Commercial Alert is a non-profit group that opposes the expansion of advertising into formerly ad-free environments, such as schools and public buildings. Current campaigns fight prescription drug advertising, product placement, and advertising on school busses.

**Adland: The Commercial Archive**

http://commercial-archive.com/

Launched in 2000, this is a quirky, highly entertaining compilation of new television and print advertising from around the world, presented in a blog format. New ads are shown free, and a paid archive contains copies of thousands of television commercials going back to the 1970s.

**Campaign for a Commercial-Free Childhood**

http://www.commercialfreechildhood.org/

This is a non-profit organization that opposes the commercial exploitation of children. Headquartered in Boston, the group has current efforts against the sexualization of children in advertising and entertainment, the intrusion of advertising into schools, and the commercialization of children's web sites such as Webkinz.

**Blog: The Cool Hunter**

http://www.thecoolhunter.net/

This blog keeps up-to-date on worldwide innovations in advertising, architecture, and fashion, among other arts. New advertising media, and new uses of traditional ad media, make early appearances here.

# Section 3

# Representation
# and Recruitment:
## Women and Minorities

# Women in Advertising:
## Representation and (Lack of) Possibilities

## by Tom Reichert

*You can tell the ideals of a nation by its advertisements.*
—Norman Douglas (1917)

DESPITE DOVE'S RECENT ad campaign that showcases "real" women, rather than super-thin models, advertising research continues to show that women are narrowcast in traditional occupations (e.g., nurse, teachers, secretaries) or as sexual objects.

The advertising profession is addressing this issue by bringing attention to particularly egregious instances of stereotyping (e.g., Advertising Women of New York's awards), and educators and scholars are addressing this issue in the context of media literacy.

The representation of women in advertising is important to consider because often it presents a distorted view of women's reality that can lead to misperceptions about women's roles in society.

## Background

Media critics argue—and research supports—that women are consistently portrayed in narrowly defined roles that overemphasize physical beauty and sexuality, while de-emphasizing intellect, ability, and occupational reality (Lazier & Kendrick, 1993).

### Debate Began in the 1960s

Much of this debate began in the 1960s during the women's liberation movement which was characterized by feminist awareness and political activism. Critics claimed that the depiction of women in advertising presented a distorted view of the reality of women's lives.

One of these critics was Betty Friedan, author of *The Feminine Mystique.* In her book, Friedan discussed the disconnect between society's prescribed roles for women and the reality of their lives. "Friedan was one of the first to raise pointed questions about the portrayal of women in women's magazines and the advertisements contained therein," noted Bowling Green State University professor Vickie Shields (1997, p. 74).

Partly in response to Friedan's observations, researchers began analyzing stereotyping and sex-role representation in advertising and the media.

These studies found that indeed women were shown in very limiting ways. For instance, women were rarely portrayed outside the roles of homemaker and decorative object. According to media researcher Linda Lazier-Smith (1989):

> In print advertising, the results of more than a dozen studies, almost all conducted in the 1970s, have shown the messages of advertising to be astonishingly similar: Woman's place is in the home; women are dependent upon men; women do not make independent and important decisions; women are shown in few occupational roles; women view themselves and are viewed by others as sex objects (p. 249).

Also during this period, Erving Goffman, in 1979, published *Gender Advertisements*, a synopsis of his analysis of women and men in ads. Trained as a sociologist, Goffman examined 500 ads and reached some interesting conclusions regarding the gender reality presented in ads.

For instance, he noticed that compared to women, men take up more space in ads and are shown as executives, whereas women defer to men, are more restricted in their movements, and that women's bodies, through the act of touching, are perceived as more delicate and precious than men's bodies.

Goffman's study and these early analyses have been replicated and extended in a number of different media and forms of advertising by media researchers. Most of their findings are surprisingly consistent, even today.

### Reality vs. "Reality"

Consider, for example, the discrepancy between the reality of the workplace for women and their "reality" as portrayed through advertising.

In 2005, 46% of the entire US labor force consisted of women. Of women in their prime working years (25–54), over 75% were in the workforce.

As important, these women did not just occupy traditionally viewed women's occupations—teachers and secretaries—but many of them were executives and CEOs. In 2006, for example, over 40% of all businesses in the US were owned by women.

Now, compare those facts to what is portrayed in advertising.

In a recent content analysis I conducted with Courtney Carpenter-Childers (2006), an advertising professor at the University of Tennessee, we found a strikingly different pattern of results. We analyzed over 956 ads in 2003 issues of six mainstream, high-circulation magazines. We found that only 3% of all women were shown in a "progressive" manner.

This means that very rarely were women shown occupying professional or managerial roles and/or aspects of their personalities were emphasized that related goals, abilities, and competencies.

A recent Plavix ad features a woman in a progressive role. The headline reads: "Running a busy E.R., Janet is a formidable woman. But she was no match for something smaller than the tip of her pen. A clot." The woman, presumably a physician, is standing outside a hospital emergency room. She's wearing a white lab coat and a stethoscope.

### 25% "Traditional"

About 25% of the portrayals were "traditional." Women in these ads were portrayed as relational partners, mothers, homemakers, or employed in traditional female-oriented occupations (e.g., secretaries, assistants, nurses).

For example, a recent Dress Barn ad in Oprah's magazine features a woman in the kitchen stirring cupcake batter with her young daughter. The headline reads: "Let yourself cook up something new," "Let yourself spill the sprinkles," and "Let yourself be stirred."

Another ad assures moms that "Every dinner should feel this good" when they serve pre-cooked lasagna.

### 73% Decorative

Most striking, 73% of the images were "decorative." These images depicted women as product adornments—women were present merely to enhance the product.

Emphasis in these ads was placed on women's bodies and their attractiveness without any mention of the women's competencies, goals, or job-related abilities.

Demonstrating this decorative approach is a recent ad for Glaceau's SmartWater featuring Jennifer Anniston. Other than the brand name, the ad consists of an appealing close up of a smiling Anniston holding the bottled water.

As the analysis demonstrates, the discrepancies are significant between women's reality and what is reflected in advertising.

## Why Do These Images Matter?

While we might be tempted to think that the twelve or so hours of media we consume each day has no effect on us, research shows that it does have both long- and short-term *indirect effects*.

This means that the media aren't intentionally trying to manipulate us in a macro-social sense, but that the nature of content does have subtle influences on people that occur incrementally over time.

### Effects of Media Images

Theories of media effects have long suggested that exposure to media images can influence social perceptions and self-concept.

Children learn much about gender roles from a very early age through observations and imitation of role models. The learning pattern of younger individuals is to first observe, then to imitate—a process called social learning.

Regarding long-term influences, sexist images in the media can influence how people view themselves.

A steady diet of these images has the power to shape appropriate and expected attitudes and behavior for women and men.

For example, young women may feel less ambitious and career worthy after years of viewing stereotypical messages where women are shown only in one-dimensional or maternal roles.

All of us want to fit in to some degree. We take cues from the media as we strive to be successful members of our culture.

## Appropriate Roles for Women

Based on what you know so far, what do the media suggest are appropriate roles for women?

A safe assumption is that physical appearance and sexual attractiveness are vital requirements for female success. Talking about the predominance of sexist messages in advertising, Shields (1997) states:

> These messages, used to sell everything from cosmetics to cars to beverages, provide prescriptions for how women should look and be looked at, how they should feel, and how they are expected to act. In short, these messages prescribe particular gender identities to which women should aspire.
>
> They also prescribe how men should relate to women (p. 72).

## "Idealized" Reality?

Secondarily, one can deduce that a woman's place is either in the home or in some sort of traditionally feminine occupation.

Now, keep in mind that advertising represents our society's "idealized" version of reality—what we dream and strive for.

Keeping that conception in mind, what type of career options are available for women?

Now, answer that question when you consider that men are predominately portrayed as successful executives, professionals, managers, and leaders.

Regarding short-term influences, images in the media can influence people immediately after exposure.

Recall that almost three-quarters of women in advertising are portrayed in a decorative manner. Several studies have shown that these same types of images can influence a woman's body image.

In addition, men have been shown to become more callous toward women after viewing images of sexualized women. Also consider that Alex Tan (1985), a media professor at Washington State University, was able to influence the value of beauty as an attribute by showing young women several cosmetics commercials.

Compared to female teens who viewed neutral commercials, the teens viewing ads for cosmetics reported that being beautiful was more important to them personally, and it was essential to be popular with boys.

## What's Being Done

Faced with the facts, why haven't marketers "cleaned up" their ads?

Despite the results of the previously described content analysis, marketers are making efforts to accurately portray women.

Well, that seems to be happening. In interviews with advertising executives, I get the impression that they are much more sensitive to portrayals of women than in the past.

### "Real Beauty"

One notable effort by the industry to address the issue of women's representation has created a tremendous level of buzz in the marketing world.

The "Real Beauty" campaign initiated by Unilever's Dove is using real women in its ads to combat what it calls narrow definitions of beauty based on only physical appearance.

The women in the ads are clad only in their intimate-wear and they are not airbrushed or retouched.

The entire focus of the campaign, initiated in 2004, has been to encourage women to broaden their definitions of beauty. Dove discovered during its pre-campaign research that most women are dissatisfied with their bodies and that they blame the media for it. Specifically, Dove found that most women think that advertising and the media set unrealistic and unachievable beauty standards.

new Dove Firming.
As tested on real curves.

Dove
Firming Range

This research also found that 13% of women are very satisfied with their bodies, and that only 2% consider themselves beautiful. In addition, the research revealed that more than half of all women said they are disgusted with their bodies.

As a result, Dove went out and hired real women to star in its ads. According to one *USA Today* reporter, the commercials "feature candid and confident images of curvy, full-bodied, real women" (Howard, 2005).

The campaign has won numerous awards—and praise—for its "real world" approach.

For example, a short video for Dove's beauty care line became a viral sensation and won the Golden Lion award at the 2007 Cannes Lions International Advertising Festival.

A winner in both the Cyber and Film categories, "Evolution" began as an Internet video before running as a television commercial. Ogilvy & Mather, Toronto, produced the video and uploaded it to YouTube where it has been viewed millions of times.

As part of the "Real Beauty" campaign, the video challenges beauty preconceptions with "time-lapse photography show[ing] the transformation of an average woman into a glamorous billboard model using beauty stylists and Photoshop enhancements" (High, Morrissey, & Parpis, 2007, p. 6).

Other brands noted for their positive images of women include L'Oreal, Nike, Curves, and Kellogg's Special K.

Whether other companies adopt a similar approach remains to be seen. Several people have noted that while they applaud Dove's overall message, its ads do promote beauty products in the form of firming creams and lotions designed to reduce the appearance of cellulite.

### An Advocate—AWNY

Also, within the industry at least one group is particularly effective at raising awareness and changing practices by publicly praising (and shaming) advertisers who do a good (bad) job representing women in ads.

The organization is Advertising Women of New York (AWNY), a professional organization designed to help women in their communications careers.

Each year the organization bestows "The Good, The Bad & The Ugly" awards. "Good" winners in 2006 included Dove, Kodak, and American Ex-

press. The ESPN ad "Running Away" won the "Grand Good" award.

Winners of the "Bad" distinction included Axe, La Perla, and GoDaddy.com, with the "Grand Ugly" going to Carl's Jr. and its spot featuring Paris Hilton.

Winning an "Ugly" award is comparable to having your name posted on the courthouse stairs for failure to pay your taxes.

I would hate to imagine you, a future communications executive, trying to explain to your client why they were publicly ridiculed for sexist advertising you approved or created.

## Guys—Listen Up

My experience, both personally and professionally, is that men outwardly nod their agreement to the points made during this discussion, but inwardly shake their heads in disagreement. Men can become reactive and think to themselves: "Just picking on guys once again."

I know what you're thinking because in 1987 I was sitting in your seat when one of my professors gave a similar presentation. I didn't say anything at the time but I also had a reactionary response.

A male professor seemed to share my perspective when he made light of the presentation and told us that he wanted to protest the negative ways men are portrayed in advertising: as bumbling idiots who need help figuring out how to empty the trash.

But after 15 years of studying the influence of mass media on people's lives, it has become clear to me that media images contribute to our sense of reality.

For me, that talk in 1987 opened the door ever so slightly to the possibility that society views women in a certain way, and that those values are both reflected and reinforced through advertising.

Little by little that door opened wider as I gained personal experience and I had the opportunity to analyze relevant academic research.

Guys, there is truth here.

At this point all that I can ask is that you keep your mind open. That you be alert. And that you look for the underlying social messages in advertising. You might want to find a copy of the video *Stale Roles and Tight Buns*. Produced by a couple of professors, the video critiques the way men are presented in advertising.

The professors present a compelling argument that men are also narrowcast in advertising (e.g., success at all cost, aloofness, extreme competitiveness), and that what advertising deems appropriate behavior for men to strive toward can have negative consequences.

## Today and Tomorrow's Ads

The future of women's images in advertising shows promise despite the findings of recent analyses. There are signs of improvement, and progressive depictions are sure to appear in more ads as women continue to move into executive roles both in corporations and advertising agencies.

Also, images will become more balanced as society increases its awareness of the effects of these distorted images. Not that all images need to

177

show women in the boardroom, but more ads will talk to women by appealing to their personalities, abilities, and their desires for achievement instead of hyping the value of beauty.

Consider a recent campaign for sports apparel marketer Under Armour. Known for its "click-clack" spots and slogans such as "Not in our house," the company is now targeting young women, ages 14 to 22, with its biggest ad campaign to date.

The ads are notable because they are emphasizing hard work and goal attainment. In an article titled "No Sugar and Spice Here," the writer describes the campaign as "a series of ads that show Under Armour–outfitted female athletes gutting and grunting their way through grueling workouts" (Mullman, 2007, p. 3).

Under Armour's approach is progressive because the emphasis is on young women practicing to develop their skills and endurance. Determination is the focus, not eye candy (or telling women how to look like eye candy). Although Under Armour's approach is hardly the feminist ideal, the ads speak to women about athleticism and personal achievement, not just looking good in athletic wear.

While Under Armour's approach—similar to ads by Nike, Asics, and other athletic marketers—could become the norm, decorative portrayals have not disappeared. Consider a recent Heineken commercial that caught the attention of *Advertising Age*'s critic Bob Garfield (2007, p. 25): "[The] new ad for the Heineken DraughtKeg… is arguably the most sexist beer commercial ever produced."

Garfield's claim is fairly strong considering the history of beer advertising.

The commercial features a female robot in a skimpy dress demonstrating the mini-keg's convenience as she stares into the camera and dances to club music. Oh, and she happens to store the keg in her abdomen. Garfield likened the depiction to an "animated image of a babelicious cyborg who looks like the issue of C3P0 and Gwen Stefani—a totally hot blonde bot."

Garfield didn't mind the model's attractiveness so much as the commercial's allusion to sexist jokes about "mute nymphomaniac[s]" and women with flat heads "to rest your beer on."

More important, he makes the point that sexist images are not only insulting, but that there is usually a price to be paid by the offending marketer: "they have reduced half the world to a man-serving beer tap… That isn't futuristic. It's retrograde," said Garfield.

"And when women see what Heineken is up to, it won't be a robot that needs to be repaired." By repaired he means a backlash by female consumers in the form of lost Heineken sales, a tarnished image, or both.

The campaigns by Under Armour and Heineken represent depictions at the extremes of female representation in contemporary advertising. Over time, the bulk of ads featuring women will continue to fall between these two end-points but should skew toward progressive as advertisers increasingly reflect the realities of women's lives.

## Questions

1.  Have you ever compared yourself to models in advertisements? How did it make you feel?

2.  Have you ever promised yourself that you would take some type of action (e.g., workout, diet, etc.) as the result of viewing an ad? Did you follow through?

3.  What magazines contain the most progressive images of women? Is that progressiveness reflected in the ads within the pages of those magazines?

## References and Recommended Reading

Busby, Linda, & G. Leichty (1993). Feminism and advertising in traditional and nontraditional women's magazines 1950s–1980s. *Journalism Quarterly*, 70 (2), 247–265.

Cortese, Anthony J. (1999). *Provocateur: Images of women and minorities in advertising*. Lanham, MD: Rowman & Littlefield.

Courtney, Alice E., & Sarah W. Lockeretz (1971). A woman's place: An analysis of the roles portrayed by women in magazine advertisements. *Journal of Marketing*, 8, 92–95.

Courtney, Alice E., & Thomas W. Whipple (1983). *Sex Stereotyping in Advertising*. Lexington, MA: Heath.

Ferguson, Jill Hicks, Peggy J. Kreshel, & Spencer F. Tinkham (1990). In the pages of *Ms.*: Sex role portrayals of women in advertising. *Journal of Advertising*, 19 (1), 40–51.

Ford, John, Michael S. LaTour, & Courtney Middleton (1999). Women's studies and advertising role portrayal sensitivity: How easy is it to raise 'feminist consciousness?' *Journal of Current Issues and Research in Advertising*, 21 (Fall), 77–87.

Friedan, Betty (1963). *The Feminine Mystique*. New York: Dell.

Garfield, Bob (2007, August 27). A Heineken spot that's so sexist it left even us feeling infuriated. *Advertising Age*, p. 25.

Goffman, Erving (1979), *Gender Advertisements*. Cambridge, MA: Harvard University Press.

Harrison, Kristine, & Joanne Cantor (1997). The relationship between media consumption and eating disorders. *Journal of Communication*, 47 (1), 40–67.

High, Kamau, Morrissey, Brian, & Parpis, Eleftheria (2007, June 25). The 'evolution' of advertising. *Adweek*, p. 6.

Howard, Theresa (2005, July 8). Ad campaign tells women to celebrate who they are. *USA Today*. Retrieved October 9, 2006, from: http://www.campaignforrealbeauty.com/press.asp?section=news&id=3073

Kendrick, Douglas T., Sara E. Gutierres, & Laurie L. Goldberg (1989). Influence of popular erotica on judgments of strangers and mates. *Journal of Experimental Social Psychology*, 25, 159–167.

Kilbourne, Jean (2000). *Can't Buy My Love: How Advertising Changes How We Think and Feel*. New York: Free Press.

Lavine, Howard, Donna Sweeney, & Stephen H. Wagner (1999). Depicting women as sex objects in television advertising: Effects on body dissatisfaction. *Personality and Social Psychology Bulletin*, 25 (August), 1049–1058.

Lindner, Katharina (2004). Images of women in general interest and fashion magazine advertisements from 1955 to 2002. *Sex Roles*, 51 (October), 409–421.

MacKay, Natalie J., & Katherine Covell (1997). The impact of women in advertisements on attitudes toward women. *Sex Roles*, 36 (9/10), 573–583.

McKenzie-Mohr, Doug, & Mark P. Zanna (1990). Treating women as sexual objects: Look to the (gender schematic) male who has viewed pornography. *Personality and Social Psychology Bulletin*, 16 (June), 296–308.

Mullman, Jeremy (2007, June 18). No sugar and spice here. *Advertising Age*, p. 3, 35.

Myers, Philip N., & Frank A. Biocca (1992). The elastic body image: The effect of television advertising and programming on body image distortions in young women. *Journal of Communication*, 42 (Summer), 108–133.

Shields, Vickie Rutledge (1997). Selling the sex that sells: Mapping the evolution of gender advertising research across three decades, in *Communication Yearbook*, Brant R. Burleson, ed., (pp. 71–109). Thousand Oaks, CA: Sage.

Signiorelli, Nancy (1993). Television, the portrayal of women, and children's attitudes, in G. L. Berry & J. K. Asamen (Eds.), *Children and Television: Images in a changing sociocultural world* (pp. 229–242). Newbury Park, CA: Sage.

Tan, Alexis (1985). *Mass Communication Theories and Research*. New York: Macmillan.

# Online Resources

### "Good, Bad & Ugly Award" Winners
http://www.aef.com/exhibits/awards/gbu/index.html

The site, sponsored by the Advertising Education Foundation, contains examples of what the Advertising Women of New York consider to contain "good" and "bad" portrayals of women.

### Gender Ads
http://genderads.com

A large site with hundreds of ads. Scott Lukas developed this site to support one of his gender courses. The ads on the site demonstrate how sex and race are portrayed in contemporary advertising.

### About-Face
http://about-face.org

A site that promotes positive self-esteem in girls and women through a "spirited" approach to media education, outreach and activism.

### Wonder Branding
http://www.wonderbranding.com

Michelle Miller claims to be an expert at understanding and reaching female consumers. Her firm is Wizard of Ads. Be sure to check her blog.

# Wanted: Sense and Sensitivity
## Regarding Race and Ethnicity in Advertising

### by Caryl Cooper

IF BEAUTY IS IN THE EYE OF THE BEHOLDER, then analyzing how race and ethnicity are portrayed in advertising is an important way to understand how advertising challenges or reinforces the way minorities are perceived. The ability to critically analyze media content can help people understand the cultural shorthand advertisers use to brand their products and services. However, not every consumer interprets advertising messages in the same way.

## "Reading" Ads

In a recent session about advertising literacy, the instructor asked students in an introductory-level mass communications course to view magazine advertisements and decide if the ads challenged or reinforced cultural stereotypes. The ad in question was for Timberland—the outdoor outfitter—and featured a young black man and a child standing by a fence in a field enjoying nature. Trees and mountaintops framed the two subjects. The text read: Saturday afternoon hike. Talked about birds and bees. Son now thinks mother is a bee.

The instructor asked the students if the ad challenged or reinforced any racial or ethnic stereotypes. A young black female student claimed that the ad challenged stereotypical images of African American men. When asked to explain her observation, she said that most mediated images do not show young black men outdoors and enjoying nature. A young white male student disagreed and said that since the ad was for rugged, outdoor boots, placing someone wearing those boots in a different setting would not be believable. "Race has nothing to do with it," the white student contended hotly. A lively discussion ensued.

Finally, after many white students voiced their agreement with their white colleague, the instructor asked all of the students to close their eyes for a moment and envision a young black man, aged 18-24. Then she asked the students to consider what the young black man was wearing, how he was speaking, and what he was doing. After asking the students to open their eyes, the instructor asked, "Did anyone think of a young black man in the woods in a nurturing relationship with a child?"

The room was silent. No one, not even the black students, raised their hands. "Do you understand why it is important to 'read' an advertisement?," the instructor asked quietly. "Because the Timberland ad challenges the images you have in your head about young, black men. It challenges a stereotype. Knowing how to 'read' an ad will help you distinguish the differences."

The response of the students demonstrates why analyzing minority images in advertisements is important for understanding the impact advertising has on society. As scholar and marketing expert Marilyn Kern-Foxworth explained in a *New York Times* interview, "Not only are we being given images of who we are supposed to be, but others are also formulating their images of us based on that" (Peters, 2006).

However, the way students responded to the exercise demonstrates how difficult it may be for them to appreciate the salience of the topic. After all, today's student has never known a time when African Americans and other minorities were not in advertisements. For the most part, they've never been asked to consider how the roles and relationships of people in ads can influence our purchases or reinforce our beliefs. In addition, students may not know that advertisers consider minority consumers important to the survival of their companies.

## Shifting Demos and Market Power

Consider these facts about the consumption of the two largest minority groups in the US; African Americans and Hispanics. According to 2006 data provided by the U.S. Census Bureau (2007), minority representation is growing as is its buying power.

- The nation's minority population is more than 100 million.
- The African American population is 40.7 million.
- African Americans have an expendable income of $800 billion—the highest of any minority group.
- African Americans are extremely brand loyal and trust the brands they buy.
- African-American women make many major purchasing decisions.
- The Hispanic expendable income was $686 billion in 2004 and is expected to reach $1 trillion by 2010.
- Hispanics make up 14.8 percent of the total U.S. population.
- The Hispanic population topped 44.3 million and is considered the fastest growing consumer group in the US.
- The Hispanic population is not a homogenous group. It includes people whose origins are in Mexico, Cuba, Puerto Rico, the Caribbean, Central America, South America, and other Spanish-speaking countries or regions. As a result, understanding language and cultural nuances is important.

As scholar Barbara Mueller notes, the population changes and increases in minority expendable incomes will "have a direct influence on the products and services that will be offered to consumer groups in the future, the media used to communicate with them, and the agencies employed to create the messages appearing in those media" (Mueller, 2008, p. 16).

With so much money at stake, advertisers want to make sure that the creative strategies used in ads resonate with and do not offend minority consumers. But achieving these goals is not as simple as it sounds. Not only do these issues concern the content of the ad, they also pertain to the creator of the ad. Ironically, these concerns did not emanate from the advertising community. They have been an issue within the African American community since the early 1800s.

## Brief Historical Perspective

Images of African Americans in advertising found in general market media have changed over time. Advertising for slaves dominated advertising space in early American newspapers. Slave owners placed advertisements in newspapers urging the recapture of runaway slaves in newspapers during the 1700s and 1800s.

GOOD MORNING! Have you used PEARS' SOAP?

Kern-Foxworth (1994) notes that advertising played an important role in maintaining slavery by letting potential buyers know when and where slaves could be bought and sold. In addition, these advertisements contained information about the attributes of slaves, such as gender and skill.

Although most advertisers did not value the minority market, by the late 1800s, African American images began to appear in advertisements for a variety of consumer products. In the 1890s, an artist's rendition of Nancy Green, a former slave, was created to serve as a trademark for pancake flour. The Aunt Jemima trademark is considered by *Advertising Age* to be one the top 10 advertising icons and best known trademarks in advertising history (Enrico, 1999). Rastus was created for Cream of Wheat cereal and Uncle Ben was created to sell white rice. Although these images show blacks in subservient roles and recall days of slavery, these images have been used as trademarks for more than 100 years.

Although the use of African American images as trademarks proved to be effective, the successes of these companies did not encourage the advertising industry to view the African American market as lucrative nor to hire blacks. Throughout the early 20th century, the advertising industry remained predominantly white and male.

However, the post-World War II social and political environment—as well as the success of *Ebony* magazine and several prominent black newspapers—companies and their advertising agencies began to explore the value of marketing to African American consumers. Most companies, however, believed that advertising to African Americans would alienate their white consumers.

Companies that experimented with marketing to the black market found that their white consumer base was not affected. Because of this outcome, along with the social advances made by the Civil Rights Movement, economic pressure created by the activities of Jesse Jackson's Rainbow Coalition and the creation of minority advertising agencies, such as Burrell Communications and UniWorld Group, African Americans became involved in creating advertisements and developing marketing strategies for black consumers.

Although advertising agencies began hiring African Americans in the 1970s, the industry continues to struggle with low numbers of minorities in the industry and remains challenged to created culturally-relevant ads for minority audiences.

## Current State of Affairs

More than 30 years later, the advertising industry has continued to draw criticism for its use of minorities in advertising. During the later part of the 20th century, most complaints focused on the lack of minorities in advertising.

Today, there is increased criticism about the way minorities are portrayed in advertisements. For example, African Americans often complain about the way black men are portrayed. In the article, "The Potholes of Multicultural Marketing," *Washington Post* journalist Warren Brown (2007) illustrates the problem of race portrayal by describing typical automobile commercials. "The driver usually is white and male. When gender changes, the driver is white and female. Black or other vehicle occupants of color usually sit in the front passenger's seat… or they sit in the rear. But they seldom sit behind the wheel, in charge of the car."

According to Brown, seating arrangement is important because positioning symbolizes power and authority. How? Because the driver knows where he or she is going in life and is in control of the situation. Being relegated to the rear of the car consistently reinforces society's views of blacks being in subordinate and dependent positions, rarely holding positions of authority over whites

Even in commercials featuring African American couples, the man is often portrayed as ineffective and subordinate to the woman. For example, in a recent television ad for a stock brokerage firm, a black husband and wife discuss the strategies they used to secure their future. The man sat slightly behind the women and was faintly out of focus. For every strategy the man brought up, the woman not only corrected him on the proper terminology, but also took credit for executing the strategy. Again, the African-American man was in a subordinate position, in this case, to the woman of the household.

Critics have complained also about the portrayal of African American women in advertising. To its credit, the advertising industry seems to have embraced the diversity of African American women by portraying them in a variety of shapes, sizes, skin colors, hairstyles and in both dominant and subordinate positions of power.

A recent effort spearheaded by Procter & Gamble—one of the world's largest advertisers—to reach and empower women of color is the "My Black is Beautiful" campaign. According to *Advertising Age*'s Jack Neff (2007, p. 21), the goal of the campaign "is to make all black girls and women feel [beautiful] regardless of skin tone or origin." Research by P&G revealed that 77% of black women were concerned about their portrayal in media and 71% felt that they are portrayed worse than other racial groups. The campaign theme will be used across several of P&G's brands.

One caricature of the black woman, however, seems to persist—the obese, boisterous and frequently aggressive woman (Peters, 2006). From floor cleaners, to laxatives, to amusement parks, advertisers have used this image of the black woman to promote a variety of products and services. And while the campaigns using these images are considered effective, the images are considered stereotypical, offensive, and do not challenge people to look at black women in new and different ways.

## Multicultural Marketing 101

Reasons for these portrayals are varied and often relates to the strategies creative teams use to develop ads. A common strategy used by many advertisers is simply to include women and minorities in advertising developed for the general market. The formula, described by Monique Tapie, Communications Director for Global Advertising Strategies, as "Multicultural Marketing 101," is simple; "A woman here, man there, black person there, Asian here, Latino there... [It] assumes that all Asians are alike, that all African Americans are alike, that all Spanish-speaking people are alike, that we are all alike, which means that we're mainstream [white]" (Brown, 2007).

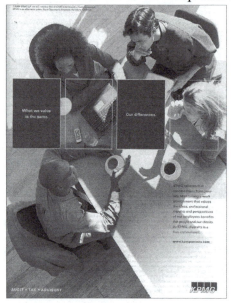

Tapie's comments reflect the concerns about the process advertising agencies use when developing advertisements. The complexity of this process was explored in a *New York Times* article by Jeremy Peters (2006). Peters included as an example a 2006 television campaign for Dairy Queen Blizzard. In one commercial an overweight black woman is featured as an irritated airline passenger. In another ad, she is featured as an airport security screener.

When asked how she was selected, Rick Cusato, executive vice president for Grey Worldwide (the agency that created the ad), said that they looked for the funniest person. "We didn't specifically cast for a black woman." Dairy Queen's chief brand officer Michael Keller supported the agency's decision. "She projected an image that was everything we wanted it to be. This is just a strong woman being herself."

Since neither Dairy Queen or Grey Worldwide received any complaints, everyone assumed the advertising was fine. No minority writers were involved in the creation of the Dairy Queen ads and some African American advertisers contend that this is the problem: Many images are created by white writers who don't understand the nuances of minority cultures.

Understanding the context of culture when creating advertising is a concern for Hispanic marketing, also. And, similar to the African American market, the issue is complex. During a 2005 appearance on CNBC's "The Big Idea with Donny Deutsch," comedian George Lopez created a stir within the advertising industry when he said that advertising targeting Hispanics and African Americans was unnecessary due to the blurring of cultural lines.

Most Hispanic advertisers contend the opposite. In a response to Lopez's comments, President-CEO of Lopez Negrete Communications, Alex Lopez Negrete (2005, p. 25), said "that the only way for brands to connect with consumers is through insight and emotion, and thus, through context and culture… The U.S. Hispanic market has grown not only in numbers, but also in its complexity, diversity and influence. Heritage, level of acculturation and geographic concentration are only a few of the nuances that are critical to understanding how to reach this increasingly coveted market segment."

## Into the Future

What can advertisers and their agencies do to make sure their advertising does not offend targeted audiences? Critics contend that the industry's lack of diversity is part of the problem. For example, African American employment in New York advertising agencies is estimated to be approximately five percent (Monahan, 2007). In 2004, New York City's Commission on Human Rights began to investigate the hiring practices of the city's advertising agencies. As a result of the investigations, several agencies signed agreements to boost minority hiring over three years. In addition,

Omnicom committed $2.5 million over five years for a plan that includes creating an advertising curriculum at a New York City college (Howard, 2006). Omnicom's plan suggests that higher education can and should play an important role in preparing students for the changing marketplace.

Students seeking entry into the advertising industry can increase their chances of being hired by demonstrating their ability to create ads for different audiences. For those wanting to be creative directors, students should consider developing portfolios with targeted versions of the same ad. As scholar Barbara Mueller explains, "Effectively communicating with black consumers means creating messages relevant to their lifestyle" (Mueller, 2008, p. 183).

Students cannot develop the kind of understanding necessary for creating targeted advertising by simply analyzing mediated images. Students would do well to develop intercultural competencies by taking courses specializing in that area. Courses in history and American culture would work well also. For those wanting to go into account service, media and research, students should be able to demonstrate their awareness of population trends, promotional techniques, media, and media strategies that can be used to target minority consumers. For example, students should know that the top ten television programs for Hispanic audiences are not the same as those for the general audience.

The issues about advertising to minority audiences will continue until advertisers and their agencies decide that cultural awareness and sensitivity is a requirement for employment. Employers, educators, and students must understand that our nation's changing demographics, and the advertising developed to reach them, require an improved set of skills for business success.

# Questions

1. How can advertisers avoid using stereotypical images in advertising?

2. Compare advertisements in magazines, such as *Ebony* and *Essence*, with those in similar general market magazines. Are the images and text different? In your opinion, are the ads effective for reaching the target audience?

3. Is developing advertisements for targeted markets part of a company's social responsibility?

4. What stereotyping can you find in advertisements in general market publications and on television?

# References and Recommended Reading

Brown, Warren (2007, June 10). The potholes of multicultural marketing. *The Washington Post*, p. G2. Retrieved January 23, 2008, from: http://www.washingtonpost.com/wp-dyn/content/article/2007/06/07/AR2007060701582.html

Chambers, Jason (2007). *Madison Avenue and the color line*. Philadelphia: University of Pennsylvania.

Enrico, Dottie (1999, March 29). Top 10 advertising icons. *Advertising Age*.

Grimes, Diane Susan (2006). "Getting a bit of the other": Sexualized stereotypes of Asian and black women in Planned Parenthood advertising. In Tom Reichert & Jacqueline Lambiase (Eds.), *Sex in Consumer Culture* (pp. 301-318). Mahwah, NJ: LEA.

Howard, Theresa (2006, September 27). N.Y. ad agencies vow to address lack of diversity: People of color hold few top jobs. *USA Today*. Retrieved, January 23, 2008, from: http://www.usatoday.com/money/advertising/2006-09-26-ad-diversity-usat_x.htm

Kern-Foxworth, Marilyn (1994). *Aunt Jemima, Uncle Ben, and Rastus: Blacks in advertising, yesterday, today, and tomorrow*. Westport, CT: Praeger.

Mastro, Dana, & Susannah Stern (2006). Race and gender in advertising: A look at sexualized images in prime-time commercials. In Tom Reichert & Jacqueline Lambiase (Eds.), *Sex in Consumer Culture* (pp. 281-299). Mahwah, NJ: LEA.

Monahan, Rachel (2007, September 23). Brooklyn borough president to create ad public school. *New York Daily News*. Retrieved January 23, 2008, from: http://www.nydailynews.com/lifestyle/education/2007/09/23/2007-09-23_brooklyn_borough_president_to_create_ad_-3.html

Mueller, Barbara (2008). *Communicating with the multicultural consumer: Theoretical and practical perspectives*. NY: Lang.

Neff, Jack (2007, August 27). 'My black is beautiful.' *Advertising Age*, p. 1, 21.

Negrete, Alex Lopez (2005, October 31). Marketers, don't assimilate your Hispanic ads. *Advertising Age*, 25.

Peters, Jeremy W. (2006, August 1). An image popular in films raises some eyebrows in ads. *New York Times*. Retrieved January 29, 2008, from: http://www.nytimes.com/2006/08/01/business/media/01adco.html

U.S. Census Bureau (2007, May 17). Minority population tops 100 million. Retrieved January 24, 2008, from: www.census.gov/Press-Release/www/releases/archives/population/010048.html

## Online Resources

### Target Market News
www.targetmarketnews.com

TMN promotes itself as a leading authority on black consumers. The site contains a wealth of information for marketers who desire to effectively target this population. Also, the site contains buying power statistics and a range of useful information related to advertising, marketing, and public relations as they relate to all media formats.

**Hispanic Market Weekly**

www.hispanicmarketweekly.com

Hispanic Market Weekly claims to be a leading authority on news and events moving the Hispanic market. The site offers information about "the people, companies and trends that influence the U.S. Latino market." Most of the information is accessible for a nominal charge per visit to the site.

**EthnoConnect**

www.ethnoconnect.com

This is the website for Michael Lee; a "multicultural" marketing consultant. Lee's specialty is educating marketers about the basics of marketing to various racial and ethnic groups. Check out the "articles" section for helpful information.

**The Root**

www.theroot.com

The Root is an online magazine published by the *Washington Post* and *Newsweek* that provides news from a black perspective. The site seeks to inform people who are interested about black culture both in the US and around the world.

# New Opportunities for Minorities:
## Today, Growth Is in Multicultural Agencies and Media, Not on Madison Avenue

**Jami Fullerton, Alice Kendrick and Tom Reichert**

IN NOVEMBER 2004, THE NEW YORK CITY Commission on Human Rights began an investigation of Madison Avenue's systematic failure to diversify its workforce. The advertising industry was publicly scrutinized for alleged discriminatory hiring practices and the New York City Council threatened to subpoena agency executives in order to grill them on the subject (Sanders, 2006a). The investigation ended in September 2006, when 16 major agencies signed memos of understanding with the Commission and released goals for minority hiring. The challenge ahead for advertising agencies is how to achieve the new hiring and retention goals.

Increasing ethnic diversity in the advertising business will require hiring more minority employees. Of even greater importance, according to some, will be an increased focus on retaining multicultural talent so that agencies can further diversify mid-level and upper management (Capps, 2007). Job satisfaction is one important factor in employee retention and promotion, but there are many other factors. This chapter describes the challenges surrounding the representation of minorities in the advertising industry. Although advertising jobs on Madison Avenue have not kept pace with diversity in America, the large growth in the diversity of US audiences is offering opportunities for graduates and professionals interested in minority agencies and media.

## Minorities in Advertising

Concern about lack of diversity in the advertising industry goes back at least three decades. According to New York City councilman Larry Seabrook, hiring practices for minorities in advertising have not improved since Watergate, and in fact, "conditions within the industry have gotten worse" (Sanders, 2006a). To this point, a 1974 industry report issued by the American Association of Advertising Agencies documented that 9.9% of all advertising agency employees were minorities compared with 8.9% in 1970. The same report stated that 4.2% of the professional and managerial positions were held by minority employees, down from 4.6% in 1970 (Donath, 1977). In 1998, less than 3% of agency managers were racial or ethnic minorities, and most of those were working in minority owned firms (Snyder, 1998).

Diversity increased slightly in 2001—blacks, Hispanics, and Asians accounted for 14.4% of total advertising employees and 7.8% of the officials and managers working in the advertising industry ("Minority employment," 2001). In the September 2003, AAF Survey of Industry Leaders on Advertising Trends, 88% of the responding industry leaders acknowledged that multiculturalism and diversity have become more important with shifts in US demographics. Nearly three-quarters of respondents to a March 2006 *Advertising Age* online poll said that there were too few minorities in advertising (Sanders, 2006b).

Anecdotal comments from industry professionals confirm this observation. Wells Davis, a planner from a Toronto agency told *Advertising Age* that he worked in the advertising business for 17 years and "I have only worked with two black males, one an account person and one a writer" (Sanders, 2006b).

## Hiring and Retention Obstacles

One obstacle cited as a reason for low numbers of entry-level minority hires is low entry-level pay. Many entry-level positions are in large cities that have a high cost of living and would require relocation. Young minority candidates are less likely than whites to have parents who can afford to help them in the early years of their careers (Sanders, 2007a). Further, the best and brightest minority graduates are lured away from advertising to better paying jobs at client companies, as well as other fields such as finance and marketing (Sanders, 2007b).

According to many agency human resource personnel, "hiring isn't the problem—retention is" (B. Rozman, personal communication, Jan. 18, 2007; Neff, 1998). Similarly, Ericka Emeruwa, a 27-year-old African

American BBDO Worldwide executive, told *Advertising Age*, "I don't think the issue is getting people in. I think it is retention. You've got to keep people in the industry" (Sanders, 2007b, p. 27).

Talented minority candidates may not stay in the industry, and hiring at mid- and senior-level positions is very difficult. Obstacles for mid- and upper-level hires are generally centered on culture and networking—minorities do not always feel welcome in the business because there are so few of them (Sanders, 2007b). Bill Gray, CEO of Ogilvy North America, told *Advertising Age* that "you've got to have senior, visible minorities who can act as validation that the industry has opportunities" (Sanders, 2007a).

Doug Alligood, also an African American BBDO executive—but with over 40 years on Madison Avenue—recently described the industry's problem retaining minority executives:

> There was an article in the *New York Times* one year that showed all the black account executives in New York at that time. I think JWT had six. I was in it; I think I was the only one from BBDO. There were a couple of others at other agencies. There were like 10 guys; 10 years later not one of them except me was in the business (Sanders, 2007b, p. 27).

Alligood believes that several reasons are responsible for lack of retention. Those reasons include lack of competitive pay, a glass ceiling, and disenchantment. Particularly enlightening, Alligood believes that Madison Avenue does a poor job compensating its best minority employees: "Many people—particularly blacks—they're high profile, well-educated, work hard, very good at what they do, and outside industries can buy them off a lot easier than advertising can" (p. 27).

Regardless of the difficulties, the major advertising agencies have committed themselves to increasing minority hires. For example, BBDO pledged to increase management minority new hires to 15% of total agency employees in 2008 and professional minority new hires to 28% (Sanders, 2007a). To reach these numbers it will be necessary for the industry executives and their human resource personnel to make advertising jobs more attractive and satisfying to employees. Tactics the agencies plan to use include tying managers' compensation to minority-hiring results, using executive-search firms to find minority leaders, long-term mentoring for younger minority hires, and creating a culture welcoming of minorities (Sanders, 2007a).

## "Most Promising Minority Students" Survey

One tactic for achieving diversity—the retention of existing minority staffers—may be achieved through understanding minority advertising professionals' current levels of job satisfaction, particularly as it compares with job satisfaction for all advertising professionals and for minorities in other industries.

The concept of job satisfaction has deep roots in the human resource and organizational behavior literature. In a 1959 landmark book called *Motivation to Work*, Herzberg, Mausner and Snyderman outlined factors affecting job satisfaction. Salary wasn't a determinant in job satisfaction, but was a major dissatisfier along with poor company policy, interpersonal relations, and working conditions. There are many definitions of job satisfaction, but it is generally defined as the level of satisfaction that individuals have toward their work and their employers.

A recent study asked former American Advertising Federation's Most Promising Minority Students in Advertising (MPMS) participants about their job satisfaction and other experiences at work (Fullerton & Kendrick, 2007). About 70% of those interviewed reported working in advertising or marketing communication. Those in the field reported annual salaries ranging from $21,000 to $175,000, with an average salary of about $54,000.

The survey revealed that minorities working in the industry are generally satisfied with their jobs. However, some respondents remarked that they had to work hard to get their opinions heard while it seemed as if those of white employees were readily adopted. "At times it seems as if the Caucasian colleagues get promoted faster or get to move throughout the company with no problems whereas you have to assertively push for career development," observed one participant.

The study also revealed that networking and establishing a mentorship is especially important for success. For example, one participant remarked that, "Some companies don't actively pursue trained college students. They hire friends or friends-of-friends." Another participant noted, "Entry level opportunities are not available unless you know somebody in the field."

## What Can be Done?

The American Advertising Federation (AAF) attempted to address the diversity hiring issue almost a decade ago. In response to industry pressure to bring top minority student talent and advertising employers together, in 1996 they launched the annual "Most Promising Minority Students" program. Each year through the AAF program as many as 50 minority advertising students from across the country are brought to New York City for three days of industry immersion that includes career workshops and a recruiting fair.

According to unpublished AAF data, the program results in the hiring of minority students by advertising agencies, media, and client companies each year. Other diversity efforts by the AAF and other organizations include regional minority career fairs, summer internship programs, and agency recruiting at historically black colleges and universities.

According to the AAF's MPMS study, the most frequently mentioned challenges for minority advertising employees were related to the issues of adequate preparation for the entry-level job and competition for entry-level positions. Although the respondents in the AAF study were honored as "top students," some respondents in this study reported that they were not always successful in overcoming the barriers to entering the advertising work force.

Advertising educators can play a key role in helping students realize the importance of both academic and professional preparation. In addition, professors can assist students in obtaining and leveraging relevant professional or pre-professional experiences such as internships, part-time jobs, advertising or marketing competitions, and even class projects for real-world clients.

Networking needs were also cited as very important to the minority advertising professionals in the MPMS study. Faculty and advertising professionals can contribute to student development in this area by inviting advertising organizations to make presentations or engage in recruiting on campus, by directing students to area or regional career fairs, and by encouraging them to get involved in academic and professional organizations.

Membership in student component societies of advertising, marketing, or communication organizations such as AAF, Public Relations Society of America, and Women in Communications can fulfill some of the networking needs of students while they are in school. Unfortunately, many students do not maintain those affiliations with professional organizations once out of school. In the AAF survey of "Most Promising Minority" students, only four reported belonging to an AAF chapter, though almost all were members of AAF student chapters while in college. The AAF, through the work of its academic committee, is taking steps to help bridge the gap between student membership and joining local advertising clubs after graduation.

Once employed in advertising, multicultural employees face challenges that often center around expanding and enhancing social and professional networks, including obtaining a mentor. When facing challenges in the workplace, a mentor can be a major factor in facilitating success of the advertising employee. Whether 'appointed,' 'discovered,' or otherwise acquired, mentors were cited as a contributor to building confidence, navigating tough situations, and setting the stage for career-long professional and personal satisfaction.

## "Off-Madison" Agency and Media Opportunities

Given America's increasing diversity, it's clear that Madison Avenue is not the only place for ethnic and racially diverse job applicants to find opportunities in the world of advertising. There are plenty of prospects to be had as marketers strive to connect with the fast-growing minority segments in the US.

To begin, it is no secret that diversity is and will continue to play a big role in the future of America. A recent analysis by the Selig Center at the University of Georgia concluded that over $2 trillion of US buying power—about 20% of the US consumer market—is accounted for by the top three minority groups (Hispanics, African Americans, and Americans of Asian ancestry; Dodson, 2007).

Hispanics are now the largest and fastest growing minority in the US. At close to 15% of the population, it is estimated that by 2012 one person out of every six living in the US will identify themselves as of Hispanic origin. Since 1990, this group has seen its buying power increase over 300%. "In 2007, the Hispanic consumer market in the United States is about the same size as Mexico's entire economy—in terms of its GDP," observed Jeff Humphreys, director of the Selig Center (Dodson, 2007).

Recently eclipsed by Hispanics, African Americans represent the second largest minority in the US with over $845 billion in buying power. The number of black-owned businesses has sharply increased, and black buying power is growing fastest in the southeast and District of Columbia. Although Asians represent the third largest group, they are the second-fastest growing minority after Hispanics. According to 2004 US Census numbers, Asians represented 5% of the US population with heaviest concentrations along the West Coast. Asian personal income is higher than the average US population.

Each year these groups and other minorities increasingly represent America's consumer market. If there are limited opportunities in general market agencies, or in advertising firms in major markets such as Chicago, Dallas, Atlanta, and San Francisco, other firms will fill the void. One area where that is occurring is advertising agencies that specialize in communicating with multicultural markets. Another opportunity is the growth of minority-oriented media.

## Multicultural Agencies

Many minority-owned agencies have emerged to service diverse and underserved markets. These agencies often have the expertise that allows them to understand these markets and to place messages in appropriate media. One such agency is Carol H. Williams Advertising, headquartered in Oakland, California. This agency specializes in reaching the African American market, and its estimated 2006 revenue was $35 million (see Table 1).

The days of independence appear to be numbered, however, as the holding companies are buying up these specialty agencies. For example, Kang & Lee, specialists in the Asian American market, is now owned by WPP Group. As Table 1 illustrates, four of the largest 11 multicultural agencies are owned by parent companies.

The same is true with agencies that specialize in the buying and placing of media. According to *Advertising Age* reporter Laurel Wentz (2007),

| Table 1: Largest Multicultural Advertising Agencies by 2006 US Revenue | | | |
|---|---|---|---|
| **Minority** | **Agency (Parent)** | **Headquarters** | **Revenue*** |
| Hispanic | Bromley Comm. (Publicis) | San Antonio | $44 |
| | GlobalHue | Southfield, MI | $42 |
| | Bravo Group (WPP) | New York | $39 |
| | | | |
| African American | GlobalHue | Southfield, MI | $41 |
| | Carol H. Williams Adv. | Oakland, CA | $35 |
| | Burrell Communications | Chicago | $28 |
| | | | |
| Asian American | PanCom International | Los Angeles | $15 |
| | Kang & Lee (WPP) | New York | $12 |
| | Admerasia | New York | $10 |
| *Millions of US Dollars | | | |
| Souce: *Advertising Age* (2007, April 30), p. S-14. | | | |

"Almost every major media-agency network now has its own multicultural unit, a big shift from just a year ago" (p. S-4). For example, media agency Starcom MediaVest recently formed two multicultural units, Tapestry and 42 Degrees at MediaVest. Similarly, in September 2006 ZenithOptimedia formed ZO Multicultural. And in February 2007, WPP Group's MindShare created MindShare Multicultural.

One of *Advertising Age*'s 2007 Top Players in Hispanic Media included Monica Gadsby, CEO of the two multicultural media-buying units at Starcom MediaVest ("Top 10 players," 2007). A native Brazilian, Gadsby oversees $750 million in media buys for clients such as General Motors and Procter & Gamble—advertisers that desire to market their many brands to ethnic and racially-diverse consumers. *Advertising Age* noted that Gadsby is often sought out for her expertise in reaching the US Hispanic market.

## Minority Media

Aside from working at agencies, a second area of opportunity is minority media. These outlets range from Asian-language newspapers on the West Coast, to African American networks such as BET and TV One, to Spanish-language networks such as Univision and Telemundo. Even conservative estimates forecast fast growth as minority audiences seek information and entertainment content tailored to their interests. For example, Spanish-language media is expected to grow—from $3.9 billion in 2006—at least twice as fast as the general market (Wentz, 2007b). Many job opportunities exist in these media, especially in the areas of marketing and sales.

One such successful Hispanic executive is Joe Uva. He rose through the sales ranks to head TV sales at Turner Broadcasting. More recently, Uva was tapped to head Univision, the largest Spanish-language network in the US. The network currently boasts a 16.5 rating and 27 share of Hispanic households. Uva is seen as someone who can boost the amount of broad-based ad support from mainstream marketers. "If anyone can get national advertisers to go from spending just 3% of their ad budgets to spending closer to 14%, mirroring the percentage of the US population that's Hispanic, it's Mr. Uva," noted a recent profile in *Advertising Age* ("Top 10 players," 2007, p. S-2). In addition to increasing its share of Hispanic viewers, Univision is making substantial progress into the online market; the network's websites are expected to generate over five billion page views in 2007.

Despite predictions that print media is dead, some of the largest growth in minority media is in magazines. Someone leading that charge is Jackie Hernadez-Fallous, the publisher of Time's *People en Espanol* ("Top 10 players," 2007). Her magazine is the undisputed leader among Hispanics both in advertising revenue and circulation. Hernadez-Fallous is attempting to leverage the magazine's content with Hispanics' heavy usage of cell phones and mobile data services by sending e-mail alerts and integrating bilingual content on the website.

Uva and Hernandez-Fallous are two very public minority media executives, but there are many others who are staking new ground in the quest to provide content to America's diverse markets. As these markets grow and the media serving those markets mature, opportunities will increase for talented recruits who share the market's values and/or language.

## Conclusion

It is difficult to know if all young advertising professionals experience the same obstacles and whether they overcome them and flourish in the business. It is clear that minority professionals are underrepresented in the industry and steps need to be taken to increase their numbers, particularly at the executive ranks. As stated, these problems are especially acute in the general market agencies on Madison Avenue.

Strategies for success cited by those who survived in the advertising industry included persistence in the face of adversity, and a continual focus on making and nurturing contacts. Those who teach advertising students can communicate to their students the importance of continuous relationship-building to career success.

Last, given the growing influence of minority consumers in the US, multicultural agencies and media are offering skilled graduates and professionals opportunities for employment and advancement. General market agencies on Madison Avenue can do the same if they increase minority representation within their ranks. If so, they'll be in a much better position to serve America's increasingly diverse marketplace.

## Questions

1.   Have you ever experienced obstacles to job performance similar to those discussed in this chapter?

2.   Regardless of your race or ethnicity, do you feel prepared for a job in advertising? What can you do to increase your chances for success?

3.   Madison Avenue is definitely perceived as a glamorous place to work. Would you consider a career in media; perhaps for a minority network or magazine?

4. Do you ever think the day will come when advertising agencies specializing in reaching white consumers become minority agencies?

5. How are you preparing for a career in a multicultural society?

## References and Recommended Readings

Capps, Brooke. (2007, February 12). Nearly one-third of AAF minority candidates vacate ad industry. *Advertising Age*, p. 2.

Dodson, David (2007, July 31). Minority groups' share of $10 trillion U.S. consumer market is growing steadily, according to annual buying power study from Terry College's Selig Center for Economic Growth [press release]. Selig Center, Athens, GA. Available: http://www.selig.uga.edu

Donath, B. (1977, October 3). Agency minority hiring slow to rise, *Advertising Age*, p. 2.

Fullerton, Jami, Kendrick, Alice, & Forsythe, J. (2006, September 17). Diversity in advertising, *New York Times Magazine*, 78 – 82.

Fullerton, Jami., & Kendrick, Alice (2007). Job satisfaction among minority advertising professionals. Paper presented to the annual meeting of the Association for Education in Journalism and Mass Communication, Chicago.

Herzberg, Frederick, Mausner, Bernard, & Snyderman, Barbara (1959). *Motivation to Work*. NY: Wiley.

Kendrick, A. (2000, December 4). Attracting best and brightest to agencies. *Advertising Age*, p. 36.

Minority employment in advertising agencies. (2001). *Advertising Age*, p. S4.

Neff, Jack (1998, February 16). Diversity. *Advertising Age*, p. S1.

Sanders, Lisa (2006a, March 6). NYC slams Mad Ave. for woeful lack of diversity. *Advertising Age*, 77.

Sanders, Lisa (2006b, March 13). Ad industry must ramp up its diversity efforts. *Advertising Age*, p. 4.

Sanders, Lisa (2007a, January 15). NYC shops scramble to hit diversity targets. *Advertising Age*, p. 1-2.

Sanders, Lisa (2007b, March 19). Being black on Madison Ave.: Tales from young and old. *Advertising Age*, p. 3, 27.

Snyder, W. (1998, February 16). A business imperative: Building for a diverse future. *Advertising Age*, p. 58.

Top 10 players in Hispanic media market. (2007, April 23). *Advertising Age*, S-2.

Wentz, Laurel (2007a, April 23). Multicultural media shops carve out more roster space. *Advertising Age*, S-4.

Wentz, Laurel (2007b, April 23). Expect more growth in '07. *Advertising Age*, S-1, S-4.

## Online Resources

### 2006 New York Commission on Human Rights
http://www.nyc.gov/html/cchr/pdf/annual06.pdf

This link connects you to the final report produced by the NY Commission on Human Rights. You will see that advertising is only one area in need of improvement.

### American Advertising Federation's Mosaic Center
http://www.aaf.org/default.asp?id=20

The AAF's Mosaic Center is a clearing house devoted to educating the industry about multiculturalism and diversity issues. The site contains links to the "Most Promising Minority Students" competition as well as links to guidelines for the industry.

### The Big Tent
http://adage.com/bigtent

Big Tent is a blog site sponsored by *Advertising Age*. The blog features timely discussion about diversity issues in advertising and related industries. Check out the viewpoints of Tiffany Warren, VP and Director of Multicultural Programs and Community Outreach at Arnold Worldwide. Warren was one of AAF's "Most Promising" minority students.

## PanCom International
http://pancom.com

PanCom is the leading full-service Asian American agency in the United States. With revenue in excess of $15 million, the agency helps marketers who want to reach Asian Americans. Some of its clients include Ford, Volvo, and AT&T.

# Section 4

# Content and Effects:
## Sex, Celebs, and America

# Sex in Advertising:
## Appeals to One of Our Basic Instincts

## by Tom Reichert

WHAT IS THE MOST RECENT sexual ad you've seen? Maybe it's the commercial featuring an almost bare Paris Hilton strutting around as she washes a car and bites into a juicy Carl's Jr. burger.

Maybe it's a billboard for Hooters.

Most likely, it's one of the thousands of scintillating fashion ads that occupy the pages of men's and women's magazines; ads for Tommy, Abercrombie, or Calvin Klein. We've all seen these ads, and each of us responds to them in a different way. Some people get offended (think women's studies professors and our parents). Some people like them (think boyfriends). And some people just shrug their shoulders.

### Diverse Reactions

Because these reactions are so diverse, sex in advertising is one of the most controversial topics in advertising. Controversy also extends to whether it works or not, and if it is degrading to women and relationships. In addition, sex in advertising is also accused of pushing the boundaries of good taste and social acceptability with regard to decency and morality.

Despite these controversies, we still don't know a lot about how sex in advertising operates and its indirect effects on viewers and society at large.

In the pages that follow, I cover the basics of what we do know and weigh in on some of the issues that surround sex in advertising.

## What is Sex in Advertising?

What is sex in advertising? Like most advertising, it is a persuasive message that contains sexual information. Advertisers try to get consumers to think, feel, or become aware of a product or idea, and sexual information can be related to that idea in greater (e.g., fragrance and fashion) or lesser degrees (e.g., horticulture and hemorrhoid cream).

211

## Clear Cut?

For the most part, sex in advertising is fairly clear cut—or is it? We know what we consider sexual when we see an ad that grabs our attention, but sometimes, when we show that ad to a friend, they may have a different opinion.

A Supreme Court justice once observed in a landmark case when he was asked to define pornography and obscenity: "I know it when I see it."

People do differ in what they consider sexual, but most agree about the more clear cut instances of sex in advertising.

To discern what people consider sex in advertising, I conducted a study with a colleague, Art Ramirez. Over several years we asked almost a thousand young adults what they considered sexual in advertising (Reichert & Ramirez, 2000).

The most prevalent answer had to do with physical characteristics of the people in the ads. This included references to physical attractiveness, desirable physiques, and clothing (or lack thereof) that accentuated those physiques.

## Model Behavior

The second most mentioned category had to do with sexual behavior.

Many of the respondents noted the way a model moved or posed, or the way a model looked into the camera. They were describing the non-verbal behavior of the models in the ads. Many times models act like they are flirting with the viewer, and many people consider those actions to be sexually inviting.

But models can engage in sexual behavior with others as well. People reported that images of couples engaged in passionate kissing or more advanced forms of sexual behavior triggered sexual thoughts and feelings.

212

## Facilitating Factors

Often physical characteristics and sexual behavior were accentuated by what we referred to as facilitating factors.

Respondents noted the ways that camera angles, black-and-white imagery, and editing influenced or contributed to the sensuality of a scene. Sometimes the setting made a scene sexual: on a rug in front of a cozy fire, in the bedroom, or by a swimming pool.

## Emotional Response

Generally, when people are exposed to sexual information they experience sexual feelings, sexual arousal (heart rate, pupil dilation, perspiration), and/or sexual thoughts. Note that feelings and arousal are common ingredients in what is referred to as an emotional response.

In many cases, people have strong visceral reactions to sexual imagery.

Those reactions might be either positive or negative depending on a series of factors such as appropriateness, taste, gender of the model(s), gender of the viewer, and relevance to the product. Also, people can recognize an ad as sexual (sexual thoughts: "Oh, look. They are about to kiss.") without them experiencing an emotional reaction one way or the other ("so what?").

## Prevalence

Sexual appeals aren't in every ad, but they are prevalent enough to be considered a common tactic in advertising.

A recent analysis of network prime-time television revealed that about 15% of commercials contain sexual content. Half of those commercials contain little more than a brief shot of a model in a bikini. In the other half, about 8% of commercials, sex is the primary theme of the spot.

It's speculated that sexy ads are more common on cable networks where FCC programming guidelines regarding decency are less restrictive.

Sexy ads are also more apt to be found in magazines, especially mainstream men's and women's titles. About 20% of full-page ads in general-interest magazines contain sex, but that figure is higher in magazines such as *Details*, *Esquire*, and *Maxim*.

Similarly, up to 20% of banner ads on high-traffic news, sports, and entertainment websites contain images of highly attractive people, many of them in revealing attire.

## How Does it Work?

Aside from people debating its use in advertising, dispute also centers on whether sex actually influences consumers. A perusal of the academic literature provides some answers.

Overall, scholars recommend that sex shouldn't be used because (1) it's not that effective and (2) it is an inherently risky advertising strategy.

### Sex Attracts Attention

In what seems like a benefit, research convincingly demonstrates that sex attracts attention to the ad.

Sex evokes a hardwired emotional response that is linked to species survival. We can't help that our eyes are drawn to it because emotional information has a way of piercing our perceptual field and getting noticed.

In a cluttered media environment with 17 minutes of commercials during every hour of programming and hundreds of ads in each magazine, something that stands out from the pack is a plus, right? Not really.

Despite the increased attention, findings support a distraction hypothesis. That is, sexual information in the ad grabs most of the viewer's attention such that he/she isn't as likely to remember the brand sponsor.

I remember interviewing a copywriter about sex in advertising and he said that just the previous evening, he had seen a commercial with two very sexy people. The ad was for toothpaste but he couldn't remember the

brand. But with a sly look on his face, he described in detail the actors and their actions.

So, sexual information gets noticed and encoded (a good thing) but people don't remember who paid a quarter of a million dollars for the ad (a bad thing).

Does that mean that Calvin Klein, Guess, and Gucci, who invest heavily in sexually oriented advertising campaigns, are wasting their money? Hardly. For these brands, you can remove the brand name from the ad and most people can still accurately guess whether the ad is for Calvin or Abercrombie, because these advertisers have maintained a consistent image for many years.

If you run one ad, sex might not be an effective strategy. But if you decide to build a long-term sexual brand image through advertising—and you are a fashion brand—sex might be an appropriate call.

## A Sex-Related Brand Benefit

But sex is used to do more than grab attention and brand products. I did some work with Jacqueline Lambiase, and we discovered that 73%, almost three-quarters, of sexual ads in magazines contained a sex-related brand benefit.

Common themes followed the "buy this, get this" formula. If you buy our product: (1) You'll be more sexually attractive, (2) have more or better sex, or (3) just feel sexier for your own self-confidence.

Recall the commercials recently used by Unilever to introduce Axe body spray. A young man sprays it on and attractive women (some are even physicians and mothers of girlfriends) find him irresistible. Credible? Doubtful. Tongue-in-cheek. Sure.

I'm convinced, however, that the agency handling Axe found through extensive research that these appeals resonated with members of the target audience (teens and young men 14–34 years old).

## Erotic Brand Identities

Sex is also used to create sexualized identities for brands. Advertisers, especially those for fragrances and fashion, attempt to create connections between sex and their brands with steamy scenarios and the revealed physiques of gorgeous models.

Calvin Klein Underwear

In the early 1980s, Calvin Klein employed this approach to introduce the world to his designer briefs. With ads featuring Tom Hintinaus, a muscular Olympic athlete, modeling Klein's new briefs, sales of the underwear went through the roof. Whether men thought the briefs would enhance their attractiveness or make them look like Hintinaus—probably both—Klein successfully imbued his brand with sex appeal.

Victoria's Secret, with its retinue of supermodels, has attained a similar status in the intimate wear and lingerie categories.

## Product Considerations

Can any brand be advertised with sex? I suppose, but research does show that sex is more effective for products that have a reasonable link to sex or sexual situations. As you can probably guess, those product categories include fragrance, fashion, travel, entertainment, alcohol, and tobacco. Beauty and some personal-care products also use sexuality in ads.

For example, ads for razors, men's body spray, deodorant, and gel often contain some appeal involving sexual attractiveness as a result of using the product. During my interviews with creative people in the advertising industry, however, almost all said that they could create a sexual ad for almost any product.

One ad director said that he could create a very effective commercial for Compound W—a product for wart removal. A young girl can't get a date to the high school prom. Compound W comes to the rescue. Now she has to fight off the offers. It's a story line we've seen a thousand times.

With that said, gratuitous uses of sex—a blatant attention getter, with no realistic connection to the brand—tend to be judged more stringently. Humor is one approach advertisers employ to mitigate criticism. For example, a common theme is poking fun at the use of sex in the commercial. Consumers are more forgiving if the leering man in the ad gets his comeuppance.

## Target Audience Considerations

Research, and personal experience, also suggest that people respond to sexual ads in different ways.

Generally, males are more favorable to uses of sexuality in advertising. However, that only applies to images of women and couples.

Men respond very negatively to images of other men, more so than women do to sexualized images of women. Research also indicates that women respond more positively to images of romance than do men.

### Differences within Gender

But we must be careful not to lump all males or all females together.

Research indicates that within gender, differences are evident when people are exposed to sexual ads. For instance, one's overall liberal/conservative orientation can affect responses.

Another study found that older men and Catholics were more favorable toward the use of sex in advertising, but there has been little follow-up research to support these findings.

New research into personality shows some promise for differentiating who responds most favorably to sexual appeals and those who do not.

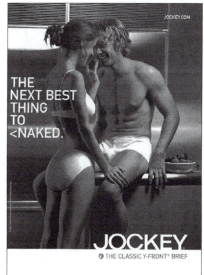

One personality characteristic is referred to as Sexual Self-Schema. Someone with a positive sexual schema is more likely to be open to sexual materials, have more sexual history, and to feel confident about their own sexuality.

The opposite is true for people with a negative sexual schema.

Recent research I conducted with Michael LaTour, a marketing professor at the University of Nevada at Las Vegas, indicates that these schemas influence whether women like sexual ads or not.

217

Schemas didn't have any effect for men.

It appears that men respond more directly to sexual information than women do, but whether that difference is genetic or learned has not been determined.

## Setting Limits

Although sexual ads aren't illegal, several curbs exist to limit patently offensive ads beyond consumer complaints.

One gatekeeper is the brand manager. These professionals are charged with protecting the brand's value. If the agency recommends a particularly risky approach that involves sex, the brand manager can step in to say "no way."

The potential always exists that a promotion strategy can harm the brand's image. As mentioned, research has shown gratuitous sexual ads can result in negative brand image and attitudes if there is no strong connection between sex and the brand.

### Media Watchdogs

The media also play a substantial role in policing ads. Networks have standards boards that preview commercials for objectionable content before they run. These committees can refuse to run ads, suggest changes, or require that commercials be aired after prime time to minimize exposure to young children.

Recently, Fox and NBC rejected several Dove commercials that showed side views of naked older women for its Pro-Age line of products (Neff, 2007).

Print versions of the Dove ads in question did appear, however, in Oprah's magazine and *Ladies' Home Journal*.

As previously discussed, sexual ads are more likely to find a home in magazines because the risk of exposure beyond circulation is limited.

Publishers make decisions about the acceptability of ad content in magazines, newspapers, and websites. Most media contain a set of advertising guidelines that prohibit lewd or egregious ads that could offend readers. Publishers of magazines with provocative content are more likely to approve provocative ads.

With regard to self-regulation, several industry groups have guidelines pertaining to sex in advertising. For example, the Distilled Spirits Council of the United States (DISCUS) strongly discourages advertising that links alcoholic beverages to sexual outcomes.

For example, its code of conduct advises its members that they "should not rely upon sexual prowess or sexual success as a selling point for the brand" ("Code of Responsible Practices," 2007).

Additionally, the code prohibits gratuitous nudity, promiscuity, overt sexual activity, and indecency.

Members usually adhere to these standards or take corrective action. But nonmembers are not as beholden to the advisory board's rulings. For example, marketers of Svedka, an up-and-coming Finnish vodka, were repeatedly rebuked for sexy ads that violated the DISCUS code. Svedka often failed to respond to the organization's calls for corrective action.

Although unlikely, extremely egregious sexual ads could face regulation if they catch the attention of policy makers. Currently, the FCC has very specific guidelines regarding decency in programming content. Violators face substantial fines.

In the United Kingdom, the Advertising Standards Authority has the power to restrict offensive ads based on the quantity and quality of complaints it receives. A similar system could gain momentum in the US if brand managers and the media fail to heed future vociferous consumer complaints about sex in advertising.

## Negative Implications of Sex in Advertising

There are some negative social implications of sex in advertising.

### Degrading Images of Women

One is that most sexual ads contain degrading images of women. In my estimation, at least 95% of sexual ads feature women, and most of those ads show women whose primary purpose is to be sexually enticing or a sexual plaything for men.

Feminists and some media scholars have argued that decorative images of women—women shown as one-dimensional objects merely present to look good—influence people's attitudes and perceptions about women's contributions and roles in society.

The research shows that they are right.

Both women and men who are exposed to these decorative images place more value on women's physical attractiveness and role as a mate, and devalue their intellect, skills, and competencies.

One ad won't do it, but who sees just one ad? We see hundreds of them everyday. Over time, and unannounced, sexist attitudes work their way into our belief system.

How does this relate to sex in advertising? Although beefcake images have made inroads in the last 20–25 years, provocatively dressed women in suggestive poses constitute a fair portion of sexual images.

In some cases women are subservient to their male counterparts. Men watch as their women strip, dance, or playfully tease them in some other manner.

As a whole, these images are unacceptable. The advertising industry is increasingly aware of the sexism inherent in these types of images, and it is cleaning up its act.

In some cases, the industry is policing itself.

## The "Grand Ugly" Award

For example, there is a very influential industry group known as Advertising Women of New York (AWNY). At their annual meeting they give out awards to advertisers who portray women in the most positive and negative ways. Several instances of sex in advertising have received the "Grand Ugly" award.

These awards publicly identify particularly offensive ads (and their sponsors), which usually results in a lot of bad press.

Several years ago Candie's won the "Grand Ugly" award for a print ad featuring Jodi Lyn O'Keefe astride a computer monitor, and Sugar Ray's Mark McGrath sitting at the keyboard. On the screen, a space shuttle is shown blasting upward toward O'Keefe's crotch.

## Targeting Teens and Young Adults

A second knock is that marketers use sex when targeting teens and young adults. Some of these advertisers include Abercrombie, Hollister, and Candie's, among many others.

For example, some have claimed, including me, that sexual ads unfairly target teens and young people.

Raging hormones, sexual discovery, and newly minted critical thinking skills can cloud judgment and make teens especially susceptible to sexual appeals that advocate brands as sexual attractants.

Advertisers who are guilty of targeting young adults obviously should be held accountable. For example, Abercrombie & Fitch has felt the heat recently as public pressure is mounting to compel them to tone down the sexual explicitness of its quarterly "magalogs" and other forms of promotion.

## What's Next?

If you look back at sex in advertising over 100 years ago—yes, sexy ads did exist back then—you'll notice that by comparison today's ads are much more graphically revealing and explicit than before.

Keep in mind that decency norms do change over time. In the early part of the 19th century, for instance, revealing a woman's ankle was considered too taboo for advertising. Compare that to recent ads for fashion and fragrance and you'll see how far we've truly come.

In the spring of 2007, Dolce & Gabbana was called to task for ads depicting what some in the media labeled a fantasy gang-rape scene.

More recently, Tom Ford, former creative director for Gucci and other designer brands, generated buzz with promotion introducing his new fragrance. The ads and flash-presentation on the cologne's website depicted the fragrance bottle strategically positioned between a naked model's breasts and pubic area.

"Just how far will it go?" is a common question.

I suspect that advertisers will continue to exert pressure on the boundaries of today's norms, just as writers and producers do the same in television programming and in movies. Industry observers and the public will let them know when they've crossed the line, even though that line continues to retreat.

# Questions

1.	What reaction do you have to sexual ads? Have you ever been influenced or offended by one?

2.	In your opinion, at what point does a sexual ad cross the line?

3.	Sexuality and reproduction are a natural part of everyone's lives. Is there anything wrong with using sexual themes to sell brands associated with increasing one's attractiveness to others? What about brands not associated with sex?

4.	If you were marketing a fragrance to men, would you consider using sex to promote your product? Does gender—your gender and that of the target audience—influence your decision? How does your personality or other factors influence your decision?

# References and Recommended Reading

Code of responsible practices for beverage alcohol advertising and marketing (2007). Distilled Spirits Council of the United States. Retrieved online October 4, 2007, from: http://www.discus.org/industry/code/code.htm

Gould, Stephen (1994). Sexuality and ethics in advertising: A research agenda and policy guideline perspective. *Journal of Advertising*, 23, 73–80.

Lambiase, Jacqueline, & Tom Reichert (2003). Promises, promises: Exploring erotic rhetoric in sexually oriented advertising, in Linda Scott and Rajeev Batra (Eds.), *Persuasive Imagery: A Consumer Perspective* (pp. 247–266). Mahwah, NJ: Erlbaum.

LaTour, Michael, & Tony L. Henthorne (2003). Nudity and sexual appeals: Understanding the arousal process and advertising response, in Tom Reichert and Jacqueline Lambiase (Eds.), *Sex in Advertising* (pp. 91–106). Mahwah, NJ: Erlbaum.

Neff, Jack (2007, February 19). Why Dove oldies aren't on the nets—or YouTube. *Advertising Age*, p. 61.

Pardun, Carol J., L'Engle, Kelly Ladin, & Brown, Jane D. (2005). Linking exposure to outcomes: Early adolescents' consumption of sexual content in six media. *Mass Communication and Society*, 8, 75–91.

Reichert, Tom (2003). *The Erotic History of Advertising*. Amherst, NY: Prometheus.

Reichert, Tom, & Art Ramirez (2000). Defining sexually oriented appeals in advertising: A grounded theory investigation, in Stephen J. Hoch & Robert J. Meyer (Eds.), *Advances in Consumer Research,* Vol. 27 (pp. 267–273). Provo, UT: Association for Consumer Research.

Reichert, Tom, & Jacqueline Lambiase (2003). How to get "kissably close": Examining how advertisers appeal to consumers' sexual needs and desires. *Sexuality and Culture*, 7 (3), 120–136.

## Online Resources

### Sex in Advertising
http://www.sexinadvertising.com

This site is an online resource for people who want good information on sex in advertising: what it is, how it works, and how it gets created. The site is created and maintained by Tom Reichert, an advertising professor at the University of Georgia.

### White Paper: How to Handle Sex in Advertising
http://www.iaany.org//sitebuildercontent/sitebuilderfiles/final_white_page.PDF

This paper summarizes a roundtable discussion between professional advertisers, marketers, lawyers, and advocates regarding issues related to sex in advertising. The paper, sponsored by the New York chapter of the International Advertising Association, provides guidelines for ad professionals considering the use of sexual content and themes.

# Celebrity Endorsement in Advertising:
## A Double-Edged Sword

## By Sejung Marina Choi

AMERICA IS OBSESSED WITH CELEBRITIES. So are marketers. As mass media and the Internet become progressively inundated with images and news of celebrities, advertising continues to be a popular venue for many famous faces to appear and sell a wide range of products from underwear to automobiles and prescription drugs. From Michael Jordan to Madonna, Jerry Seinfeld to Catherine Zeta-Zones, marketers have spent enormous sums of money to have well-known personalities promote their products. For instance, Nike paid $100 million to have golf megastar Tiger Woods endorse their products for five years.

Celebrity endorsement in advertising is not a novel concept. As far back as 1921, Babe Ruth entered into a contract as an endorser for Jockey underwear. Ever since, more and more marketers have capitalized on the power of the rich, famous, and beautiful. Yet not all celebrity endorsements have proven as effective as expected. Furthermore, a number of high-flying celebrity endorsers' involvement in negative events and scandals has put the effectiveness of this all-time favorite practice of marketers into question. As today's consumers become increasingly savvy, marketers need to understand the advantages and disadvantages of celebrity endorsement, as well as how it works in order to make sound decisions in developing their celebrity endorsement strategy.

## Who is the Celebrity Endorser?

By definition, a celebrity is anyone who is well known to the public. A celebrity endorser refers to any individual "who uses recognition on behalf of a consumer good by appearing with it in an advertisement" (Mc-Cracken, 1989, p. 310). Individuals from a variety of fields, ranging from entertainment to movies, sports, music, cuisine, and business, achieve stardom and enjoy a high profile, distinctive image, and public attention. Due to the omnipresent nature of media in today's society, the pace of earning celebrity status seems to quicken daily. Some individuals suddenly acquire fame and are elevated to celebrity status via an appearance in a reality show such as *Survivor* or *American Idol*.

Celebrities are seen everywhere these days. With a large list of magazines, television shows, tabloids, and websites devoted to celebrity news and gossip, consumers can easily keep up to date with popular stars' behaviors and lifestyles. Although most consumers never meet celebrities in real life, some fans even develop a sense of attachment to or intimacy with them. To their fans and followers, celebrities are the idols that lead a life they desire to live. In this way, celebrities represent an appealing reference group by providing high standards of achievement to which consumers aspire to, which subsequently influences the consumers' opinions and behaviors.

The overwhelming influence of celebrities is commonly observed in the consumers' consumption patterns as well. Many people hope to develop a kinship with their favorite celebrities by purchasing the same products and dressing the same way as the celebrities. Celebrity fashion and gossip columns are among the most popular sections in fashion and tabloid magazines and many teenage girls and older females follow their favorite stars' style. Marketers even try to incorporate a celebrity's name in their branding, building on this consumer motivation. A well-known example is Nike's Air Jordan shoes. Young boys admiring Michael Jordan were fascinated with the basketball shoes named after the superstar. Recently, Gatorade announced a partnership with Tiger Woods on a new sports drink that will make its debut in stores in the spring of 2008. In the fashion arena, Madonna is collaborating with H&M for her collection called "M." This alliance is an example of smart co-branding because of the good match between Madonna, a fashion icon with distinctive styles, and H&M that is known for its trendy but affordable offerings. No wonder many marketers tap the power and prestige of the famous in promoting their products despite the huge fees that celebrities command.

Among the many celebrities to appear as endorsers, sports stars are the endorsement champions, as their personas have driven sales of some products to exceptional levels of success. Well-known examples include the Air Jordan shoe carrying Michael Jordan's name and Nike golf products associated with Tiger Woods. Female athletes have emerged as a strong, new group of endorsers in proportion to the growth of the female sports market. Venus and Serena Williams, Michelle Kwan, Anna Kournikova, Annika Sorenstam, Mia Hamm, and Maria Sharapova are a few examples of high-profile endorsers. For instance, the roster of Sharapova endorse-

ment deals includes Canon, Nike, Motorola, Tag Heuer, Colgate-Palmolive, Gatorade, Land Rover, and Tropicana. Kournikova has served as an endorser for Adidas, Charles-Schwab, Lycos, Microsoft's XSN Sports, Multiway Sports Bra, Omega Watches, Pegasus Cell Phones, and Yonex Rackets.

## Why is Celebrity Endorsement Used?

The common use of celebrity endorsement in advertising ascribes to its potential benefits which include increased salience in a cluttered environment, increased influence, increased profits, and more. Celebrity endorsement is more influential than other types of strategies in several ways (Erdogan, 1999). First, ads featuring celebrities draw more attention than ads without celebrities. In other words, when celebrities appear in advertising, the message is more likely to rise above the consumers' attention thresholds than when unknown actors are shown. Likewise, celebrities help ads break through the surrounding and otherwise busy clutter.

Since celebrities embody a bundle of distinctive images that many consumers find relevant, celebrities are also used to create, enhance, and change brand images. For example, in the late 1990s Madonna helped the cosmetics brand Max Factor revive its image from dull and old-fashioned to youthful and sexy.

Moreover, celebrities with worldwide recognition and popularity can help overcome cultural barriers and appeal to consumers around the globe. Pepsi, for instance, successfully increased its market share on the global scale when its advertising campaigns featured Michael Jackson and, later, the Spice Girls. The universal fame and appeal of those music stars transcended cultural boundaries and contributed to the brand's image of youthful vitality. In addition, a number of Hollywood stars such as Kevin Costner, Brad Pitt, and Cameron Diaz have taken advantage of their global appeal and successfully endorsed various brands in Japanese advertising.

More important, celebrity endorsement boosts sales and profits. For instance, Michael Jackson's contract with Pepsi resulted in an eight percent increase in sales in 1984, although he turned out to be a regretful choice for the company due to his alleged child molestation (Gabor, Jeannye, & Wienner, 1997). Celebrity endorsements were also found to produce positive effects on stock returns and increased the profitability of the client firms. When announcements of 110 celebrity endorsement contracts were analyzed, the involved firms gained on average half a percentage point in market value on the day of announcement (Agrawal & Kamakura, 1995). To put this in perspective, Google's value would rise by $1 billion if it announced a celebrity endorsement deal.

In another study, Michael Jordan's expected return to the Chicago Bulls from playing baseball in the minor leagues in 1993 was found to generate an increase of over $1 billion in total stock market values of his five client firms (Mathur, Mathur, & Rangan, 1997).

## How Does Celebrity Endorsement Work?

Many scholars have attempted to theorize the effects of celebrity endorsement in advertising. Originated from research by Carl Hovland and his associates in the early 1950s (Hovland, Janis, & Kelley, 1953), studies have explained the effectiveness of celebrities via the credibility they render to the messages. That is, celebrities bring instant credibility to the messages they convey through an established reputable image derived from wide recognition and esteem.

Roobina Ohanian (1990), an advertising scholar, invented a scale for measuring a celebrity's credibility, which is comprised of three dimensions: expertise, trustworthiness, and attractiveness. Expertise is the extent to which a celebrity is perceived to know about the product area and be able to make valid assertions. The celebrity's "expertise" is largely based on his/her knowledge, experience, or training in the related field. Trustworthiness refers to a consumer's confidence in the celebrity to provide information or opinions in an objective and honest manner. Attractiveness is related to how likable or physically attractive the celebrity is to the consumer.

To illustrate, when a consumer perceives a celebrity as attractive, genuine, and possessing some expertise on the product the celebrity endorses, she is more likely to view the product in a highly favorable light and purchase it. For instance, Jennifer Aniston with her "girl next door" image is a favorite star for  many fans. Her physical attractiveness as well as attributes of friendliness, fitness, familiarity, and sincerity makes her an effective endorser, which recently led Smartwater to add her as an endorser. Aniston became the official face of the natural, vapor-distilled water with electrolytes and now appears in its advertising campaigns.

Another theoretical explanation for celebrity endorsement effects is the Meaning Transfer Model proposed by McCracken (1989). In this model, celebrities are understood as cultural icons that represent a bundle of various symbolic properties and meanings. A celebrity develops such images and meanings based on her recordings, pubic performances, and media appearances. When a celebrity associates herself with a product through endorsement, the meanings the celebrity possesses are transferred to the product. For example, Max Factor keeps the brand's image updated by associating it with celebrities who exude the desired image facets of "modern, charming and glamorous." Their current endorser, sexy film star Carmen Electra, fulfills this task by transmitting her meanings to the brand. Similarly, actor Pierce Brosnan conjures images of James Bond, and projects those images in endorsements for Omega watches and Erickson mobile phones. Next, the images and meanings of the product are shifted to consumers who purchase and consume the product. McCracken noted that some celebrity endorsements work better than others due to a natural match between the celebrity and the product which facilitates the meaning transfer process.

The idea of fit between the celebrity and the product has been further studied and a number of reports have shown that a good match-up between a celebrity and the product is important. Generally, a good match is more effective than a bad one (Kahle & Homer, 1985; Kamins & Gupta, 1994). In other words, when consumers perceive the image of the celebrity as congruent with that of the product the celebrity promotes, they are more likely to trust the celebrity's endorsement and have favorable attitudinal and behavioral responses to the product.

In light of the theoretical accounts, marketers should be careful to select the right celebrity, one who holds a credible image and has appropriate meanings consistent with the desired images of the product. Although a few superstars with exceptional charisma, such as Michael Jordan and Tiger Woods, have proven to be quite effective endorsers for a wide array of products, a celebrity with a successful endorsement history can be a disappointment when tied to other products. For example, when Bill Cosby—an effective endorser for Jell-O, Coke, and Kodak—was hired to endorse E. F. Hutton and Texas Instruments, the outcomes were not satisfactory.

Marketers must also understand the nature of celebrity images. Some celebrities might have obvious, distinctive meanings whereas others have rather unclear meanings. The cultural meanings of a celebrity can change over time. For instance, a celebrity can attempt to recreate her image as the original image loses appeal. Or, a celebrity's meanings can become negative as she falls from public favor due to misconduct and scandal.

## The Dark Side of Celebrity Endorsement

Obviously, celebrity endorsement is not a risk-free strategy. Although marketers spend large sums of money securing relationships between celebrities and their brands, the investment can be unrewarding and seriously damaging when the celebrity becomes involved in allegations of illicit or unethical behavior. For example, Magic Johnson lost his endorsement contracts when he announced in 1991 that he was HIV-positive. The infamous murder case involving O.J. Simpson concerned Hertz car rental, whose name was linked with him through endorsement. More recently, Kobe Bryant, the NBA superstar with the spotless reputation and multimillion dollar endorsement deals, was charged with felony sexual assault. While the charge was subsequently dropped, Bryant's public image has not been the same.

Consumers quickly learn about celebrities' negative incidents due to the real-time media circus surrounding celebrities. Consequentially, the reputation and images of the associated companies and products might suffer from the damage, whether or not they drop the endorsements.

At least one study found that negative information about a celebrity endorser unfavorably influenced consumer perceptions of both the celebrity and the endorsed product (Till & Shimp, 1998). For example, in 2005 the tabloid press published photos of supermodel Kate Moss allegedly using cocaine. The Swedish clothing giant H&M, whose upcoming advertising campaign was to feature Kate Moss, initially responded that it would keep her. Yet H&M reversed its position soon after, announcing that Kate Moss and the campaign would be dropped together in response to furious customers who maintained that the retailer—that markets its inexpensive clothing to teenagers and young adults—had a social responsibility to publically disapprove of such behavior.

Following suit were Burberry and Chanel, two fashion brands in Moss' portfolio of endorsements. Burberry dismissed Moss from its advertising campaign, and Chanel decided not to continue the relationship after their contract with her ends. More recently, Atlanta Falcons quarterback Michael Vick was indicted on charges of being involved in dog-fighting. Advertisers quickly acted on the public outcry about Vick's behavior; Nike, Reebok, and Rawlings all suspended their respective associations with him.

As much as consumers are fascinated with celebrities, they never forget what celebrities have done wrong. Marketers must take every caution to protect their own reputation. More and more advertisers are running detailed background checks on celebrities being considered for endorsements and have begun to include morals clauses in their agreements. These are seen as necessary pre-emptive measures, and the nature of the clauses can vary from general integrity to much more specific parameters. Back to the earlier example, Kate Moss signed a written statement with her clients in which she promised to remain "healthy, wholesome, and sound" when her alleged cocaine use went public.

Yet not all marketers seem to back down on endorsement contracts with troubled celebrities. Several celebrities who have put themselves in crises have managed to keep endorsement deals and regained their public images in recent years. Despite her troubles with Chanel and Burberry, Kate Moss reappeared in advertising campaigns for fashions brands such as Dior. She also inked a new deal with Canon. In addition, Moss successfully launched her own line of clothing at the London-based retailer Topshop.

Model and actress Paris Hilton has reaped notoriety as a result of several legal incidents including her recent DUI offense, the aftermath of which caused her in 2007 to serve time—measured in days—in a correctional facility. What's intriguing about Hilton is that the increased publicity and attention she generates appears to contribute to her endorsement career.

Apparently, her involvement with DUI charges and a sex-tape revelation seem to resonate, refuel, and augment her rebellious and wild image, and endorsements congruent with those image dimensions remain intact. Actually, new endorsement opportunities arose for Hilton involving Hilton and Guess after the sex-tape revelation. Perhaps these brands tried to draw upon her bad-girl image in order to reach certain consumers who find that image appealing.

Another concern is the influence of multiple endorsements. When a celebrity endorses more than one product simultaneously, for example, the effectiveness of the celebrity endorsement may be diluted (Tripp, Jensen, & Carlson, 1994). In addition, consumers might be more distrustful of the celebrity's true motive for her endorsements. They may believe that she is only doing deals for the compensation she receives, rather than sincerely believing in the merits of the product. The obvious monetary motivations underlying the celebrity's endorsement deals should lessen the perceived credibility of the celebrity as an endorser. Even worse is when a celebrity switches endorsement to a rival brand. For instance, British soccer star David Beckham signed an endorsement deal with Adidas in 2006 after he endorsed Asics for several years.

From a legal standpoint, endorsements and testimonials in advertising are considered a special type of product claim and Federal Trade Commission (FTC) guidelines stipulate specific parameters for their use (Guides §255.1 (a)). As discussed earlier, consumers often rely on the credibility of celebrity endorsers, and if the endorsers' statements are untrue or misleading, then the endorsement could be deemed deceptive thus exposing the advertiser and endorser to fraud claims. As consumers believe that endorsers are expressing their true opinions based upon their own knowledge or experience with the products, it would jeopardize the believability of product claims and endorsements if the endorsers were to make differing statements elsewhere. Furthermore, consumers assume that endorsers are genuine users of the products, at least throughout the period of advertising. Celebrity behavior inconsistent with such a belief would cause consumer distrust in the endorsements and the products. Advertisers should ensure that celebrity endorsers learn and follow the FTC guidelines in order to avoid any backlash and liability problems for both parties.

In many cases, the pitfalls of celebrity endorsement are often underestimated. Marketers must carefully examine potential pros and cons of each celebrity when selecting the right star to endorse their product.

## Branching Out

Marketers' use of celebrities is no longer limited to 30-second commercials and full-page glossy magazine ads. Today's marketers are moving beyond standard endorsements in traditional advertising as they seek both cost-efficient channels of marketing communications and new venues and forms to publicize the relationship. For instance, John Nardone, MMA's (a unit of Aegis Group) Chief Client Officer, notes the blurring of celebrity endorsement, sponsorship, and product placement by noting Coca-Cola's integration into *American Idol*. Simon Cowell is seen with a Coke cup on the show, and he appears in Coke commercials aired during the program's commercial breaks (Hanas, 2006).

Another emerging strategy that capitalizes on celebrity power is "celebrity seeding." This practice refers to disseminating free products to celebrities in the hope that they will wear or use them. Although people naturally assume that celebrities independently choose what brands to use, the impact can be substantial if a celebrity is seen using a particular brand. For example, the popularity of Ugg boots in the US began with a simple shipment to Hollywood stars during Ugg's introductory phase. The brand was literally placed on the feet of celebrities instead of in magazine ads or TV spots. Many celebrities, including Pamela Anderson, were seen wearing the distinctive boots. Look around any campus today and you'll see that "celebrity seeding" was successful for the Australian boot marketer. Celebrity seeding is considered a cost-effective strategy because it generates "free" exposure within editorial content—photos and stories of celebrities—instead of paid advertising insertions. Further, "seeding" is a more subtle form of persuasion compared to advertising.

Last, there is a trend toward treating and managing celebrities as brands, similar to the management of branded goods and services. In addition, a growing number of celebrities launch their own businesses, leveraging their personal assets and name value. Big names from Madonna to Oprah Winfrey, Sean Combs, Hank Aaron, and Clint Eastwood have successfully licensed their names to businesses in various fields from clothing to perfume, restaurants, entertainment, and car dealerships. Similarly, co-branding efforts between celebrities and marketers are on the rise. Through such partnerships, both parties can benefit from each other's appeal, target markets, and profits.

## Summary

The use of celebrity endorsement will take on different forms and continues to evolve, but the use of celebrities in advertising and other promotions will not disappear. The relationship between goods and celebrities will remain strong as long as society's fascination with celebrities perpetuates. As previously mentioned, celebrity endorsement can be financially fruitful if the right celebrity is selected and the strategy is executed correctly and under the appropriate circumstances.

As several cases of failure suggest, however, it is crucial for advertisers to understand the complex configuration underlying celebrity endorsement and the multitude of elements involved, including a celebrity's expertise, trustworthiness, attractiveness, symbolic meanings, public and/or private persona, and match between the celebrity and their brand. A more extensive, systematic tool is needed for advertisers to avoid arbitrary decisions and enhance the strategic value of celebrity endorsement decisions before they connect the branded celebrity to their precious branded product.

## Questions

1.   Are you influenced by celebrity endorsements? What about your friends? Do you think younger consumers are more accepting of or susceptible to celebrity endorsements?

2.   Does the impact of celebrity endorsements vary with product categories? What makes a perfect match between the celebrity and the product in an endorsement? Imagine that Scarlett Johansson and Orlando Bloom are being considered for endorsement deals. What products would make good (bad) matches for each celebrity?

3.   In your opinion, what types of celebrities are most influential as endorsers? What are the qualities a successful celebrity endorser should possess?

4.   What ethical or legal responsibilities do you think celebrity endorsers should have?

5.  What do you think about celebrities appearing in endorsements for various products at the same time? How does it affect the believability of the celebrity or the endorsements?

6.  Do you think the impact of celebrity endorsements varies around the world? What would be the cultural factors influencing the influence of celebrities?

## References and Recommended Reading

Agrawal, Jagdish and Wagner A. Kamakura (1995). The economic worth of celebrity endorsers: An event study analysis. *Journal of Marketing*, 59 (3), 56-63.

Choi, Sejung Marina, Wei-Na Lee, and Hee-Jung Kim (2005). Lessons from the rich and famous: A cross-cultural comparison of celebrity endorsement in advertising. *Journal of Advertising*, 34 (2), 85-98.

Erdogan, B. Zafer (1999). Celebrity endorsement: A literature review. *Journal of Marketing Management*, 15 (4), 291-314.

Erdogan, B. Zafer, Michael J. Baker and Stephen Tagg (2001). Selecting celebrity endorsers: the practitioner's perspective. *Journal of Advertising Research*, 41 (3), 39-48.

Fortini, Amanda (2005, September 27), Kate Moss: The ironies of her downfall. *Slate*. Retrieved November 13, 2007, from: http://www.slate.com/id/2126381

Gabor, Andrea, Thorton Jeannye, and Daniel P. Wienner (1987, December 7). Star turns that can turn star-crossed. *U. S. News and World Report*, 103, 57.

Guides Concerning Use of Endorsements and Testimonials in Advertising (1980). 16 C.F.R. Pt. 255.

Hanas, Jim (2006, February 20). Star power. *Advertising Age*, 77 (8), S1-S2.

Johnson, Allison R. (2005). When a celebrity is tied to immoral behavior: Consumer reactions to Michael Jackson and Kobe Bryant. *Advance in Consumer Research*, 32, 100-101.

Kahle, Lynn R., and Pamela M. Homer (1985). Physical attractiveness of the celebrity endorser: A social adaptation perspective. *Journal of Consumer Research*, 11 (4), 954-961.

Kamins, Michael A., and Kamal Gupta (1994). Congruence between spokesperson and product types: A matchup hypothesis perspective. *Psychology and Marketing*, 11 (6), 569-586.

Louie, Therese A., Robert L. Kulik, and Robert Jacobson (2001). When bad things happen to the endorsers of good products. *Marketing Letters*, 12 (1), 13-23.

Louie, Therese A., and Carl Obermiller (2002). Consumer response to a firm's endorser (dis)association decisions. *Journal of Advertising*, 31 (4), 41-52.

Mathur, Lynette Knowles, Ike Mather and Nanda Rangan (1997). The wealth effects associated with a celebrity endorser: The Michael Jordan phenomenon. *Journal of Advertising Research*, 37 (3), 67-73.

McCracken, Grant (1989). Who is the celebrity endorser? Cultural foundations of the endorsement process. *Journal of Consumer Research*, 16 (3), 310-321.

Money, R. Bruce, Terence A. Shimp, and Tomoaki Sakano (2006). Celebrity endorsements in Japan and the United States: Is negative information all that harmful?" *Journal of Advertising Research*, 46 (1), 113-123.

Ohanian, Roobina (1990). Construction and validation of a scale to measure celebrity endorsers' perceived expertise, trustworthiness, and attractiveness. *Journal of Advertising*, 19 (3), 39-52.

Pringle, Hamish (2004). *Celebrity Sells*. Hoboken, NJ: John, Wiley & Sons, Inc.

Till, Brian D. and Terence Shimp (1998), Endorsers in advertising: The case of negative celebrity information. *Journal of Advertising*, 27 (1), 67-82.

Tripp, Carolyn, Jensen, Thomas D., and Carlson, Les (1994). The effect of multiple product endorsements by celebrities on consumer attitudes and intentions. *Journal of Consumer Research*, 20 (4), 535-547.

## Online Resources

### Q-Scores
http://www.qscores.com/

Q-scores (aka Q-ratings) are intended to inform advertisers of potential celebrity success when endorsing products based on two criteria: familiarity and likeability. Beginning in the 1960s, the New-York based company Marketing Evaluations began annually collecting data on approximately 1,500 celebrities. The results are Q-scores. Higher Q-scores are generally associated with more recognized and likeable celebrities.

### Davie Brown Index
http://www.dbireport.com/

Since 2006 the Davie Brown Index (DBI) has served as a tool for marketers to determine a celebrity's ability to influence their brand. The DBI evaluates more than 1,500 celebrities four times a year in terms of seven key attributes including appeal, notice, trendsetter, influence, trust, endorsement, and aspiration.

### Celebrity 100 Ranking
http://www.forbes.com/lists/2007/53/07celebrities_The-Celebrity-100_Rank.html

*Forbes* magazine publishes annual listings of the 100 most influential celebrities. In determining the celebrity rankings, *Forbes* analyzes celebrity earnings and media metrics such as Google hits, press mentions, TV/radio mentions, and the number of appearances on the cover of 32 major consumer magazines.

## Hollywood-Madison Group

http://www.hollywood-madison.com/

The Hollywood-Madison Group is one of the leading agencies that recruit celebrities for endorsement, product placement, and other types of appearances. With its "The Fame Index®," the agency considers over 10,000 celebrities.

# Political Advertising:
## A Formidable Weapon in Battleground States and Beyond

## by Tom Reichert

THE 2004 PRESIDENTIAL election was especially notable for the immense attention placed on a select group of 16 to 21 states that included Ohio, Pennsylvania, and Florida.

These states were identified as "battleground" states—places where the election was so close that crucial blocks of electoral votes could swing the election to either presidential candidate.

As a result, most of the $547 million spent on spot television ads in the presidential campaign was pumped into these states with the average viewer seeing hundreds of political commercials during a relatively short period of time.

### An Effective Means of Influencing Voters

In essence, the question of who would occupy the White House in 2004 was partially decided by ads—30-second persuasive messages advocating the election or defeat of Bush or Kerry.

But wait a minute. Isn't democracy about one person, one vote? Of course it is. But political advertising has evolved into one of the fastest and most effective means of influencing significant groups of voters in a campaign.

Far from being limited to presidential campaigns, polispots (another term for political advertising) are used in elections at all levels from Congress to local city councils. Because political advertising is so pervasive and powerful, it is important to understand what it is and how it influences voters.

## Political Advertising

Today's political ads look like slick Hollywood productions compared to those first broadcast in the 1952 presidential campaign.

The first political commercials, aired by the Eisenhower campaign, featured Ike telling citizens how he was going to "clean up Washington."

He appeared awkward and scripted but it didn't matter because Ike "cleaned up" against his opponent, Adlai Stevenson. Stevenson didn't believe in this new form of campaigning and decided not to run any political spots. He observed, "The idea that you can merchandise candidates for high office like breakfast cereal is the ultimate indignity to the democratic process."

While some politicians may agree with his sentiments, few successful ones have repeated Stevenson's mistake. Since Eisenhower's era, political advertising has matured to represent a dominant force in political campaigns.

Many people are surprised to discover that political advertising usually represents the bulk of campaign war-chest expenditures. For example, over $1.85 billion went to campaign advertising in 2004, which represents about 68% of all campaign spending. As far back as the presidential election of 1992 (Bill Clinton vs. George H.W. Bush), over 60% of the total presidential campaign budgets of both candidates was invested in advertising (West, 1993).

As the saying goes, a politician can reach more voters in one 30-second spot than they can reach in one month of shaking hands on a local street corner.

## Tremendous Growth

Political advertising also is experiencing tremendous growth. For example, there was a 112% increase in ad spending from 2000 to 2004. Looking only at the 2004 presidential election, over $600 million was invested to elect the nominees, which was about a three-fold increase over 2000. The amount reached $2 billion in 2006—an amount unprecedented for a mid-term election year.

Considering the early beginning of the 2008 presidential race and the large number of candidates on both sides, 2008 spending on advertising and other forms of marketing is expected to exceed $4.5 billion.

Lynda Lee Kaid and Daniela Dimitrova (2005), political advertising experts, attribute much of that increase to activity by 527 organizations, independent political action committees, and the Democratic and Republican National Committees.

For example, America Coming Together, a pro-Kerry group, spent $62 million on the campaign, whereas the Bush-friendly Swift Boat Veterans for Truth spent close to $26 million.

## Traditional Connections Dissolving

The rise of political advertising is coming at a time when traditional means of connecting with voters is dissolving. Not that long ago, people in the community who were connected with one of the political parties went door-to-door talking to constituents. Voters knew these people and were influenced by who they endorsed.

But party affiliation has declined in recent years with more people reporting that they are "independent."

You might hear someone say that they don't vote exclusively Republican or Democrat—that they vote for the "best person for the job."

Today, how do we know who is the best person for the job? We get that information from several sources such as friends, family, talk radio, news, and from political advertising. Today, we take fewer cues from the parties and more from candidates and their campaign ads.

## Selling Soap vs. Selling Candidates

Some critics don't consider political advertising to be a true form of advertising. They say selling soap is not the same as selling a candidate.

While technically true, the promotion of candidates through 30-second commercials does qualify as advertising. By most definitions, advertising is the paid placement of persuasive messages in the media about products, services, and ideas that are targeted to specific audiences.

Obviously, a polispot is a 30-second persuasive message that seeks to create a difference between candidates. The ads are paid for by identifiable sponsors, and the ads appear on television, radio, and on the Internet.

As important, polispots are directed toward specific target audiences such as groups of likely voters—or undecided voters in the "battleground" states.

For example, advertising scholars Patrick Quinn and Leo Kivijarv (2005) report that presidential ads only ran in 96 of 210 DMAs (Dominant Market Areas) in the US.

If you lived in Georgia or Texas, you probably didn't see a presidential campaign ad because both states were predicted to "go Republican." The Kerry campaign wanted to concentrate on swaying Democrats and undecided voters to support Kerry, and viewed any advertising outside swing states as a waste of precious resources.

### "Don't Call it Advertising"

Even if some professionals in the advertising industry don't want to be associated with political advertising, there isn't much they can do about it—except to run an ad.

For example, Ketchum Advertising ran a full-page ad in the *Wall Street Journal* titled "Don't call it advertising" after the 1994 elections. The ad took issue with a few vicious attack ads, calling them "filth" and "trash" because they were full of "lies" and "character assassination."

Political ads can go overboard, but taking issue with all political advertising because of a few extreme instances is the same as derogating the entire advertising industry over a few sexist or misleading commercials.

## Political Advertising Makes an Impact

Political advertising is prevalent because it works.

It has the power to influence campaigns.

Believe it or not, political ads are often the primary source of information about the election. In one study, political advertising was the most important source of information for voters about the issues and candidates in a campaign (Kaid, 1976).

Information from news, talk radio, and interpersonal sources still is important, but facts about the issues and candidates are still most likely to come from advertising.

It's easy to see why. In the 2004 election season *Campaigns & Elections* magazine reported that there were over 630,000 campaign commercials. This equates to five ads for each campaign news story ("By the Numbers," 2006).

## An Effective Means of Persuasion

Political ads are an effective means of persuasion. Research shows that political advertising can influence people's perceptions, beliefs, and feelings toward candidates.

Ads can influence how voters perceive a candidate.

For example, ads that show a candidate surrounded by family members, children at a school, and workers at a factory give voters the impression that the candidate is a good family man, that he cares about education, and he cares about jobs.

Also, candidates and their political consultants try to communicate issue information to the electorate. If the candidate is an incumbent, for instance, his or her ads might describe votes on certain bills. Alternately, a challenger can attack an incumbent's record and show how the challenger will do a better job.

Not only can polispots influence how people feel about candidates, but these ads get noticed and remembered.

According to a study by political scientists C. Richard Hofstetter and Terry Buss (1980), 79% of respondents remembered seeing short political ads (30-second spots) during the campaign.

## Generating Buzz

Particularly daring ads create buzz and get picked up and re-aired in newscasts and websites. These ads can be very successful because they generate impressions beyond the media buy.

One such ad, recently aired by Hillary Clinton's campaign in summer 2007, led *Adweek* critic Barbara Lippert to compare it to one of the most infamous political ads of all time: "[It's] the most audacious political ad since LBJ's 'Daisy'" (p. 23).

Lippert was referring to a spot supporting Lyndon Johnson's 1964 campaign featuring a cute little girl picking petals from a daisy. The scene abruptly cuts to a countdown followed by a mushroom cloud produced by a nuclear explosion.

Interestingly, "Daisy Girl" aired in a small local market but because of its effrontery, was picked up by the networks and broadcast for several days—free of charge.

244

The Clinton spot was notable because it spoofs the last scene in the final episode of the *Sopranos*, with Hillary as Tony and Bill Clinton as Carmella. The spot aired soon after the last episode.

Similar to "Daisy Girl," Clinton's ad was picked up and aired on network, cable, and Internet newscasts. Mentions in late-night monologues drew even more attention to the polispot.

Lippert noted that Clinton's ad had "pitch-perfect timing" as it coincided with the ambiguous and controversial ending of the final episode: "It hit a nerve, partly because *Sopranos* addicts are still reeling from, and arguing about, the original [ending]" (p. 23).

## Not Regulated for Truthfulness

Perhaps most important of all, political ads are not regulated for truthfulness, although most people believe that they are.

For instance, communication researchers Annie Lang and Elizabeth Krueger (1993) discovered that most respondents believed that political advertising was regulated for truthfulness by the government.

The First Amendment, which governs Free Speech, grants broad protection to those seeking office. It is up to voters and opposing candidates to sort out the facts and act accordingly. Government regulations do exist for candidate spending limits, but not for inaccuracies and distortion.

In Lang and Krueger's study, most people thought that information in political ads was completely true, and that if it wasn't, the government would remove the ads.

# Types of Political Ads

There are many variations of political ads but most of them can be categorized into three types: positive, attack, and refutational ads.

## Positive Ads

Positive ads are those that extol a candidate's virtues. In these ads you might hear something like: "Chuck Jones is the man for the job. He's a family man with good values who will stand up for us in Washington."

Positive ads are run by the campaign or by groups that support the candidate. These ads focus almost exclusively on the candidate. They help to define who the candidate is and what he or she stands for.

Common themes in these ads include flattering images with family, and images that portray the candidate as a leader. Testimonials from the "man-on-the-street" and leading citizens also are common.

Rarely, however, is the competing candidate mentioned.

Positive ads are usually most prevalent in the early stages of a campaign as candidates try to characterize themselves to voters.

Early in the 2008 primary season, for instance, many candidates used humor to define themselves in their political ads.

Bill Hillsman, a political advertising consultant who made a name for himself with funny ads for Senator Paul Wellstone's successful 1990 election, believes that humorous ads can be very effective because they "can be used to raise visibility, inoculate a candidate against expected negative ads, ease the impact of a gaffe or soften a candidate's image" (Teinowitz, 2007, p. 33).

For example, John Edwards' campaign makes use of self-deprecation in a video called "What really matters." The video makes fun of stories about Edwards' $400 haircut. After a few light-hearted jabs, the video makes the point that voters should be more concerned about Edwards' stances on meaningful issues.

In addition, New Mexico Governor Bill Richardson's campaign produced several ads featuring him in a job interview situation.

Pahl Shipley, Richardson's campaign spokesperson said the humorous approach was a "way to stand out, to stand apart, but with a serious message of: Give him a look before you make up your mind" (Teinowitz, 2007, p. 33).

## Attack Ads—"Mudslinging"

Attack ads get the most attention in campaigns because they violate norms of civility. These ads are often referred to as negative because they condemn, attack, and/or question the integrity and qualifications of an opponent.

Attack ads are also referred to as "mudslinging."

Whereas many people say that they don't like this type of ad and that they tune it out, research shows that attack ads are very effective.

Candidates can be attacked on their positions on issues, their voting record, their character, and their association with other notable people such as unpopular political figures.

For example, in attack ads during the 2006 Congressional races, many Republican candidates were labeled as supporting Bush's war on Iraq.

According to political advertising scholars Judy Trent and Bob Friedenberg (1995, p. 129): "These ads are designed to place the opponent in an unfavorable light or in an uncomfortable position. They focus on the shortcomings (real or imagined) of the opponent rather than attributes of the candidate."

Not only do attack ads create questions about the targeted candidate in voters' minds, but attacks force the opponent to respond to allegations.

Responding to attack ads keeps a campaign on the defensive.

Political consultants have learned that attack ads must be responded to in a timely fashion. Otherwise, even overtly outlandish claims can—over time—gain credibility in voters' minds.

Research conducted by University of Georgia professors Ruthann Lariscy and Spencer Tinkham (1999) has shown this "sleeper effect" to be potentially damaging to candidates who fail to respond to an opponent's accusations.

### Refutational Ads

The third type of political spot is the refutational ad. These are ads that respond to both attacks and innuendo. They also provide damage control by giving the targeted candidate an opportunity to respond to allegations or misrepresentation.

For example, you might hear in one of these ads: "Cindy Chavez says that I took campaign money from USGA Insurance. That's just not true. Maybe Ms. Chavez is attacking me because she's ashamed of her own record on crime, unemployment, and the environment."

Research shows that candidates must respond quickly to attacks. Targeted candidates can either chose to rebut the allegations, to attack the opponent's motives, or to use humor to play down the issue.

## Future of Political Advertising

The future looks bright for political advertising. As previously mentioned, spending in 2008 will be a banner year as candidates and interest groups invest increasingly large sums to influence voters.

The Internet is one of the biggest factors changing the face of political advertising. Campaigns are taking advantage of increases in online connectivity and interactivity, especially video viewing and social networking.

Online political advertising grew from about 1% of ad dollars in the 2004 election to about $12 million in 2006. Spending in 2008 looks to increase exponentially. With that said, however, 95% of political advertising is still expected to go into local television. That percentage is not expected to drastically change in the foreseeable future.

Candidates can also save a lot of media costs by posting their ads online where they can be viewed an unlimited number of times. Google's Peter Greenberger says that posting ads and videos on YouTube and related sites "provides candidates an incredible opportunity to speak directly to voters" (Klaassen, 2007, p. 23).

"The best way to do it is not just upload campaign commercials and walk away and say, 'We've used YouTube,'" says Greenberger, "but to use it to open up a dialogue." Greenberger notes that Mitt Romney has been attacked in several YouTube videos, but that Romney has very effectively used video to answer those charges.

Being at the forefront of technology says a lot about a candidate's ability to grasp and take advantage of new trends. One such candidate is Hillary Clinton. "No one has outvideoed Hillary," observed Lippert.

"She and her team have used the Web brilliantly, especially to highlight her easier, looser side" (2007, p. 23).

In addition to online advertising, campaigns can use the web for related activities such as search marketing, blogging, and social networking. Not all of these activities are advertising per se, but they do represent forms of candidate promotion. And they represent ways that candidates can reach voters beyond the television screen.

With regard to search expenditures, Peter Greenberger speculates that "each one of the top six candidates have probably spent more than Kerry and Bush spent combined" (p. 23).

Considering social networking and UGC (user-generated-content) sites, campaigns are mining these as well. For example, MySpace has a channel featuring pages created by presidential campaigns.

Rudy Giuliani's campaign, as well as all the major candidates, has a channel at YouTube and networking platforms at MySpace and Face-book.

These channels allow Giuliani's people to post and organize ads and other videos from the campaign. For example, video on Giuliani's You-Tube channel contains rebuttals to recent attacks by Moveon.org.

## Obama Girl

Not to be left out, viral videos have the potential to influence campaigns as well. Much buzz and media attention surrounded a video viewed millions of times in the summer of 2007. The music video resembled a gushing ode to Barack Obama by a bikini-clad fan.

"I've got a crush on Obama," featured "Obama Girl" Amber Lee Ettinger lip-synching words such as: "I cannot wait / till two thousand and eight / baby, you're the best candidate."

Reporter Ken Wheaton described the video as "campaign gold," and that "the video was so hot and steamy, it imme-diately jumped from the interwebs to local and cable news" (2007, p. 36).

It was soon revealed that the ad was produced not by the Obama campaign, but by political satirists BarelyPolitical.com. Before long, Obama Girl began appearing in other videos and getting into pillow fights and dance offs with the "Romney Girls" and "Giuliani Girls."

Given the popularity of Obama Girl, it appears that campaigns—or organizations supporting a campaign—can generate a lot of attention and favorability with a compelling viral video.

## VOD

Last, some in the cable industry believe that video on demand (VOD) will play a much larger role as the technology is made available to cable subscribers. Andrew Capone, an executive with National Cable Communications, recently told *USA Today* that candidates' speeches and longer-format videos and presentations will be made available to viewers in the upcoming election.

"VOD is in 30 million homes," notes Capone. "That will be the biggest new technology platform for political advertising in 2008" (Lieberman, 2007).

## Questions

1.      Do you think political advertising would influence you if you were exposed to it? Why? What is it about you that makes you open or invulnerable to political ads?

2.      What type of people, in your opinion, are most likely to be persuaded by political advertising?

3.      If you were running for office, what would you say about yourself in a "positive" ad?

4.      Why are the rules different for female candidates and attack advertising? For instance, research shows that female candidates must be careful when attacking an opponent. Also, male candidates must be very careful when attacking a female opponent.

## References and Recommended Reading

By the Numbers (2006). *Campaigns & Elections*, 27 (7), 14.

Diamond, Edwin, and Stephen Banks (1993). *The Spot: The Rise of Political Advertising on Television* (3rd ed.). Cambridge, MA: MIT Press.

Hofstetter, C. Richard, and Terry Buss (1980). Politics and last minute political television. *Western Political Quarterly*, 33 (1), 24-37.

Jamieson, Kathleen Hall (1996). *Packaging the Presidency: A History and Criticism of Presidential Campaign Advertising*. Oxford University Press.

Kaid, Lynda Lee, and Daniela Dimitrova (2005). The television advertising battleground in the 2004 Presidential election. *Journalism Studies*, 6 (2), 165-175.

Klaassen, Abbey (2007, August 13). Google's political guru talks campaign 2008. *Advertising Age*, p. 23.

Lang, Annie, and Elizabeth Krueger (1993). Candidate's commercials and the law: The public perception. *Journal of Broadcasting & Electronic Media*, 37 (2), 209-218.

Lariscy, Ruthann Weaver, and Spencer F. Tinkham (1999). The sleeper effect and negative political advertising. *Journal of Advertising*, 28 (4), 13-30.

Lieberman, David (2007, August 9). Fight is on for campaign TV ad dollars. *USA Today*. Retrieved September 12, 2007, from LexisNexis.

Lippert, Barbara (2007, June 25). Married to the mob. *Adweek*, p. 23.

Quinn, Patrick, and Leo Kivijarv (2005). US political media buying 2004. *International Journal of Advertising*, 24 (1), 131-140.

Teinowitz, Ira (2007, July 30). A funny thing happened on the way to the White House. *Advertising Age*, p. 3, 33.

Trent, Judith S., and Robert V. Friedenberg (1995). *Political Campaign Communication: Principles and Practices* (3rd ed.). Westport, CT: Praeger.

Welke, Bob (1999, September 2). Why we should get rid of political advertising—now. Salon.com. Retrieved October 12 from: http://salon.com/media/feature/1999/09/02/advertising/

West, Darrell M. (1993). Air wars: Television advertising in election campaigns, 1952-1992. Washington, DC: *Congressional Quarterly*.

Wheaton, Ken (2007, June 18). Barack Obama just might like this kind of cynicism. *Advertising Age*, p. 36.

## Online Resources

### The Living Room Candidate

http://livingroomcandidate.movingimage.us/index.php

This online exhibition is housed at the American Museum of the Moving Image. It is a valuable storehouse for historic ads such as the 1952 Eisenhower ads and the "Daisy Girl" spot run to support the Johnson campaign.

### "Mixed Messages"

http://projects.washingtonpost.com/politicalads/

This site sponsored by the *Washington Post* contains a large political advertising database primarily from Federal and Gubernatorial races across the US.

### *National Journal*

http://nationaljournal.com

You can also find a large number of recent ads on the *National Journal*'s website. Look for the "Ad Spotlight" link at the top of the right-hand column.

### Julian P. Kanter Political Commercial Archive

http://www.ou.edu/pccenter/

The archive housed at the University of Oklahoma's Political Communication Center is a valuable starting point for investigating political advertising. It contains links to other sites and a catalog of thousands of political ads.

### You Choose

http://youtube.com/youchoose

YouTube is a tremendous resource for candidate polispots. The "You Choose" site is essentially a video clearing house; each major candidate has a channel. In addition, you can view extended videos and polispots on specific issues such as healthcare, Iraq, and education.

# Can Advertising Sell America?
## Winning Hearts and Minds in the Muslim World

## by Jami Fullerton and Alice Kendrick

ADVERTISING IS PERSUASIVE COMMUNICATION used to *change consumers' attitudes* toward a particular product, brand, person, or idea. Ideally advertising leads to buying a product, voting for a political candidate, or accepting an idea, such as "only you can prevent forest fires."

But can advertising be used to "sell" or promote America? Can it change attitudes toward the United States in other countries? Can it lessen the hatred that some people, particularly those in predominantly Muslim countries of the Middle East and Asia, feel toward the US government and America in general?

Former Secretary of State Colin Powell thought so. He was so convinced that he told the US Congress in early 2001 that he was bringing people to Washington who were experts at persuasive communication to "brand" America and market American values to the world.

And he did. Shortly after the September 11th attacks, Powell hired star advertising executive Charlotte Beers to head up public diplomacy at the US State Department. She was immediately charged with the daunting task of selling America's core values to the Arab and Muslim world.

## Charlotte Beers & the Shared Values Initiative

Called out of retirement at 66 after a remarkable career in the advertising business, Charlotte Beers was sworn in as Under Secretary of State for Public Diplomacy and Public Affairs on October 2, 2001, only weeks after the 9/11 attacks. Beers was widely known on Madison Avenue as the only advertising executive ever (male or female) to serve as head of two of the top 10 worldwide advertising agencies, Ogilvy and Mather and J. Walter Thompson.

Beers did not shrink from the challenge of branding America. Her tenure at the State Department can be credited for several new and aggressive communication programs. Her most notable and publicized campaign was known as the Shared Values Initiative (SVI).

SVI consisted of numerous communication elements. It featured speeches by diplomats and American Muslims to international audiences, "town hall" events in several countries, Internet sites and chat rooms, and various mass media messages. Among these was a 60-page, four-color magazine titled *Muslim Life in America* and a series of newspaper advertisements. The campaign was produced in English and various Middle-Eastern languages and dialects such as Arabic, Farsi, and Urdu.

The most visible mass media component of SVI was a series of five television commercials that the State Department called "mini-documentaries."

The testimonial-style commercials used a "slice-of-life" format that showed happy and prosperous American Muslims in various personal and professional roles. All of the spots featured actual American Muslims actively practicing their religion and commenting positively on the tolerance Americans have for the Muslim faith. Below is a brief description of each.

"Baker" profiles an average day in a busy family-run bakery/restaurant in Toledo, Ohio, which is owned by a Lebanese family, and highlights the interaction between the Muslim owners and their non-American Muslim clientele. The accompanying frame illustrates how the "straight path" can be followed in America by showing the baker's family praying during a visit to a local amusement park.

American Muslim family stops to pray while enjoying an evening at an amusement park in Toledo, Ohio.

"Doctor" showcases the accomplishments of Dr. Elias Zerhouni, whom President George W. Bush had named as Director of the National Institutes of Health. Dr. Zerhouni, born in Algeria, describes his life as a successful government official and respected American Muslim. During the spot, Dr. Zerhouni is shown shaking hands and speaking with President Bush.

*Dr. E. Zerhouni shakes hands with President Bush and is thanked for his outstanding contribution to medicine.*

"School Teacher" features Rawai Ismail working as a public school teacher in Toledo, Ohio. The spot shows her wearing a hijab while teaching elementary school children and later holding Saturday Koran classes in her home.

*Rawai Ismail teaches elementary school in America.*

"Journalist" follows an Indonesian journalism student at the University of Missouri through a typical day as a reporter for the school's television newscast, as a college student, and as a practicing Muslim.

*Faridz is a journalism student at the University of Missouri and works as a reporter on a local newscast.*

"Firefighter" focuses on two New York City employees—a young, Muslim firefighter who shares his experiences since September 11th, and a Muslim chaplain who explains how he meets the needs of the people who work for the city. In the spot, the young firefighter describes the closeness he feels to both his Muslim and non-Muslim co-workers and community around a New York City fire station.

*Farooq Muhammad is a firefighter for the city of New York.*

At the end of each commercial the viewer sees the line "A message from The Council of American Muslims for Understanding." The image dissolves to a final frame of all black with the words, "And the American People."

Presented by the Council of American Muslims for Understanding

Beers hired advertising agency McCann-Erickson to produce the SVI spots and buy the media time and space in the targeted countries using some of a $15 million State Department budget—a relatively small sum when compared with other international branding campaigns.

According to Beers, the ultimate goal for the SVI campaign was to cause "discussion and debate," and not to automatically change minds about US foreign policy. She believed that the primary target audience for SVI was "the people." Specifically Beers cited the importance of reaching women in the target countries; "the mothers and teachers." To do so, she employed mainstream media such as television. The messages were "from the people and to the people" as opposed to from-government-to-government or from-elite-to-elite, the way most US public diplomacy efforts had been in the past.

True to her consumer marketing training, Beers drew upon consumer opinion research to help understand her audience and formulate the campaign. She used a RoperASW Worldwide research tool known as Value-Scope™, which employs ongoing international consumer research that uncovers "core belief systems based on personal values." The research identifies 57 discrete values that exist throughout the world. These values are ranked by randomly selected citizens in various countries and combined to provide a composite ranking of values for each country.

The 2002 ValueScope™ data showed vast differences between the United States and Muslim countries such as Saudi Arabia and Indonesia on values such as modesty, obedience, duty, perseverance, and freedom. The same research revealed significant agreement among people of predominantly Muslim nations and the United States regarding the values of faith, family and learning. Based on these findings, Beers designed a campaign to focus on the common interests or "Shared Values" of Americans and Muslims—namely *family*, *religion*, and *education*.

## Execution of the SVI Television Campaign

The SVI television schedule began October 29, 2002, in Indonesia—the largest target nation, with 80 percent of its 220 million people who are Muslim—followed by what the State Department described as a "sequential rollout" to other Muslim countries. Ultimately only about $5 million of the total $15 million campaign budget was spent on television airtime. Most of the Arab countries, including US-friendly countries such as Egypt and Jordan, refused to run the spots. Beers later told PBS anchor Jim Lehrer that the decision to refuse the SVI spots was probably because they were thought to be "based on propaganda" ("Public Diplomacy," 2003).

Al Jazeera, the pan-Arab station sometimes referred to as "the CNN of the Arab World," initially said it would consider it "an honor" to accept the US anti-terror message, but later refused to air the spots. A State Department spokesperson said at a press briefing that Al Jazeera "wanted too much money" (Boucher, 2003).

Even though Al Jazeera was not included in the media buy, the spots aired on a number of state-run media systems, including those in Pakistan, Malaysia, Indonesia, and Kuwait. Viewers in other countries, such as Jordan, Egypt, Saudi Arabia, Bahrain, Oman, Qatar, Lebanon, and the United Arab Emirates, were reached via pan-Arab satellite. SVI spots ran in Kenya and Tanzania through embassy placement. Other embassy placements were not secured, possibly due to lack of support from US ambassadors in those countries.

In early 2003 a number of conflicting reports about the status and future of SVI were circulating. McCann's media flowcharts and internal State Department documents indicate that SVI commercials were scheduled to run only through early December 2002. However, on January 16, 2003, *The Wall Street Journal* wrote that SVI was discontinued by the State Department because it failed to register with Muslim audiences and had been prevented from being aired by host governments.

On February 3, 2003, the State Department said that the spots had stopped running in December, as planned, and that they would be revised before airing again. They never again aired.

## SVI Criticism

Immediately after the mini-documentaries aired in late October 2002, the US media reported that the campaign was not well received. In news reports, which typically consisted of person-on-the-street interviews, the chief complaint was that the spots did not explain US foreign policy.

American Muslim and university professor Mamoun Fandy told PBS that the campaign had "contributed to anti-Americanism in the region" ("Public Diplomacy," 2003). *Advertising Age*, a well-read industry magazine said, "This is no job for commercials" (Garfield, 2002).

The international media also were critical of SVI. One Malaysian newspaper called the campaign a "waste of time." A Pakistani newspaper labeled it "another Zionist propaganda tool" (Lau, 2002). A London-based Saudi commentator said that the campaign caused incitement against US policy in several Islamic countries, including demonstrations denouncing US policy in Indonesia (US State Department, 2002).

An often-repeated quote came from William Drake of the Carnegie Endowment for International Peace who said, "the notion that you can sell Uncle Sam like Uncle Ben's (rice) is highly problematic" (in reference to Beers' former client; Starr, 2001). Secretary of State Colin Powell responded to the remark in a widely publicized speech defending Beers and her ideas by saying, "She got me to buy Uncle Ben's rice. And so there is nothing wrong with getting somebody who knows how to sell something" ("International Campaign," 2001). To which Margaret Carlson of *Time* replied: "Uncle Sam is harder to sell these days than Uncle Ben's ever was" (Carlson, 2002).

## Did SVI Work?

The State Department was frequently asked if the campaign "worked" and how it would be measured, but no definitive answers were provided. According to Beers, any and all responses to the campaign would be considered good. She told CNN that the campaign would be successful if it started a dialogue "about things which we have in common." For example, Beers said people who saw the spots in other countries were surprised that the United States had mosques and that a teacher could work with her head covered.

Post-campaign survey research conducted by McCann-Erickson in Indonesia revealed that 288 million people throughout the Arab and Muslim world saw the SVI spots and that they scored higher on message recall and retention than commercials for "a typical soft drink campaign run at higher spending levels for more months."

But the ultimate question, *did the SVI spots work?* was never directly answered by the State Department. Why not?

Advertisers acknowledge the difficulty of linking advertising to specific sales levels or behavior. The purpose of most advertising is to sell products, but determining specific return-on-investment (ROI) for each dollar of advertising expenditure continues to elude most advertisers, even the ones who spend tens of millions of dollars per year on television commercials. Why is this so? The answer is that several factors, of which advertising is only one, contribute to whether a consumer will purchase a product or service or take some other action. Advertising is joined and sometimes upstaged by such forces as product pricing, advertising by competitive brands, weather conditions, and word-of-mouth recommendations from friends or family. Isolating the degree to which advertising results in sales or other action can be a very tricky process.

In the case of SVI, determining whether the campaign *worked* must take into account that its primary objective was not to increase the sales of anything. The SVI spots were not tourism videos intended to promote travel to the United States, but rather to inform an audience about America and to potentially affect audience attitudes. The high campaign recall scores in Indonesia suggest that these objectives may have been accomplished.

The US State Department never measured the potential of the SVI spots to affect attitude toward America—but we did shortly after the SVI campaign ended.

As advertising professors and researchers, we wanted to know if advertising, such as the SVI spots, could help improve international citizens' attitudes toward America.

To find out, we designed a simple pre-post experiment to test the potential of the commercials to improve attitudes toward the US government, the Americans, and how Muslims are treated in the United States. Our studies were conducted in laboratory settings under highly controlled conditions to more closely examine the effect of the SVI spots on viewers. We showed the commercials to international college students in London, Singapore, and Cairo. In total, more than 500 international students were tested.

## Pre-Post Test SVI Experiment

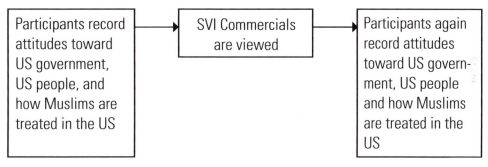

Students who participated in the experiment first completed a written questionnaire regarding their attitudes toward America and how Muslims are treated in America. Students were then shown the SVI commercials, after which they completed a post-test questionnaire containing the same attitudinal questions.

In all of the samples, attitudes toward the US government was more positive *after* the SVI commercials were viewed. The change in attitude was found to be statistically significant, which means that the change was great enough to support the contention that they were not simply due to *chance*, but rather to the experimental stimulus—the SVI spots.

And in Singapore, though not in London or Cairo, students also showed significantly more positive attitudes toward the "US people" after viewing the SVI spots.

The greatest magnitude of difference was found in the shift in attitudes about how Muslims are treated in the United States. Put another way, though exposure to SVI messages succeeded in improving both attitudes toward the US government and in some cases toward the US people, the spots were most successful in changing perceptions and attitudes regarding the life that Muslims lead in the United States. This finding indicates that the objective of changing attitudes about Muslim life in America was met.

Students with different demographic characteristics often had quite different reactions to the SVI commercials. After viewing the commercials, women overall had more positive attitudes than men toward the objects of interest, though prior to ad exposure their attitudes were similar to those of men.

Among religious groups, Muslims had the most positive attitudes after seeing the commercials. These findings indicate that the SVI commercials successfully communicated the intended information to the target audience, which was women and Muslims.

Laboratory experiments such as the ones reported here are uniquely suited to show cause and effect. In this case, the experiments demonstrated that the SVI commercials resulted in more positive attitudes toward the United States among international college students.

Findings suggest that despite the controversy surrounding SVI, the commercials demonstrated the ability to both inform and change attitudes among international audiences. When subjected to generally accepted advertising measures, the SVI campaign was in fact effective.

## Conclusion

Charlotte Beers and the Shared Values Initiative are now merely a part of US public diplomacy history; however, the lessons learned from this unique public diplomacy case are yet to be fully appreciated. Most State Department employees who worked with Beers distance themselves from both her and the campaign, privately scoffing at the notion that advertising professionals or their techniques have a place at the State Department. Members of Congress, the press, the advertising industry, and former diplomats continue to refer to the SVI campaign as a failure, especially when advertising is mentioned as a way to convey a pro-American message.

So the answer to the question of whether advertising can be used to sell an idea such as American values is that it depends. It depends on whom you ask. If you ask citizens in other nations who saw the campaign, the answer may be "yes." However, if you ask political decision-makers and the press, the answer will likely be "no." Perhaps the lesson is that an advertising campaign, using the right message and the right medium with ample frequency, can play a significant role in changing attitudes and opinions about America.

## Questions

1. Given the experimental and survey measures described in the chapter, why hasn't advertising, such as the Shared Values Initiative, been used again by the State Department for public diplomacy?

2. In your opinion, why was the campaign so harshly criticized in the press and by politicians in Washington?

3. Now that you know the story, do you think that advertising can be used to improve attitudes toward America?

4. Is advertising an appropriate tool for such an important task or are these efforts a form of "propaganda" that will never work in selling brand America?

5. If you were hired by the State Department to improve America's image abroad, what would you do?

## References and Recommended Reading

Boucher, Richard (2003, January 16). *State Department daily press briefing*. Retrieved November 1, 2005, from: http://www.state.gov/r/pa/prs/dpb/2003/16717.htm

Carlson, Margaret (2001, November 14). Can Charlotte Beers sell Uncle Sam? *Time* [on-line edition]. Retrieved July 3, 2007, from: www. time.com/time/nation/article/1,8599,184536.html

Garfield, Bob (2002, November 25). State Department effort asks the impossible of advertising. *Advertising Age*, 33.

International Campaign Against Terrorism (2001, October 25). *Hearing of the Senate foreign relations committee.* Retrieved from Federal News Service through LexisNexis.

Lau, Leslie (2002, November 6). U.S. Muslim ad drive on Malaysian TV 'a waste of time.' *Straits Times Singapore*. Retrieved January 30, 2003 from: http://www.straitstimes.com.sg/asia

Public Diplomacy (2003, January 21). *NewsHour* [on-line transcript]. Retrieved February 6, 2003, from: http://www.pbs.org/newshour/bb/media/janjune03/diplomacy_1-21.html

Starr, Alexandra (2001, December 17). Charlotte Beers' toughest sell. *Business Week*, 56.

U.S. State Department, Office of Research, (2002, November 26). *U.S. image in the Islamic world: Policy is the problem.* Ben Goldberg (ed). Retrieved October 28, 2003, from: http://www.globalsecurity. org/military/library/news/2002/11/mil-021126-wwwh21126.htm

## Online Resources

### Book Site: Shared Values Initiative
http://www.svibook.com

Visit this site to learn more about the Shared Values Initiative campaign and to see the SVI spots created by Charlotte Beers and her team.


This chapter is excerpted by Dr. Fullerton and Dr. Kendrick from their book *Advertising's War on Terrorism: The Story of the U.S. State Department's Shared Values Initiative*, published in 2006 by Marquette Books. For more information on their book, go to www.svibook.com.

# Beyond Obligation:
## Advertising's Grand Potential to Do Good

## By W. Glenn Griffin and Deborah K. Morrison

*All of us who professionally use the mass media are shapers of society. We can vulgarize that society. We can brutalize it. Or, we can help lift it onto a higher level.*

— Bill Bernbach (1911-1982)
Co-founder of Doyle Dane Bernbach and advertising icon

BILL BERNBACH HAD IT RIGHT: The folks who make advertising create work that spans a continuum from the brilliant—even the inspirational—to the stuff that makes us wonder *just what were they thinking to produce something so awful*. And that becomes the question: *What were they thinking?*

Of course, many of the creative people who write and design ads do feel a responsibility to serve the interests of both client and culture, in keeping with Bernbach's vision. They consider the implications of the images and messages crafted to sell products. They push for solutions that respect consumers and promote positive social values. They enjoy the good night's sleep that accompanies a clear conscience. Which raises another question: *Why isn't everyone else doing the same?*

Why can't advertising do more good? Is the selling of products and services somehow incompatible with a pledge to "do no harm" in the process? It's time we had this conversation.

As you contemplate a career in advertising—joining the ranks of those who Bernbach called "shapers of society"—it's important that you start thinking about how you'll answer these questions: Are you willing to do the hard (yet rewarding) work to lift the practice of advertising to a higher level? Do you think it's possible?

Read on and consider the idea that advertising's greatest contributions are still ahead and that you might play a part in changing an industry for the better.

## Advertising and Ethics? (Yes, Ethics)

Media ethicist Tom Bivins (2004), a professor at the University of Oregon, studies how professionals in advertising, public relations, and journalism do their jobs and make decisions about doing the "right thing." Recognizing that media can do harm to both individuals and society as a whole, Bivins suggests that one of the keys to acting ethically is to first care about doing so. Developmental psychologist Carol Gilligan (1982) calls this the "ethic of care." Presumably, when professionals bring that personal concern to the workplace every day, it will influence the decisions they make and the things that they do.

But why should advertising writers and art directors *care*? It's easier to understand how this might work in the context of other disciplines. In journalism, it makes sense that the world wants its reporters to be trustworthy and more like Tom Brokaw than the brawling paparazzi. And aren't the people who work in public relations required to be kind and optimistic as part of their job descriptions?

Which brings us back to Bernbach's idea: Should the people who create advertising aspire to do anything more than sell? We don't often consider that question. Perhaps, we do not because it seems silly to do so when no one is expecting more. In fact, the advertising industry is looked upon by most people with a great deal of suspicion and scorn. The 2006 annual Gallup Poll reported that just 11 percent of Americans rate the honesty and ethical standards of advertising practitioners as "very high" or "high." That's a slightly lower rating than your Congressional representative and just a bit better than a car salesman.

Besides, creativity—the lifeblood of our business—is about being edgy, taking risks, and reveling in the notion that anything is possible. Some advertising professionals take that reputation and run with it: "Nobody likes us anyway," they explain, "so we'll do whatever's necessary to make the consumer pay attention. We can't worry about the consequences of the work we do," they'll say. "This is how things are and we're not obligated to make everyone happy. We're obligated only to the client and the bottom line."

## The Industry as Its Own Worst Enemy

Let's face it, advertising deserves much of the criticism it receives. In 2005, Blockbuster Video stores across the country celebrated "Life After Late Fees" on giant posters in bright yellow letters. Of course, it was too good to be true, as many customers discovered when charged the replacement cost of any video kept out too long. The company settled complaints in 47 states and refunded charges for a lot of angry people. Despite the company's arguments to the contrary, "Life After Late Fees" was based on a lie.

Sometimes, ads can do worse than simply mislead. Calvin Klein's 1995 jeans campaign incorporated all the visual characteristics of 1970s-era child pornography, featuring very young models in vulnerable poses and various stages of undress. In the television spots, an off-screen photographer coached the models to strip down as they reluctantly obliged.

We also have ads that stereotype and denigrate. Consider the Snickers ad aired during the 2007 Super Bowl. In the television spot—and in alternative versions viewable on the web—two male actors react in disgust when they unintentionally engage in a kiss. Mars, Inc. stopped airing the ad and removed it from its website when the Human Rights Campaign and the Gay and Lesbian Alliance Against Defamation (GLAAD) charged that the spot was homophobic and endorsed anti-gay bullying.

Then there's the formulaic spot for Pine-Sol household cleaner that portrays a sassy, heavy-set black woman as its presumptive champion. Pine-Sol spokeswoman Diane Amos has touted the household cleaning brand since 1993. One industry observer called her portrayal "a walking, talking negative stereotype."

Advertising is responsible for these and other episodes. To this mix, throw in demeaning portrayals of women, dads, the elderly, Southerners, or just about any other stereotyped group. Recall the ads that show kids it pays to lie and cheat. Remember the many commercials that exalt body image over intellect or sexual longing over love. What you get is a toxic collection of bad ideas run amuck.

Lawyers and government agencies can sort out the damage done by false or misleading ads, but inside the "gray areas"—where the rules are not absolute for what's tasteful, respectful, life affirming, and reflective of reality—it is difficult to address the harm done by carelessly-crafted ads. Maybe because these ads seem less harmful than the ones that tell lies, we see a continual drip, drip, drip of promotional messages into the culture that pollute and degrade. These ads don't continue to sink the reputation of an industry and corrupt its priorities; these ads hurt people, divide society, endanger the helpless, and trivialize what's really important.

And consumers are left to ask: *What were they thinking?*

## "Moral Myopia" Obscures Our View

Are the creative people who develop and produce advertising trying to destroy the culture? Regardless of how the industry's worst critics might respond to that question, we can confidently speak for the vast majority of ad folks when we say, "No." In fact, some of the best people you'll ever meet make ads. And most of them say they care passionately about the impact their work has on the world around them. So how does so much of the bad work get out there?

As marketing researchers Minette Drumwright and Patrick Murphy (2004) suggest, too many in the advertising profession are "morally myopic" or too shortsighted to appreciate whether or not their work has a negative influence on society. Instead, ad pros focus on producing work that satisfies the client. The ad people aren't bad people, they're just distracted. Often this level of distraction can rob busy professionals of the necessary perspective to recognize that the work they've created isn't right.

Kat Lam, an art director at The Martin Agency in Richmond, Virginia, describes the conflict between career demands and conscience:

Inside the industry, you're in a kind of advertising vacuum and you get so busy that you become oblivious to things that are going on around you. But I do think it's important to take responsibility for the work that you do (March 2, 2007).

Don't get us wrong. There are people in this business who intentionally incorporate shock value, insensitivity, misogyny, racism, and other vices into their work to bring attention to their work. These people exist and they understand that controversy generates free media attention for a client's brand. *Advertising Age*'s Bob Garfield derisively refers to some of the worst examples as "shockvertising," or advertising that "generat[es] outrage to generate publicity to generate consumer buzz."

Also, it's true that some ads simply disappoint. There is much advertising that squanders opportunities to do more, that misses the mark on moral grounds, or otherwise falls short when viewed through an ethical lens. But, even though there is work that ranges from the "cringe-worthy" to the "could've-been-better," there also are wonderful examples of ads that exceed expectations and show the world what's possible when ad folks play at the top of their game. This good work reflects a mission to rehabilitate the industry's image and to *take responsibility for the influence it wields within the culture*. Most important, it's the type of advertising you can be proud to bring to the world.

## Beyond Obligation: A Mindset for Change

Consider the word *responsibility*. As political theorist Joan Tronto (1993) observes, inherent to the definition of that word is the implication that we assume some culpability for existing circumstances and recognize our need to effect change. As previously discussed, it is difficult to argue that the advertising industry has always acted in the best interests of society. In its efforts to please clients and meet their needs, those goals are sometimes met at others' expense. Because the client is the customer, professionalism rightly incorporates an obligation to give them the best work possible. This is what we're hired to do and it's why we get paid.

The term *social responsibility* better addresses the broad scope of advertising's impact on society. The term also offers those in the industry who want to do better two routes to get there.

First, those who create advertising should always take into account the possible consequences of their work. Clients expect that a campaign will fulfill their objectives, but as that constituency is satisfied, is another helped or harmed? Second, ad professionals should look for opportunities in their day-to-day work to effect positive social change. Can the work that is done on behalf of clients support an even greater purpose than it was originally designed to achieve? Ad folks who consider these questions can make a difference.

When we use our talents to create advertising while considering its impact on society during that process, we are serving interests that match, but also transcend those of the agency and the client. We are doing work *beyond obligation*, reaching past *pro forma* (expected) professional functions and making decisions based on a commitment to social responsibility. As revolutionary as it sounds, this mindset is not new but it is largely absent in our field. Is this socially responsible perspective a practical idea? Absolutely. Doing so does not require sacrificing any of the tools of the advertising trade. Instead, it affords the opportunity to use our creativity and expertise to do some good in the world.

Social responsibility is already happening in bright pockets of the industry, but how? Let's spend some time figuring it out.

## Change Agents: If Not You, Then Who?

Inside the advertising agency, the professionals most directly responsible for the crafting of the work that the world sees are the *art director* and *copywriter*, who typically work in teams. Just a step up the organizational food chain, the *creative director* guides the work of art directors and writers. Better known by those in the business as "creatives," these people are on the front lines of any effort to both raise consciousness and implement the *beyond obligation* philosophy.

The field of advertising attracts highly creative people. They are smart and intellectually curious. The best of them have been trained to think analytically and to develop strategy that infuses art with great persuasive power. They are the vanguards of cool and they drive trends in the business. They are arguably better positioned than the highest-ranking agency executives to be the agents of meaningful social responsibility, because they generate the work that is our face to the world.

The *beyond obligation* mindset, as previously noted, transcends obligation. Creatives can find opportunities in the work that they do, and a growing number are seizing them with great effect. Their leadership as change agents makes sense given what we know about creative people.

## The Creative Individual

Legendary graphic designer Milton Glaser argues that creatives' perspective on the world must include "doubt and ambiguity, as well as generosity and optimism." In other words, the creative person possesses both the capacity to see and understand problems as well as an abiding belief that they can be solved.

Harvard Business School professor and creativity scholar Teresa Amabile (1988) asserts that the creative person's *intrinsic motivation* (self-motivation) to solve a problem is the most powerful factor in doing so successfully.

Creatives derive a great deal of personal satisfaction from confronting problems and grappling with them. In fact, multiple theories of the creative process understand it as a dynamic operation; that is, a process energized through a constant cycle of problem identification and solution, particularly those solutions that are superior to ones previously offered. The creative person is positioned as challenger to the status quo. Taken together, these findings suggest that as advertising professionals, creative directors, art directors, and writers are psychologically predisposed to engage in beyond obligation thinking and can change the way that they approach their own work.

## The Social System

Of course, the members of the creative team act as individuals within a larger *social system*. In advertising, this system operates at the agency level and as a profession. Mihaly Csikszentmihalyi (1990), a noted expert on creativity and innovation, tells us that creative persons operate within a social system, in which they will (to some degree) become immersed and use that culture as part of their process.

For purposes of this discussion about social responsibility, you should recognize the different ways that immersion into one's own professional culture can impact a person's ability to be a change agent. Some young creatives enter the business with the right intentions but quickly become discouraged when the *beyond obligation* mindset is smothered by deadlines and profit motive. Many become cynical and give up the fight. Rexanna McCubbin, a writer at The Martin Agency, remembers what things were like at her first agency job:

Young people sometimes have trouble standing up for everything they believe in. The only way we can change things is to be a part of them, but getting fired or being taken out of your position won't help. Sometimes it's hard to be heard, or to know how far to push things, but you have to choose those battles and fight them daily (March 2, 2007).

It is possible, of course, to successfully navigate the agency environment and learn to negotiate it in ways that yield good socially responsible work. Art director Jason Ambrose and writer Dustin Ballard, who worked as a creative team at Crispin Porter + Bogusky in Miami on the American Legacy Foundation's (an antismoking advocacy group) "Truth" campaign, credit CP+B's "push the edge" culture as an essential complement to their own social ideologies. Their work for Truth featured sitcom-style treat-

ments of actors scripted by actual transcripts from "big tobacco" company meetings (complete with a cheesy laugh track). Their project is illustrative of the powerful synergy created when both client and agency share a commitment to positive social change.

When we find responsible, sensitive, and even courageous work being produced for clients, it usually begins with a vision for doing something different and a commitment to champion that approach.

## It Takes a Visionary

The term *corporate social entrepreneur* was coined to describe a person whose actions within a social system (think: agency, company, organization, industry, world) are primarily motivated by an agenda to benefit the social system. Nearly every occupation celebrates its visionaries, the people whose imagination change business practices for the better.

Bill Bernbach, the writer-turned-agency-principal who co-founded the agency Doyle Dane Bernbach (DDB) in the 1950s, is generally celebrated as one of the field's greatest pioneers. The Bernbach approach to

272

advertising requires that the work we do should make us proud. More than a simple philosophy, it has become a mission to some. As a case in point, creatives at DDB were among the first to incorporate racially diverse portrayals into their campaigns, most notably in a series of subway posters for Levy's Real Jewish Rye bread. Whereas diversity in ad portrayals probably wasn't a client objective, the pioneers at DDB saw an opportunity both to sell and to serve the culture.

Jelly Helm, Executive Creative Director at Wieden + Kennedy in Portland, Oregon, shook up the business in 2000 with the publication of his essay, *Saving Advertising*. In that piece, he dared to ask: "If our clients are leading us down a path that is not socially or ecologically sustainable, or that is harmful to human nature, do we resist, and how?"

Although many of his arguments are critical of advertising and its ill effects on society, his opinion is rooted in the proposition that the same people who make ads have the power to reverse a good deal of the damage it caused. In 2001, Helm was appointed to a United Nations panel charged with addressing overconsumption of the planet's natural resources. Today, he teaches aspiring art directors and writers and travels widely to lecture about sustainability and consumerism.

TBWA\Chiat\Day Chairman Lee Clow, the creative mind behind some of the most memorable ads for Apple Computer ("1984," "Think Different"), Energizer ("Energizer Bunny") and a host of other household names, recognizes that consumers are becoming increasingly knowledgeable about how advertising works, citing a "new age of transparency." As consumers turn an even more critical eye upon companies, their brands, and their advertising messages, "[ads] need to be done artfully, truthfully and intelligently" with the proper amount of respect. Clow was named one of *Advertising Age*'s Top 100 People of the Century. The publication credited his powerful influence on the profession and his strong advocacy for meaningful creative work.

Bernbach, Helm, and Clow are just a few of the people who've pushed the industry in the right direction. In so doing, they've encouraged their colleagues to produce work that they can be proud to own and to share with the world.

There are other voices calling for similar outcomes. Changing how the world sees advertising as an industry is a cause that finds many champions within its own ranks. Will you be one of them?

### *Beyond Obligation*: A Case Study

Client:      Citigroup Global Consumer Group

Agency:      Fallon Worldwide, Minneapolis, MN

Concept:    Citi is an active partner in achieving perspective, balance, and peace of mind in finances and in life for its customers.

Since 2001, the "Live Richly" campaign for Citigroup Global Consumer Group (a major division of the company encompassing credit cards, consumer lending, small business, and Internet banking) has attracted a great deal of industry attention. In addition, the campaign has won several awards, including the Global EFFIE, an honor reserved for work that is both creative and effective in achieving client goals.

The clean and simply rendered ads remind people that everything in life, including money, is best enjoyed when kept in the proper perspective. The ads offer a surprising point of view, considering that they were created for a financial services company.

Fallon Worldwide group creative director Steve Driggs recalls that the campaign was developed on the heels of the "dot com bust" in the summer of 2000 and "reflected—maybe even nurtured—a feeling that money was not the priority in people's lives."

The strategy here is fascinatingly counterintuitive, and raises the following questions: Is it possible to build a financial services brand by reminding consumers that so many other things in life are just as important as money? Can an advertising campaign do its part to counteract the problems of greed and materialism in American culture?

The "Live Richly" campaign is a prime example of advertising that serves the client and benefits society. Consider, for example, a few of the campaign's headlines:

You are not silver, gold or platinum. You are you.

Healthy credit is good, but keep an eye on your cholesterol, too.

Some of the most exciting growth charts are on the pantry door.

Contrary to popular belief, you are not what you drive.

## Is Beyond Obligation a Movement in the Making?

This *beyond obligation* mindset is finding support across the country and around the world. Perhaps it's smaller ad agencies—that are leaner and more flexible—that find this mission easiest to adopt. At New York City's Amalgamated, for example, they are no longer making advertising. Instead, they're now in the business of "cultural branding," a creative philosophy rooted in cultural ideals and a vision for "how society should be." Their work is brightly optimistic and calls for reinvention to cure what is wrong in the agency world.

Across the pond in London, St. Luke's—an ad agency named for the patron saint of artists—creates campaigns for Filofax and IKEA suited to the agency mission statement: "Your audience will only love you … when you show that you love them." But it's not only their work that is *beyond obligation*: The agency's organizational structure and leadership believe that doing the right thing in business is policy to follow, even when it's difficult.

The Austin, Texas-based agency Enviro-Media is led by principals Kevin Tuerff and Valerie Davis, who insist that paying attention to social responsibility is no longer an option for advertisers. At their shop, they pick and choose the brands they want to work with: those that want to make change for the better. Some clients on the agency's roster, such as the Texas Department of Transportation, are already noted for their commitment to the greater good; the state office launched its famous "Don't Mess With Texas" campaign in 1986. Other clients were attracted by the company's growing reputation. Dell Computer sought EnviroMedia's help to educate consumers about environmentally friendly disposal of unwanted desktop and laptop machines.

When agencies and their clients share a commitment to effect positive change, this meeting of minds isn't simply synergistic but also potentially profitable—for both agency and client. EnviroMedia, Ethos (Toronto),

Green Team (NYC) and other "social marketers" are getting plenty of press and helping set the agenda for responsible business practices.

## Conclusion

In a recent address to the 54th International Advertising Festival in Cannes, France, former U.S. Vice President Al Gore called upon an audience of advertising professionals from around the world to consider the power that they possess, arguing that "advertising is playing a much larger role than it ever has in all of history." During his appeal to the industry for a greater focus on sustainability, he cited "a great hunger for authenticity in messaging … in products … in policies" among consumers.

Clearly, those who create advertising do influence society and culture with their work.

For advertising professionals, it can be difficult to align the clients' best interests with those of the world with which we communicate. In reality, people make mistakes. They make compromises. But what an amazing step forward it would be to regularly ask ourselves the question: *Is this advertising responsible?*

As Drumwright and Murphy (2004) remind us, the right thing to do "is sometimes debatable," but that doesn't mean we shouldn't "be best prepared to wrestle with it." Our hope is that your generation of ad men and women will consider the *beyond obligation* mindset as a higher standard of professional practice.

## Questions

1. Consider all of the reasons that people might offer for considering advertising to be one of the least honest and ethical professions. How many of those reasons could be addressed by changes in the way we create advertising messages?

2. Can you describe an example of "shockvertising" (fitting Bob Garfield's definition) that you've encountered? What was your reaction to the message(s)?

3.  In relationship to the subject matter discussed in this chapter, what's the difference between obligation and responsibility?

4.  Do you agree or disagree with former Vice President Gore's suggestion that "advertising is playing a much larger role than it ever has in all of history?" Explain why or why not.

## References and Recommended Reading

Amabile, Teresa (1988). A model of creativity and innovation in organizations. *Research in Organizational Behavior*, 10, 123-167.

Bivins, Thomas (2004). *Mixed media: Moral distinctions in advertising, public relations, and journalism*, Mahwah, NJ: LEA.

Csikszentmihalyi, Mihaly (1996). *Creativity: Flow and the psychology of discovery and invention*, NY: Harper Perennial.

Csikszentmihalyi, Mihaly (1990). The domain of creativity. In Mark Runco and R. Albert (Eds.), *Theories of Creativity*, Newbury Park, CA: Sage.

Drumwright, Minette and Patrick E. Murphy (2004). How advertising practitioners view ethics: Moral muteness, moral myopia, and moral imagination. *Journal of Advertising*, 33 (June), 7-25.

Garfield, Bob (2007). Lee Clow on what's changed since '1984.' *Advertising Age* [online edition]. Retrieved June 16, 2007, from: http://adage.com/images/random/0607/garfield-clow061107.pdf

Garfield, Bob (2005). Top 100 advertising campaigns of the century. *Advertising Age* [online edition]. Retrieved June 16, 2007, from: http://adage.com/century/campaigns.html

Gilligan, Carol (1982). *In a Different Voice*, Cambridge, MA: Harvard University Press.

Gore, Albert (2007). Al Gore speech at Cannes Advertising Festival, parts 1-3. Retrieved July 27, 2007, from: http://youtube.com/watch?v=TiTOp6Yf3AQ

The Gallup Poll (2006). Honesty / ethics in professions. Retrieved June 16, 2007, from: http://www.galluppoll.com/content/?ci=1654&pg=1

Hemingway, Christine A. (2005). Personal values as a catalyst for corporate social entrepreneurship. *Journal of Business Ethics*, 60, 233-249.

Naumes, Margaret J., and William Naumes (1999). Calvin Klein, Inc. and the kiddie porn ads. *North America Case Research Association / Case Research Journal*. (Summer), 1-14.

Pollay, Richard (1986). The distorted mirror: Reflections on the unintended consequences of advertising, *Journal of Advertising*, 50, 18-36.

Tronto, Joan (1993). *Moral boundaries*. NY: Routledge.

## Online Resources

### Adbusters
http://www.adbusters.org/home/

This self-described media foundation/magazine/advocacy group is dedicated to highlighting "the erosion of our physical and cultural environments by commercial forces" and is collectively one of the ad industry's most ardent critics.

### After These Messages
http://www.afterthesemessages.com/obe/about

Anyone who signs on as a member of this free site is invited to "share, review and reflect" about ads as well as their ethical implications. "The Big Picture" section of the site offers a terrific map of the ads site members are discussing and how they are being evaluated. The site is a project of the New York City-based ad agency Green Team.

### *Good*
http://www.goodmagazine.com/

Both the online and newsstand versions of *Good* magazine are intended to offer "a platform for the ideas, people, and businesses that are driving change in the world." The editorial staff also refers to this concept as "the sensibility of giving a damn."

## Change This

http://www.changethis.com/

A site based on the hypothesis that "a significant portion of the population wants to hear thoughtful, rational, constructive arguments about important issues" and encourages readers to contribute their own "manifestos" for positive societal change. There is much content here relevant to advertising and marketing practices.

## Marketing for Good

http://marketingforgood.net/

An agency president dares to ask the question: Can marketing actually make life a little better? This site offers evidence to support answering "yes."

## "Saving Advertising" Article

http://www.emigre.com/Editorial.php?sect=1&id=25

Here you'll find Jelly Helm's landmark 2000 editorial, "Saving Advertising."

## Amalgamated, NY

http://www.amalgamatednyc.com/home.htm

Here is the website of NYC ad agency Amalgamated, discussed in this chapter.

## EnviroMedia

http://www.enviromedia.com/home.php

Here is the website of Austin, TX ad agency EnviroMedia, discussed in this chapter.

## Ethos, JWT

http://www.ethosjwt.com/who_ethos_01.html

A spin-off of agency giant JWT, Toronto-based Ethos is also courting socially conscious clients.

## Green Team
http://www.greenteamusa.com/website/index.html
Here is the website of NYC ad agency Green Team (mentioned in this chapter), the sponsor of the aforementioned "After These Messages" site.

## St. Luke's, London
http://www.stlukes.co.uk/
Here's the website of London, UK agency St. Luke's, discussed in this chapter.

# If It Feels Good, Watch It:
## Emotion in Advertising

## by Tom Reichert

EMOTIONS ARE FUNDAMENTAL to the human experience, so it is not surprising that advertisers employ emotional appeals to evoke specific feelings in consumers.

Today's commercials, print ads, and Internet interstitials generate a range of emotional reactions from humor and elation to shame and disgust, and from arousal and fear to sorrow and pity. In fact, some in the industry believe that today's advertising has swung too far into the realm of emotion and fails to deliver the useful knowledge consumers need to make brand decisions. As a result, many clients are unhappy with sizzling campaigns but sizzle-less sales. And agencies are left with compelling reels that they then use to lure the next set of clients.

A look at recent books in the field reveals the interest marketers are taking toward the emotional imperative. *Emotional Branding*, *Emotion Marketing*, and *Passion Branding* are just a few of the titles imploring the power of emotion as the key to consumer response.

Scholars and practitioners are realizing the powerful role emotion can play in getting ads noticed and establishing strong links between brands and consumers. This chapter discusses these issues while also defining and describing how emotion is used and measured in advertising.

## Emotion + Advertising

Aristotle identified "pathos" as emotion-based argument designed to play upon the audience's fears and desires.

Advertising, as we know, is a paid form of persuasive communication—compact 30-second arguments—conveyed through the media by an identified sponsor.

Marketers use advertising to create awareness, to inform, and to position their goods and services as they attempt to convince consumers that their brands are preferable to the competition.

## An Aroused Mental State

Emotion is often defined as strong feelings or an aroused mental state directed toward a specific object. There are, however, several competing conceptualizations of emotion.

In the 1980s, work in consumer behavior, borrowing from discrete emotion models, identified several basic emotions such as joy, elation, fear, and surprise.

Dan Hill, consultant and author of *Emotionomics*, believes that there are six core emotions that transcend cultures. Those emotions are happiness, surprise, anger, disgust, sadness, and fear. Moreover, these core emotions can be crossed with each other to produce secondary emotions. For example, combining happiness and surprise results in feelings of delight or relief.

Recent work by scholars shows that these fundamental emotions generally map within a two-dimensional space consisting of arousal (high/low) and pleasure (positive/negative).

It is generally thought that emotion is responsible for the human propensity to move toward stimuli and situations that are pleasurable and to move away from or avoid information that signals danger.

## How it Works

Emotions serve several roles in advertising.

An important function of emotional stimuli is to attract viewers by capturing their attention. Advertisers only have a few moments to hook viewers before they switch channels, turn the page, or scroll down a website, and emotional information is particularly adroit at getting noticed.

During the 1980s, consumer behavior researchers reported that attitude toward the ad, the feelings consumers experience when viewing an ad, could both directly and indirectly influence thoughts and feelings toward the brand as well as purchase intention, especially for low-involvement and previously unknown products.

More current research, some of it using brain imaging technology, suggests that emotion colors most experiences and influences many decisions.

To elaborate, brands are essentially an assortment of reactions. Part of the reaction consumers have to brands is rational or knowledge-based (e.g., this brand performs well in these conditions). In a related sense, brands also have personalities that come to mind when a brand is considered. But, as many are beginning to believe, emotion is the most important reaction to a brand. When one considers a brand, all these experiences are triggered—brand knowledge, personality, and emotions.

Emotion is receiving a lot of attention because scholars and practitioners think the emotional component of our reactions is the most powerful. "Brands are bundles of experiences," says Paul Price (2007, p. 20), an executive with DDB Worldwide. "The more emotionally engaging your brand experience, the more unique, intangible value you grow."

Dan Hill believes that emotions come first, before thinking. "Not only does the rational argument—persuasion—come after the emotional connection has been made, rationality is furthermore limited in that it is really best suited to address needs," states Hill (2007, p. 12). "In contrast, emotionally imbued wants are superior because they're more immediate and serve as the gateway to stopping power—an ad's ability to stop people in their tracks."

According to Hill, some of the advantages of emotion-based advertising are its ability to cut through the clutter and resonate with consumers: "…your advertising is more likely to be seen, read, believed, remembered," states Hill.

Another advantage is that a strong positive emotional connection between consumers and brands can provide a hedge against competitive brands. "When emotions get tapped, the ensuing relationship between a company and that customer acts as a barrier to conquest by competitors because loyalty is a feeling," notes Hill (p. 12).

Often advertisers simply use narratives to entertain consumers with the intention that consumers will return the favor with a purchase.

However, Leslie Picot-Zane, the founder of The Center for Emotional Marketing, suggests that today's advertisers have gone overboard with their infatuation with emotion. Today we have "advertising that is mostly fluff and little meat," argues Picot-Zane (2006).

Picot-Zane, a former cosmetics marketer for Proctor & Gamble, argues that good advertising can't rely on emotion alone. She analyzed some of the latest academic research and determined the following: "It turns out that logic and emotion work in concert to help us make decisions," says Picot-Zane. "You can't have one without the other. Effective advertising needs to convey both seamlessly."

## Advertising Taps Emotions

Advertisers use an arsenal of narrative devices and creative techniques to grab attention and imbue brands with specific feelings.

Those creative tools include images, symbols, music, color, sound, and editing techniques such as pacing, rhythm, angles, and perspective.

Once advertisers have the consumer's attention, feelings are used to associate a product or service with a particular emotion.

Dan Hill is very prescriptive in how he thinks this should be done: "CMOs (Chief Marketing Officers) should identify which emotions they're most eager to inspire in the target market… Then they should work with the [advertising] agency to identify which core visuals will best convey those emotions" (p. 12). Hill believes that images are one of the most effective tools for evoking specific emotions.

Evocative images are exactly what Honda used in 2006 to reenergize its CR-V. Honda found through consumer research that CR-V owners liked the car, and considered it practical and reliable. However, a strong emotional connection was missing. Based on these findings, Honda introduced a restyled CR-V with the emotion-based "Crave" campaign.

In magazine ads and commercials, the CR-V was creatively associated with common cravings: hot chocolate, microwave popcorn, specialty coffee, and burgers on the grill. The feelings evoked by these tasty foods were meant to transfer to the automobile so that the CR-V would come to evoke similar feelings. By most measures, the campaign was a success.

Not surprisingly, some of the most memorable commercials are those that evoked powerful feelings.

# The Early Days

Early advertising was not as emotion-evoking as it is today. From the beginnings of modern advertising through the early 1900s, advertising was chiefly informational in nature.

Ads were simple and primarily consisted of text, much like today's classified ads, as advertisers announced new services or the availability of products and informed potential consumers how to procure those products. The only images in early ads consisted of simple wood engravings, which pale in comparison to the vibrancy of today's images.

## AIDA

As advertising developed into a profession during the second half of the nineteenth century, the AIDA approach (attention, interest, desire, and action), a hierarchy-of-effects model, guided much advertising thinking.

Desire represented the emotional component of the persuasion process that was considered necessary to move consumers to take action. Much training in advertising and persuasion-based professions, such as advertising sales, continues to utilize AIDA-type models.

## Improved Technology

In the early 1900s the look of advertising was altered by printing technology as well as by several creative directors who believed it was important to use evocative images to evoke feelings such as status and patriotism, among other emotions.

At this point, advertisers could adorn their ads with colorful illustrations and photographs.

Glossy magazine ads for Cadillac emphasized the feelings of status and prestige associated with ownership.

Television was a transforming technology in the 1950s. It was a powerful means of combining images and audio in commercial messages to evoke emotions.

## Unlikable Advertising

An early commercial for the pain reliever Anacin was both annoying and highly successful. In the view of many, it gave viewers a headache as they watched an animated mallet pound repeatedly onscreen.

The Anacin commercial, created by television advertising pioneer Rosser Reeves, is often cited as an example that ads don't have to be liked to be effective.

Other successful ad campaigns that annoyed many viewers include "Don't Squeeze the Charmin," featuring Mr. Whipple admonishing shoppers not to squeeze toilet tissue in the supermarket, and a campaign for Wisk laundry detergent that removed "Ring around the collar."

The role of emotion in advertising increased as many products achieved parity and consumer behavior research became more sophisticated.

For example, today many commercials for investment brokers such as Merrill Lynch strive to emphasize security and comfort as a means for differentiation.

## Emotion Today

Today, emotions are considered an essential tool for marketing success.

"There has never been a greater need for marketers to unleash the emotional power of their brands," notes Paul Price (2007, p. 20). "Marketing sameness, media fragmentation, and confusing choices call for inspirational emotional experiences to engage consumers and create revenue growth."

As Price argues, a value of emotion is that it serves as a point of distinction between parity products. In other words, if two products perform essentially the same, the edge goes to the brand with a compelling emotional identity.

"What is the difference between an Apple iPod and a Samsung Yepp if they functionally play the same amount of music with equal portability?" asks Price (p. 20). "The distinction is the emotionally inspiring elegance, hipness, and simplicity iPod fans pay a premium to have."

Apple's recent iPod commercials definitely evoke emotions of hipness and energy with upbeat music, vibrant color, and silhouettes of dancing listeners plugged into their iPods.

## Emotion in Political Advertising

Emotion plays a significant role in political advertising as well. Tony Schwartz created several notable political ads that evoked strong emotions about candidates.

In one memorable spot for Lyndon Johnson's US presidential reelection, the image of a girl pulling petals from a daisy was juxtaposed with a countdown to a nuclear explosion.

The commercial was designed to evoke fear and doubt about the candidacy of Johnson's opponent, Barry Goldwater.

Political advertising can either seek to foster positive feelings toward the sponsoring candidate or to disparage an opponent by evoking fear and distrust.

## Going Negative

Much research has found negative advertising to be very effective in political campaigns because the negative emotions come to be associated with the targeted candidate.

In fact, recent industry research shows that voters' feelings toward candidates are very good indicators of who will win the campaign.

As reporter Jack Neff explains, "how people feel about candidates and their ads predicts how they'll vote far better than polls in which they declare their voting intentions" (2007, p. 3).

As the research from Harris Interactive demonstrates, how people feel about candidates is a more accurate predictor of who they'll vote for than what they think about a candidate or the candidate's stand on certain issues. Low favorability, thanks to an opponent's negative attack ads, will hurt at the voting booth.

In the early phase of the 2008 US presidential election, however, everyone appears to be smiling because the candidates are relying on humor to get their messages across instead of negative attacks. Candidates are less likely to alienate voters so early in the election season.

Negative political attacks usually surface as the stakes increase.

# Common Appeals

Although advertisers attempt to appeal to a range of emotions that include pleasantness, elation, accomplishment, and guilt, three emotional appeals represent the majority of emotional appeals in consumer advertising.

## Humor

Estimates indicate that up to 50% of mainstream consumer advertising is humor based. These messages contain instances of slapstick humor, self-disparaging spokespeople, and funny slice-of-life stories.

Humor is thought to work by attracting and maintaining attention, enhancing liking for the brand, and by creating favorable feelings that can become associated with the brand.

Not surprisingly, humor is thought to be more effective for low-involvement products. "Where's the beef?" was a very popular campaign from the mid-1980s that Wendy's restaurants used to compare its hamburgers to those of its competitors.

In the signature commercial, a grandmotherly woman continually asks an employee, "Where's the beef?"

## Fear

On the other end of the spectrum, marketers endeavor to persuade consumers by creating feelings of tension and fear. Similar to the concept of fear appeals in the communication field, ad creators attempt to scare consumers by creating fear and perceptions of threat.

As a result, consumers become more vigilant in their search for alternatives to reduce their vulnerability.

Usually, toward the end of the commercial, the marketer's brand or service is positioned as a preferable alternative to reducing the threat and to protect oneself and family.

Products such as auto and home insurance, retirement savings, and theft prevention devices are often advocated with threatening appeals.

Ads for personal-care products also employ fear appeals. For many decades, Listerine executives emphasized the social ostracism, loss of romance, and dead-end careers caused by halitosis. The mouthwash was touted as a proven way to avoid such undesirable outcomes.

## Sex

It is estimated that from 10 to 20% of mainstream advertising contains sexual images and references.

These images mostly consist of images of scantily clad women in provocative poses or couples in heated embraces.

Research shows that sexual information evokes an emotional response that, depending on the receiver and contextual variables, is positively arousing.

Sexy images attract and maintain attention and often serve as a compelling benefit for buying and using a brand.

Research supports a distraction hypothesis such that sexual information is more likely to be remembered at the expense of brand information (e.g., brand name, headlines).

However, consistent use of ads that contain sex can serve to imbue brand identities with sexual meaning.

For example, Calvin Klein and Victoria's Secret are brands that evoke sexual thoughts and feelings because of their long-running use of sexualized ad images.

As expected, sexual appeals most often appear in ads for low-involvement and expressive products (e.g., fashion, fragrance, entertainment).

## Measuring Emotional Responses

Emotional reactions to advertising are assessed several ways in industry and academic research.

The most common method involves asking participants to view a commercial and to respond to semantic differential items, adjective checklists, or visual representations of feeling states.

In some industry research settings, commonly referred to as copy-testing, viewers are verbally asked to rate their feelings on an interval scale.

A closely related method, often used in political advertising research, requires respondents to register their feelings in real-time by turning a dial.

A criticism of these methods is that they introduce potential bias and inaccuracy because it forces viewers to cognitively assess their emotional state.

### Physiological Indicators

To avoid response bias, researchers have increasingly employed physiological indicators to assess emotion.

Feelings can be measured by monitoring perspiration (e.g., galvanic skin response), facial muscle contractions, pupil dilation, and heart rate.

Although these methods are costly and require expertise to administer, they are considered to offer a more reliable reflection of the emotional responses consumers experience when viewing advertising compared to paper-and-pencil based measures.

More recently, researchers are beginning to look to brain science and brain imaging to assess emotion in response to advertising.

MRI technology is used to determine areas of the brain that are stimulated by certain advertising features.

These methods hold promise but are prohibitive to most researchers.

However, brain imaging and other advanced methods answer calls from within the field, from both practitioners and scholars, to better understand the role of emotion and consumer response.

For example, in 2003 the Advertising Research Foundation joined with the American Association of Advertising Agencies to sponsor research designed to enhance emotion assessment and to increase understanding of the role of emotion in the consumer behavior process.

## Conclusion

Imagine someone from 100 years ago watching a few hours of today's prime time television fare. Aside from the sex and violence in the programming itself, that person would be awash in a sea of emotional commercials.

Long gone are the informational ads of that person's era, or the product demonstrations so common in the early days of television. Today, marketing has (de)evolved to the point of using emotion to stand out in a cluttered media environment, and to differentiate the seemingly endless choices of essentially identical products.

If it feels good, people will watch it. But the information consumers are actually gleaning from today's commercials is little beyond a panache of feelings and gut reactions.

## Questions

1.    What is your favorite emotion-based commercial? What emotion(s) does it evoke?

2.    Many ads aimed toward college students employ humor. Why, in your opinion, is that so?

3.    What do you think: Is it ethical for marketers to intentionally play upon people's emotions without them being aware of its use?

## References and Recommended Reading

Batra, R., and M. L. Ray (1986). Affective responses mediating acceptance of advertising. *Journal of Consumer Research*, 13, 234-249.

Brown, S. P., P. M. Homer, and J. J. Inman (1998). A meta-analysis of relationships between ad-evoked feelings and advertising responses. *Journal of Marketing Research*, 35, 114-126.

Du Plessis, E., and M. Brown (2005). *The Advertised Mind: Groundbreaking Insights into How Our Brains Respond to Advertising*. Philadelphia, PA: Krogen Page.

Duffy, Neill (2003). *Passion Branding: Harnessing the Power of Emotion to Build Strong Brands*. Hoboken, NJ: Wiley.

Edell, J. A., and M. C. Burke (1987). The power of feelings in understanding advertising effects. *Journal of Consumer Research*, 14, 421-433.

Gobe, Marc (2001). *Emotional Branding: The New Paradigm for Connecting Brands to People*. NY: Allworth.

Gordon, W. (2006), What do consumers do emotionally with advertising? *Journal of Advertising Research*, 46 (1), 2-10.

Hill, Dan (2007, August 27). CMOs win big by letting emotions drive advertising. *Advertising Age*, p. 12.

Hill, Dan (2007). *Emotionomics: Winning Hearts and Minds*. Edina, MN: Adams.

Neff, Jack (2007, September 3). Engagement could hinder Hillary. *Advertising Age*, p. 3, 25.

Picot-Zane, Leslie (2006, January 9). Is advertising too emotional? *Brandweek*. Retrieved September 21, 2007, from http://www. brandweek.com/bw/magazine/article_display.jsp?vnu_content_ id=10018008092

Poels, K., and S. DeWitte (2006). How to capture the heart? Reviewing 20 years of emotion measurement in advertising. *Journal of Advertising Research*, 46 (1), 18-27.

Price, Paul (2007, March 12). Unleash emotions for business growth. *Advertising Age*, p. 20.

Smit, E. G., L. Van Meurs, and P. C. Neijens (2006). Effects of advertising likeability: A 10-year perspective. *Journal of Advertising Research*, 46 (1), 73-83.

Stewart, D. M., and D. H. Furse (1986). *Effective Television Advertising*. Lexington, MA: DC Heath.

## Online Resources

### Emotions in Advertising FAQs

http://www.ciadvertising.org/studies/student/98_fall/theory/weirtz/Inner.htm

This site is a bit dated but it provides a brief discussion of how emotion in advertising works and how it is measured. Be sure to visit the "Hall of Fame" for examples of what this site considers some of the most emotionally charged ads of all time.

### Research PowerPoint

http://www.arfsite.org/downloads/2005-09-27_adweek_ARF.pdf

This PowerPoint presentation represents an initiative within the industry to better understand how emotion works in advertising. The slides summarize how practitioners have measured advertising in the past, and provides ideas for future analysis.

This chapter is adapted, with permission, from: Reichert, Tom (in press). Advertising, Emotion in, in *International Encyclopedia of Communication*, Wolfgang Donsbach, ed., Oxford, England: Blackwell.

# Index

**A**

about-face.org: 182

Adbusters: 279

Addressable advertising: 162

Adidas: 232

Adland: 166

Advergames: 88

Advertising 2.0: 140–41

*Advertising Age*: 1, 3, 106, 107, 117, 119, 121, 152, 160, 163, 189, 197, 204, 207, 269

Advertising Agencies, Multicultural Opportunities: 9

Advertising clutter: 154–56, 226, 284

Advertising Education Foundation (AEF): 182

Advertising exposure: 152–54

Advertising Research Foundation (ARF): 292, 294

Advertising saturation: 7, 152–63
    Avoidance: 160
    Responses to: 158–61

Advertising spending: 2, 154

Advertising Standards Authority: 219

Advertising to Children: 5–6

Advertising Women of New York (AWNY): 169, 176, 182, 220

African American agencies: 202

African American population: 185, 202

African Americans in advertising: 183–84, 190–92
    Historical representation: 186–89

AIDA (attention, interest, desire, approach): 286

Al Jazeera: 258

Alcohol Advertising: 5, 57–67, 219
    Future of: 66–67

Moderation messages: 65

Online: 64–65

Overexposure of youth: 61–64

Self regulation: 58–59

Spending: 58, 65

Alli: 43

Altria: 79

Amabile, Teresa: 271

Amazon.com: 33–34

Ambrose, Jason: 272

America Coming Together: 241

America Online (AOL): 114, 139

American Academy of Pediatrics: 61

American Advertising Federation (AAF): 197, 199, 200–201, 207

American Association of Advertising Agencies (4As): 197, 292

American Broadcasting Company (ABC): 109

American Express: 33, 176

*American Idol*: 225, 233

American Medical Association (AMA): 47

American Psychological Association (APA): 92

American Tobacco Company: 72

Anacin: 287

Anderson, Pamela: 233

Andrews, Amanda: 109

Anheuser-Busch: 57, 58, 115

Aniston, Jennifer: 172, 228

Antismoking campaigns: 77–78

Apple Computer: 115, 139, 273

*The Apprentice*: 130

Arens, Bill: 26

Asian-American agencies: 202

Asian-American population: 202

AT&T: 34
Atkin, Charles: 60, 62
Aunt Jemima: 186–87
Austin, Erica: 60, 62, 63, 65
AWNY "Grand Ugly" award: 176, 220
Axe Body Spray: 115, 145, 146, 176, 215

**B**

Baker, Mike: 110
Balasubramanian, Siva: 127, 131
Ballard, Dustin: 272
Barbie: 86
BarelyPolitical.com: 249–50
Bartle Bogle Hegarty (BBH): 115
BBDO Worldwide: 198
Beckham, David: 232
Beer Institute: 59, 70
    Advertising and Marketing
    Code: 59, 65
    Code Compliance Review Board
      (CCRB): 57
Beers, Charlotte: 253–54, 257–60,
    262, 264
Belch, Michael: 129, 130
Below-the-line advertising: 106
Bernays, Edward L.: 74
Bernbach, Bill: 265, 266, 272–74
Better Business Bureau: 96
Bivins, Tom: 266
Black Entertainment Television (BET): 204
Blockbuster Video: 267
Bounds, Gwendolyn: 112
Brand Channel: 165
Brandeis, Louis: 30
brandhype.org: 133, 137
Bree, Joël: 5, 85
*Bride's Magazine*: 154
Brown, Warren: 188–89
Bryant, Kobe: 230

Budweiser: 57, 58, 61, 62, 65, 66
    BudTV: 66–67, 70
*The Bulgari Connection*: 135
Burger King: 115
Burns, Whitney: 114
Burrell Communications: 187
Bush, George H.W.: 240
Bush, George W.: 239, 247, 255
Buss, Terry: 244
Bzzagent: 145–46, 151

**C**

Calvin Klein: 215, 216, 267, 290–91
Camel: see R.J. Reynolds
Campaign for a Commercial-Free
    Childhood: 166
CAN SPAM Act: 157, 159
Cannes Lions International Advertising
    Festival: 118, 175, 277
Capone, Andrew: 250
Cappo, Joe: 3, 11, 119
Captain Morgan: 63
Carl's Jr.: 176, 211, 231
Carlson, Margaret: 259
Carlyle, Thomas: 153
Carnegie Endowment for International
    Peace: 259
Carol H. Williams Advertising: 202
Carpenter-Childers, Courtney: 171
Castengera, Michael: 106, 107, 114
*Cathy's Girl*: 134
Celebrity Endorsement: 10, 224–34
    Celebrity as brand: 233
    Celebrity seeding: 233
    Congruence with product: 229
    Credibility of:227–29, 232
    Morals clauses and: 231
Center for Emotional Marketing: 284
Center for Media Research: 124

Center for Science in the Public Inter-
est: 97, 99
Center on Alcohol Marketing and
Youth: 65, 70
*Central Hudson Corp. v. Public Ser-
vice Commission*: 58
Channel One: 93–94
Childhood obesity: 92–93
Children's Advertising: 85–97
Attitudes towards: 90
New Media: 88
Print media: 87–88
Processing: 89–91
Radio: 88
Spending: 92
Television: 89
Children's Advertising Review Unit
(CARU): 96, 97, 99
Children's Online Privacy Protection
Act (COPPA): 32, 95
Children's Television Act of 1990
(CTA): 95
Choi, Sejung Marina: 10, 224
Ciesinski, David: 116
Citigroup: 274–75
Civil Rights movement: 187
Clear Channel: 160
Clinton, Bill: 240
Clinton, Hillary: 244–45, 248
Cloaking: 146
Clow, Lee: 273–74
Coca-Cola: 93, 120, 135, 229, 233
Cohen, David: 103, 104
Combs, Sean: 233
Commercial Alert: 134, 165
Commercial-free media: 161
Competitrack: 115
*Consumer Reports*: 19
The Cool Hunter: 166

Cooper, Caryl: 8, 183
Corporate social entrepreneur: 272
Cosby, Bill: 229
*Cosmo Girl*: 87–88
Courvoisier: 66
Cover Girl: 134–35
Cowell, Simon: 233
Craigslist: 105
Cream of Wheat: 186
Creamer, Matthew: 3, 11, 152, 163
Crispin Porter + Bogusky (CP+B):
115, 272
Cultural branding: 276
Curran, Catharine: 5, 32, 36, 38, 85,
93, 95
Curves: 176
Cusato, Rick: 190

**D**

Dairy Queen: 190
Daisy Girl: 244–45, 288
Davie Brown Index: 237
Davis, Welles: 197
Dell Computer: 276
Diesel Clothing: 118–19
DiFranza, Joseph: 76
Digital Video Recording (DVR):
107–108, 132, 160
Dimitrova, Daniela: 241
Direct Marketing: 33, 162
Direct-to-consumer (DTC):
41–53, *see also* Pharmaceutical
Distilled Spirits Council of the United
States (DISCUS): 59, 70, 219
Dolce & Gabbana: 221
Domino's Pizza: 147
Donaton, Scott: 127, 133
Do-not-call registry: 110, 159
Doritos: 116

Douglas, Norman: 169
Dove: 8, 169, 174–76, 218
Doyle Dane Bernbach: 272–73, 284
Drake, William: 259
Driggs, Steve: 274
Drumwright, Minette: 268, 277
Dunkin' Donuts: 146

## E

*E.T.: The Extraterrestrial*: 128
eBay: 33, 105
*Ebony*: 187
Edwards, John: 246
Eisenhower, Dwight D.: 240
Electronic Privacy Information Center: 39
Ellison, Carol: 114–15
E-Loan: 26
Emeruwa, Ericka: 197
Emotion in Advertising: 11, 282–92
   Attack ads and: 289
   Fear and: 290
   How it works: 283–86
   Humor and: 289–90
   Physiological indicators: 291
   Response to: 291–92
Energizer: 273
Enpocket: 110
EnviroMedia: 276, 281
Ethics in advertising: 266
EthnoConnect: 195

## F

Facebook: 4, 7, 88, 139, 249
Fallon Worldwide: 274
Family Education Rights and Privacy Act (FERPA): 31
Fandy, Mamoun: 259
FCC Fairness Doctrine: 76

Federal Communications Commission (FCC): 76, 95, 134, 159, 213, 219
Federal Trade Commission (FTC): 16, 32–33, 44, 57, 93, 95, 97, 100, 134, 159, 232
First Amendment: 58, 96, 245
Fischer, Paul: 76
Food advertising: 6
Food and Drug Administration (FDA): 41, 43, 44, 45, 48–50, 52, 55, 56
Food, Drug, and Cosmetic Act: 444
*Forbes'* Celebrity 100 Ranking: 237
Ford, Tom: 221
Foster, Susan: 64
FOX Television: 111, 120, 218
Friedan, Betty: 169–70
Fullerton, Jami: 9, 10, 196, 253, 264

## G

Gadsby, Monica: 203
Gallup Poll: 23, 266
Garfield, Bob: 11, 178–79, 259, 269
Garga, Sunnil: 108
Gates, Bill: 113
Gatorade: 225, 226
Gay and Lesbian Alliance Against Defamation (GLAAD): 267
General Motors: 203
Gilligan, Carol: 266
Gilman, Spencer: 144–45
Gitlin, Todd: 154, 156
Giuliani, Rudolph: 248–49
Gladwell, Malcolm: 138, 148
Glaser, Milton: 271
Global Advertising Strategies, Inc.: 190
Goffman, Erving: 170
*Good Magazine*: 279
Google: 4, 32, 112–13, 157, 248
   Adwords: 112–13

Gray, Bill: 198
Green, Nancy: 186
Grey Worldwide: 190
Griffin, Glenn: 11, 265
Gucci: 215, 221
Guerilla marketing: 138
Guess Clothing: 215, 232

**H**
Ha, Louisa: 154, 156
Hall, Emma: 119
Halter, Mark: 30
Handler, Ruth: 86
Harris Interactive: 289
Health Insurance Portability and Ac-
    countability Act (HIPAA): 31
Heineken: 178–79
Heinz: 116
Helm, Jelly: 273
Hernandez-Fallous, Jackie: 204
Herron, Brad: 116
Hershey: 128
Hertz: 230
Hill, Dan: 283, 285
Hillsman, Bill: 246
Hilton, Paris: 176, 211, 231–32
Hintinaus, Tom: 216
Hispanic Market Weekly: 195
Hispanic population: 185, 201–2, 204
Hispanics in advertising: 191
Hofstetter, C. Richard: 244
Holahan, Catherine: 115
Hollywood-Madison Group: 238
Honda: 143–44, 285–86
Hovland, Carl: 227
Human Rights Campaign: 267
Hust, Stacey: 5, 57, 60, 62, 63, 65
Hye-Jin Paek: 5, 71, 76

**I**
Iger, Robert: 110
IKEA: 276
Interactive Advertising Bureau (IAB):
    113, 124
iPod: 287–88
iTunes: 109

**J**
J. Walter Thompson: 253
Jackson, Michael: 227
James Bond: 228
Jim Beam: 66
Jockey: 224
Joe Camel: 71, 73, 75, 76, 85, 100
Johnson & Johnson: 51, 120, 144
Johnson, Brad: 107
Johnson, Lyndon: 244, 288
Johnson, Magic: 229–30
Jordan, Michael: 224, 225–27, 229

**K**
Kadlec, Kim: 119–20
Kaid, Lynda Lee: 241
Kaltschnee, Michael: 139
Kang & Lee: 202
Keller, Michael: 190
Kellogg's: 39, 85, 176
Kendrick, Alice: 9, 169, 196, 253, 264
Kern-Foxworth, Marilyn: 184, 186
Kerry, John: 239, 241, 242, 243
Ketchum Advertising: 242
Kimberly-Clark: 116
Kivijarv, Leo: 242
Koop, C. Everett: 75
Kournikova, Anna: 226
Kraft Foods: 88, 97
Krueger, Elizabeth: 245
Krugman, Dean: 79

# L

*Ladies Home Journal*: 218
Lam, Kat: 268
Lambiase, Jacqueline: viii, 7, 138, 215
Lang, Annie: 245
Lansing, Paul: 30
Lariscy, Ruthann: 247
LaTour, Michael: 217
Lazier-Smith, Linda: 170
Lehrer, Jim: 258
Leo Burnett: 73
Life Cereal: 89
Lippert, Barbara: 244, 248
LonelyGirl15: 144–45
Lopez Negrete Communications: 191
Lopez, George: 191
L'Oreal: 176
Lorillard: 71, 72
Lucky Strike: 72, 74
Lukas, Scott: 182
Lunesta: 45, 56

# M

Macias, Wendy: 5, 41
*Madison and Vine*: 127
Madonna: 224, 225, 226, 233
Marlboro Man: 71, 73, 76,
Marlboro: 72, 73, 78, 79
Mars, Inc.: 267
Martin Agency: 268, 271
Mashups: 140, 144
Mattel: 86, 96
Max Factor: 226, 228
McCann-Erickson: 257, 260
McClellan, Mark: 48
McCracken, Grant: 228
McCubbin, Rexanna: 271–72
McDonald's: 88

Meaning Transfer Model: 228–29
Media Post: 125
Men in advertising: 177
Messages, explicit: 16
Messages, implied: 16
Meyers, Bob: 105
Microsoft: 33, 115, 144, 226
Miller, Clayton: 139
Miller, Michelle: 182
Milwaukee's Best: 1–2, 6
MindShare: 203
Minority employment in advertising:
    196–205
    Hiring obstacles: 197–99
    Job Satisfaction: 199
    Retention obstacles: 197–99
Minorities, representation of: 8–9
Minority markets: 185
Minority media: 204–5
Mintzes, Barbara: 47, 53
Mobile marketing: 88, 109–10, 157
    Spending: 110
Monster.com: 105
Morrison, Deborah: 11, 265
Moss, Kate: 230, 231
Most Promising Minority Students
    Initiative (MPMS): 9, 199, 200–201
Motion Picture Association of America
    (MPAA): 79
Moveon.org: 249
Mueller, Barbara: 185, 192
Mullman, Jeremy: 2, 11
Multicultural Agencies: 202–3
Multicultural marketing: 190–91
Murphy, Patrick: 268, 277
*Muslim Life in America*: 254
*My Black is Beautiful* campaign:189
MySpace: 4, 88, 113–14, 118, 119,
    139, 143–45, 248–49

## N

*Nacho Libre*: 121
National Broadcasting Company (NBC): 59, 120, 161, 218
National Center for Health Statistics (NCHS): 78
National Household Survey on Drug Abuse: 61
*National Journal*: 252
National Minimum Drinking Age Act: 61–62
Neff, Jack: 189, 218, 289
Nelson, Jon: 58
Nesvig, Jon: 111
Neutrogena: 144–45
New Media: 6, 103–121
   Downloaded programming: 108–9
   Exposure: 111–12
   Fragmentation: 106–7
   Online advertising: 104–5, 113–14
   Spending: 115
   Online video: 114
   Search marketing: 112–13
   Video-sharing: 116–17
New York City Commission on Human Rights: 191, 196, 207
Newell, Jay: 7, 152
Nexium: 41, 43, 45, 56
Nielsen Media Research: 105, 111, 160
Nielsen, BuzzMetrics: 147
Nielsen, Measurement: 111
Nike: 8, 115, 118, 176, 178, 224, 225, 226, 231
Nintendo: 88

## O

Obama, Barack: 249
Ogilvy & Mather: 175, 198, 253
Ohanian, Roobina: 227

*Olmstead v. United States*: 30
Omnicom: 192
Opt-in approach: 36
Opt-out approach: 36
Ortho Evra: 50, 51, 53, 56
Outdoor advertising: 156, 158

## P

PanCom International: 208
Patent medicines: 43–44
PayPal: 33
Pepsi: 93, 130
Percy, Larry: 131
Permission marketing: 36
Peters, Jeremy: 189, 190
Petrecca, Laura: 116
Petrone, Gerard S.: 72
Pfizer: 52
Pharmaceutical advertising: 4–5, 41–53
   Brief summary: 42, 48
   Consumer-friendly language in: 49, 53
   Fair balance in: 49–50, 52
   Growth of: 44–46
   Guidelines: 48–50
   History of: 43–44
   Lifestyle drugs: 42
   Maintenance drugs: 42
   Over-the-counter (OTC): 42–43
   Presentation of side effects: 50
   Spending: 45–46
Pharmaceutical Research and Manufacturers of America: 52
Phillip Morris: 73, 74, 77, 79
Picot-Zane, Leslie: 284–85
Pine-Sol: 267
*Playboy*: 105
Podcast: 117–18
Polispots: *see* Political Advertising

Political Advertising: 10, 239–50, 288–89
  Buzz generation and: 244–45
  Mudslinging: 246–47
  Online spending: 248
  Persuasion and: 243–44
  Refutational: 247
  Regulation of: 245
  Spending: 240–41
  Types of: 245–47
Pop Tarts: 85
Powell, Amy: 120–21
Powell, Colin: 253, 259
*Premiere*: 105
Preston, Ivan: 4, 15, 16, 27
Price, Paul: 284, 287
Prilosec: 43
Privacy Rights Clearinghouse: 39
Privacy: 29–38
  Constitutional rights to: 30—31
  Corporate policy: 36–37
Procter & Gamble: 135, 189, 203, 284
Product placement: 6–7, 126–35, 162
  "Hero placement": 130
  Full disclosure: 133–34
  Prominence: 130–32
  Video games: 135
Public Relations Society of America: 201
Public Service Announcements (PSAs): 65, 76
Puffery: 4, 15–26
  Types of: 17–18
Pure Food and Drug Act: 44

**Q**
Q-scores: 237
Quinn, Patrick: 242

**R**
R.J. Reynolds: 72, 75, 80, 100
Race and ethnicity in advertising: 183–92
Radio Frequency Identification (RFID): 35
Rainbow Coalition: 187
Ramirez, Art: 212
Really Simple Syndication (RSS): 142
Reeves, Rosser: 287
Reichert, Tom: 103, 126, 169, 196, 211, 282, 294
Richards, Jef: 4, 7, 29, 32, 36, 95
Richardson, Bill: 246
Ries, Al: 107, 153
Robinson, Ed: 115
Romney, Mitt: 248
RoperASW Worldwide: 257
Rubel, Steve: 117
Russell, Cristel: 127, 129, 130
Ruth, Babe: 224

**S**
Sauza: 66
Sazerac Company: 66
Seabrook, Larry: 196
Second Life: 146
Selig Center: 201–2
Sex in Advertising: 9, 61, 211–21, 223, 290–91
  Attention getting: 214–15
  Brand benefits of: 215
  Distraction hypothesis: 214, 290
  Emotional response to: 213
  Facilitating factors: 213
  Negative implications of: 219–21
  Physical characteristics: 212
  Prevalence of: 213
  Product considerations: 216–17

Regulation of: 218–19
Sexual behavior: 212
Target audience considerations: 217–18
Teens and young adults as target: 220–21
Sexual self-schema: 217
Sexualized identities: 215–16
Shared Values Initiative: 10, 253–63
Shields, Vickie: 170, 173
Shipley, Pahl: 246
Simpson, O.J.: 230
Sirius Satellite Radio: 161
Smirnoff: 115
*Snakes on a Plane*: 120
Soar, Matthew: 133, 137
Sober Truth on Preventing Underage Drinking Act: 66
Social networking: 4, 7, 138–48
   Infiltration: 146–47
   Technology: 142
Social Responsibility: 11, 262–78
Sony PSP: 88, 121
*The Sopranos*: 245
SPAM: 31
*SpongeBob SquarePants*: 85
*Sports Illustrated*: 60, 61, 87
Spyware: 37
Starcom Mediavest: 155, 203
Stavchansky Lewis, Liza: 5, 41
Sternberg, Brian: 111
Stevenson, Adlai: 240
Super Bowl: 116
Sutherland, Max: 131, 133–34
Svedka: 219
Swift Boat Veterans for Truth: 241
Swift, John: 111–12

**T**

Tan, Alex: 174

Tapie, Monique: 190
Target Market News: 194
TBWA\Chiat\Day: 273
*Teen Vogue*: 87
Telemundo: 204
*The Terminal*: 126
*The Future of Advertising*: 3
The Living Room Candidate: 252
theroot.com: 195
Third Screen: *see* Mobile marketing
Timberland: 183–84
Timeshifting: 117
Tinkham, Spencer: 247
TiVo: 107–108, 111, 160
TNS Media Research: 111
Tobacco Advertising: 5, 71–80, 158–59
   As social evil: 75–76
   Origin and Growth of: 71–72
   Smokeless tobacco: 80
   Spending: 71
   Warning labels: 76
Tronto, Joan: 269
Truth campaign: 77–78, 272
Tuerff, Kevin: 276
Turnbull, Jenny: 126, 132
Turner Broadcasting: 204
TV One: 204

**U**

Ugg Boots: 233
Uncle Ben: 186
Under Armour: 178, 179, 192
Uniform Commercial Code: 23
Universal McCann: 103, 104, 106, 120
Universal Studios: 79
Univision: 204
UniWorld Group: 187

US Census Bureau: 185
US General Accounting Office (US-GAO): 47, 55
US State Department: 253–54, 257–62
US Surgeon General: 66
User-generated content (UGC): 114, 116, 139
Uva, Joe: 204
Valerie, Davis: 276
ValueScope: 257–58
Vence, Deborah: 134
Verizon: 120
Viacom: 85
Viagra: 41–42, 47, 49
Vick, Michael: 10, 230–31
Victoria's Secret: 216, 290–91
Video on demand (VOD): 249–50
Viral Factory: 115, 146
Viral marketing: 138
Viral video: 1–2, 103, 114–16, 249
Virginia Slims: 71, 73, 74–75, 76, 78–79
Volkswagen: 115
Vytorin: 45–46

**W**

*Wall Street Journal*: 112, 242
Wal-Mart: 146–47
Walt Disney: 39, 79, 110
Warren, Samuel: 30
WebMD: 53
Weldon, Fay: 135
Wellstone, Paul: 246
Wendy's: 289
Wentz, Laura: 202, 204
Wheaton, Ken: 249
Widgets: 117
Wieden + Kennedy: 273
Wine Institute: 59

Winfrey, Oprah: 171, 218, 233
Women in advertising: 169–79
    "Idealized" reality: 173–74
    "Traditional" portrayals of: 171–72
    Degrading images of: 219–20
    Effects on consumers: 172–74
    Progressive portrayals of: 171
    Representation of: 8, 169–79
    Stereotyping: 170
Wonder Branding: 182
Woods, Tiger: 224, 226, 228
Word of Mouth Marketing Association (WOMMA): 146, 150
Word-of-mouth: 7, 138–48
    Credibility of: 142
    Professionalized buzz: 145–46
    Spending: 161
Working Families for Wal-Mart: 146–47
WPP Group: 202
Wurtzel, Alan: 108

**X**
Xenical: 43

**Y**
Yahoo: 33, 117
YouTube: 1, 32, 114, 116, 140, 144, 175, 248–49, 252
Yo-Yo: 91, 94

**Z**
Zapzyt: 113–14
Zenith Media: 120, 203
Zerhouni, Elias: 255

# About the Contributors

**Joël Bree**, PhD, is Professor at the University of Caen (France) and at the Rouen Business School where he created and chairs a Masters Degree program in Children's Marketing. His primary research area seeks to understand children as consumers. He has served as the President of the French Marketing Association (AFM) from 2004 to 2006. He serves on a number of French and European committees about children, advertising, and marketing and is regularly consulted as an expert on this topic. He is the author of many books on consumer behavior and on children's consumption. Currently, he is working on a grant from the French government exploring the link between marketing to children and obesity.

**Sejung Marina Choi**, PhD, is an Assistant Professor of Advertising at the University of Texas at Austin. Her research interests are in the areas of source credibility, cause-related marketing, advertising on the Internet, and cross-cultural consumer behavior. Her work has appeared in *Journal of Advertising*, *Psychology & Marketing*, *Journal of Consumer Affairs*, *Journal of Popular Culture*, *Journal of Current Issues and Research in Advertising*, *Journal of Computer Mediated Communication*, *International Journal of Advertising*, and various conference proceedings. Prior to her graduate degrees she worked in the advertising agency business, particularly in account management.

**Caryl Cooper**, PhD, is an Associate Professor in the Department of Advertising and Public Relations at the University of Alabama. She teaches advertising courses such as media planning, as well as mass media history and introductory courses. Her research interests include African Americans in advertising and the history of the black press. Professionally, Dr. Cooper worked six years as a Media Planner/Buyer at several advertising agencies, including Doyle, Dane and Bernbach and Compton Advertising in New York City. Her background also includes seven years in media sales at Gannett-owned radio stations KUSA/KSD, and CBS-TV affiliate KMOV-TV in St. Louis.

**Catharine Curran**, PhD, is an Associate Professor of Marketing at the Charlton College of Business at the University of Massachusetts Dartmouth. She teaches the Marketing Communication courses, including Integrated Marketing Communication and Advertising. Her primary research area is the regulation of marketing and advertising to children. She has also conducted research on the impact of the imposition of market based models on traditionally non-market professions such as law, medicine, and education. Dr. Curran has authored numerous papers for the *Journal of Advertising*, the *Journal of Consumer Marketing*, and for *Young Consumers*. She is currently working on a grant from the French government exploring the link between marketing to children and obesity.

**Jami Fullerton**, PhD, is an Associate Professor at Oklahoma State University, where she teaches advertising and mass communication research and theory. Dr. Fullerton, who is the recipient of one State Department grant and a participant in two others, often spends her summers abroad teaching and conducting research on cross-cultural communication and media globalization. She is the author (with Alice Kendrick) of *Advertising's War on Terrorism* (2006).

**Glenn Griffin**, PhD, is an Assistant Professor at the Temerlin Advertising Institute at SMU in Dallas and the leader of Method Creative, the program's portfolio arm. He teaches courses in creativity and portfolio development and his research interests include the creative process, social responsibility in advertising, and the impact of new media. His students' work has been recognized by The One Club for Art & Copy and featured in *CMYK Magazine*, in addition to many other award shows.

**Stacey J. T. Hust**, PhD, is Assistant Professor of communication at Washington State University. Her primary research area is media's effects on substance abuse. Her work also explores whether the mass media can be used for health promotion through strategies such as entertainment education and media advocacy. She has published manuscripts in a variety of journals including the *Journal of Health Communication*, *Mass Communication & Society*, and the *Journal of International Advertising*.

**Alice Kendrick**, PhD, is Professor of Advertising in the Temerlin Advertising Institute at Southern Methodist University in Dallas, where she teaches advertising research and account planning. Her research interests are advertising effectiveness, advertising and public diplomacy, and advertising education and diversity issues. She is a member of the American Advertising Federation Mosaic Advisory Board, and in 2007 received the Advertising Research Foundation's Research Innovation Award.

**Jacqueline Lambiase**, PhD, is an Associate Professor in the Department of Journalism and the Mayborn Graduate School of Journalism at the University of North Texas. She teaches courses in strategic communications, ethics, qualitative research, and race and gender in media. With Tom Reichert, she is co-editor and contributor to *Sex in Advertising* (2003) and *Sex in Consumer Culture* (2006).

**Hye-Jin Paek**, PhD, is an Assistant Professor in the Department of Advertising and Public Relations at the University of Georgia. She teaches various advertising courses, including research methods in mass communication, and media and health. Her research focuses on social, cultural, and health-related issues in advertising and media messages. She has published numerous papers in leading communication journals. Her smoking research earned her several academic awards and was covered widely in the international, national, and local media.

**Liza Stavchansky Lewis**, PhD, is a Lecturer in the Department of Advertising at the University of Texas at Austin. She teaches integrated communication management and campaigns courses. Her research interest includes DTC prescription drug marketing and other health communication issues. She also worked as a marketing consultant at Schering Plough Laboratories for almost five years before returning to teach.

**Wendy Macias**, PhD, is an Associate Professor in the Department of Advertising and Public Relations at the University of Georgia where she teaches advertising courses. Her research focuses on consumer behavior issues related to interactive advertising, direct-to-consumer pharmaceutical advertising, and online health communication. She has published her research in venues such as the *Journal of Advertising*, *Health Communication*, *Journal of Health Communication*, and *Health Marketing Quarterly*.

**Deborah Morrison**, PhD, is the Chambers Distinguished Professor of Advertising at the University of Oregon's School of Journalism and Communication. She teaches conceptual thinking, creativity and content, portfolio, and campaigns courses from a social responsibility perspective. Prior to the University of Oregon, Deborah was the leader of Texas Creative at the University of Texas at Austin for 18 years. Her research concerns professional creativity, social responsibility in advertising, and the creative process. Importantly, she believes that good advertising can be one way to save the world. Morrison is a member of the Board of Directors for The One Club for Art & Copy in New York, the only university educator to hold that honor.

**Jay Newell**, PhD, researches media saturation at Iowa State University's Greenlee School of Journalism and Communication. Prior to receiving a PhD in mass media from Michigan State University, Newell directed advertising, promotion, and public relations campaigns for cable networks such as CNN, TNT, and Nickelodeon, and has won multiple Clio awards for his advertising creative work. His research has been covered in the *New York Times*, *USA Today*, and *Advertising Age*.

**Ivan L. Preston**, PhD, is a retired University of Wisconsin professor of advertising. He presented many analyses and research findings in consumer behavior and consumer law through books and articles and also through activities with academic and government organizations. Dr. Preston is also the author of *The Great American Blow-Up: Puffery in Advertising and Selling* and *The Tangled Web They Weave: Truth, Falsity and Advertisers*.

**Tom Reichert**, PhD, is an Associate Professor in the Department of Advertising and Public Relations at the University of Georgia. He teaches advertising courses and his research interests include media and politics, and the content and effects of sex in the media. Reichert authored *The Erotic

*History of Advertising* (2003) and with Jacqueline Lambiase co-edited *Sex in Advertising* (2003) and *Sex in Consumer Culture* (2006). He also maintains the website sexinadvertising.com.

**Jef I. Richards**, JD, PhD, is a Professor in the Department of Advertising at the University of Texas. His research involves advertising policy and regulation, as well as advertising education. He teaches courses in advertising law and ethics, as well as advertising and public relations campaign planning. He is on the board of directors of the Advertising Educational Foundation, on the editorial boards of several journals, and in 2008 is president of the American Academy of Advertising.

# Acknowledgements

Ads are wonderful indicators of life. In them we see our dreams, our goals and our problems.

Like life, ads also present a paradox.

We learn from them and we ignore them.

We laugh at them and we zap them.

And in them we see ourselves and we see others.

For creating and sponsoring such intriguing material, I extend my appreciation to the advertising community. Your heart is in the right place.

If anything is lost, it's in the translation.

Second, for their invaluable insights I thank my students and colleagues in the Department of Advertising and Public Relations at the University of Georgia.

Much appreciation goes to Peggy Kreshel for forwarding me interesting articles, to Michael Castengara for sending me his weekly newsletter, and to Tom Russell for giving me his copies of *Advertising Age*.

For her assistance, I thank my graduate student Jackie Ayrault.

Also, many thanks to Bruce Bendinger, Patrick Aylward, and the team at The Copy Workshop—always open to new ideas.

Last, I thank my wife and little boy for their enthusiasm and patience.

# BOOKS FROM **THE COPY WORKSHOP**

adbuzz.com | 773-871-1179 | FAX 773-281-4643 | thecopyworkshop@aol.com

We publish some of the leading books in advertising and marketing. Our authors are leading educators and industry professionals. These books are designed for those with jobs in the creative department.

## DESCRIPTION

This is the #1 book on copywriting. Agencies use it as a training resource. It's used by universities, art schools, and the American Management Association (it's the basic book for their copywriting seminar). The Really New Edition features more great examples of ads that work, a practical approach to integrated communication - The MarCom Matrix - and new chapters on Sales Promotion, Direct, and "MPR" (Marketing Public Relations). Also available in Chinese and Korean.

From the Beetle to the Mini. From "Eat Mor Chikin" to the AFLAC Duck. From "Think Different" to "Got Milk." This completely revised and expanded 2nd edition includes life lessons from 18 of advertising's most important talents.

Even in this economy, you can still get a job. But you need a good "book" (that's what the industry calls a portfolio of your work). And this is the book that tells you how to do it. Updated for today's tougher job market and changing technology. Features smart career and book-building advice from top industry professionals.
[Note: Ms. Paetro is now a top-selling novelist, co-authoring books w. James Patterson.]

This is a book about and by "The Socrates of San Francisco," Howard Gossage, the copywriter who introduced the world to Marshall McLuhan, helped start Friends of the Earth and brought interactivity to his unique brand of advertising.
He was 30 years ahead of his time, so the world may be ready.
The Second Edition also features **The Disc of Gossage** - packed with extras; a radio address, an ad gallery, and more.

We are pleased to present Professor Elaine Wagner's clear and reader-friendly book clarifying the often complicated process of preparing computer-based graphic files for printing or for sending to a publication.
This is a critical issue and Professor Wagner, with the assistance of printing professional Amy Desiderio, makes this complicated area crystal clear with principles that apply while technology evolves.

## INFORMATION

### The Copy Workshop Workbook
by Bruce Bendinger

440 pages, $37.50

ISBN# 978-1-887229-12-5

### How To Succeed In Advertising When All You Have Is Talent
by Laurence Minsky

480 pages, $47.50

ISBN# 978-1-887229-20-3

### How To Put Your Book Together And Get A Job In Advertising
*21st Century Edition*
by Maxine Paetro

272 pages, $27.95

ISBN# 978-1-887229-13-5

### The Book of Gossage
by Howard Luck Gossage
Introduction by Jeff Goodby, w. Stan Freberg, Kim Rotzoll, John Steinbeck, and Tom Wolfe.

2nd Edition - Includes the Disc of Gossage. 400 pages. $50.00

ISBN# 978-1-887229-28-9

### From File To Finish:
*A Prepress Guide*
by Elaine Wagner &
Amy Desiderio

282 pages, $37.50

ISBN# 978-1-887229-32

For more information and to Save 20% on these titles, go to the Book Shop at www.adbuzz.com

# BOOKS FROM THE COPY WORKSHOP

adbuzz.com | 773-871-1179 | FAX 773-281-4643 | thecopyworkshop@aol.com

We publish some of the leading books in advertising and marketing. Our authors are leading educators and industry professionals. These books are designed for those in research, media, and account management.

## DESCRIPTION

## INFORMATION

Agencies need to do for themselves what they do for their clients: build a distinctive brand. But they are usually so eager to be a "full-service integrated agency" that they try to stand for everything. Take a Stand for Your Brand shows how agencies can develop a clear positioning that builds on the agency's unique strengths, differentiates the agency in the marketplace, and makes the agency more intensely appealing to prospective clients.

### Take A Stand For Your Brand:
*Building A Great Agency Brand From The Inside Out*
by Tim Williams

213 pages, $29.95

ISBN# 978-1-887229-25-9

A smart book about one of the most challenging jobs in business - account management.
Use as a core text for a management course, or as a supplement for your student agency.

### The New Account Manager
by Don Dickinson

524 pages, $60

ISBN# 978-1-887229-07-4

The Consumer Insight Classic.
Clear and engaging - written by one of the top professionals in consumer insight. The book takes you through the process step by step - from Data to Information to Insight to Inspiration.
This book is used worldwide by both students and professionals.

### Hitting the Sweet Spot:
*How Consumer Insights Can Inspire Better Marketing and Advertising*
by Marian Azzaro

257 pages, $29.95

ISBN# 978-1-887229-09-8

Welcome to the world of media - the $300 billion business end of the ad business. Learn how it works from some of media's top professors and professionals. This is a book in touch with today —packed with genuine substance and contemporary best practices in a clear, easy-to-read format. A student workbook is available FREE on the MediaBuzz Web site.

### Strategic Media Decisions:
*Understanding The Business End Of The Advertising Business*
by Marian Azzaro, w. Carla Lloyd, Mary Alice Shaver, Dan Binder, Robb Clawson, and Olaf Werder
524 pages, $60

ISBN# 978-1-887229-17-3

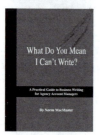

Years ago, top ad agency executive Norm Macmaster wrote a guide for beginning account executives.
It became legendary - with copies handed down from generation to generation. With the author's permission, we bring this underground classic to light - clear and practical, it provides beginners with the information they need to do the job.

### What Do You Mean I Can't Write?
*A Practical Guide To Business Writing For Agency Account Managers*
by Norm MacMaster

74 pages, $11.75

ISBN # 978-1-887229-29-6

For more information and to Save 20% on these titles, go to the Book Shop at www.adbuzz.com